AMANDA
I'm still here
BARRIE

WITH HILARY BONNER

m
B

MIRROR BOOKS

Written with Hilary Bonner

1

First published in hardback in Great Britain and Ireland
in 2025 by Mirror Books, a Reach PLC business.

www.mirrorbooks.co.uk
@TheMirrorBooks

ISBN: 9781917439367
eBook ISBN: 9781917439374

Photographic acknowledgements:
Alamy, MirrorPix, Amanda Barrie Personal Collection

Every effort has been made to trace copyright. Any
oversights will be rectified in future editions.

Editing and Production: Christine Costello
Cover Design: Chris Collins

Printed and bound by CPI Group (UK) Ltd,
Croydon, CR0 4YY.

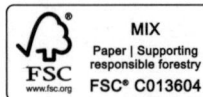

FSC
www.fsc.org

MIX
Paper | Supporting
responsible forestry
FSC® C013604

AMANDA
BARRIE

I'm still here

WITH HILARY BONNER

m
B

MIRROR BOOKS

Contents

PART FOUR: My 90th Year

I imagined a life in the theatre, I imagined a happy home life, I imagined a life without fear.

The book is dedicated to everyone who helped make it possible for my imaginings to become reality.

PART ONE

Rebirth

1

—

My Inner Fox

Twenty-five years ago, the world celebrated the start of a new millennium. For me, a whole new life was beginning. A life I had never imagined would be possible. A life which gave me freedom from the constraints I had always taken for granted. I was already in my mid-60s, and yet I was to experience what I can only describe as a rebirth. All my adult life I had kept my true self hidden. I felt I had no choice. Now, finally, I could be myself.

I came out as homosexual with a bang – which may not be the best way to put it – right across the tabloid press and on TV. And for a while I was probably more afraid of what might happen to me because of my sexuality than ever before.

I honestly wondered if I might be stoned in the street. But I noticed the world was changing. The law of the land was continuing to change.

People around me had changed. And these changes kept coming. As fate would have it, I seemed to have extremely good timing. Suddenly, everybody was coming out. It was almost fashionable. So much so, that as someone who was accustomed to being regarded as 'different', and had been told off for it at school by various headmistresses, I did consider going back in again…

Madonna kissed women on stage and it didn't seem to damage her career. So why had I been in such a state? Gay Pride was becoming a phenomenon. People were singing and shouting that they were glad to be gay. It seemed that I may have missed something! And my coming out proved to be not at all how I had anticipated it.

Now, in the UK and many other countries, gay couples can marry. Then gay men went to jail and gay women were ostracised.

I have been a small part of a transformation. I am now married to a woman. Our 11th anniversary falls on September 12 2025, two days before my 90th birthday. Miracles do happen… I have been astonished at what life has presented me with over the first quarter of a century of the new millennium.

Because, without a doubt, the most extraordinary part of my story has come about since I decided to stand up and be counted.

To young people today there will seem nothing remarkable in any of it, and they could be forgiven for questioning why it took me so long. The thousands of other gay men and women who had to deal with the world the way it used to be would never need to ask that question. Even as an actress, within an industry known for its liberal attitudes, tolerance, and acceptance of people who are different, I found that it was not always possible to be open. I firmly believed during my time in *Coronation Street* that I would have been sacked if my sexuality had become public knowledge. Actors and their characters often become as one in soap operas. And it would almost certainly have been felt that our viewers would not accept a gay Alma.

Now *Coronation Street* abounds with gay characters, to the extent that I have wondered if it should be renamed Canal

Street, after Manchester's famous gay area. Also, it seems almost irrelevant whether or not the actors who portray them are gay themselves. Which is how it should be.

Then everything was so very different. Have you ever seen a fox lurking about in your garden? You may have noticed that it has its head lowered down, that it looks furtive and frightened. And if you make any move towards it, it will disappear into the shadows. The fox knows, absolutely knows, it is going to be exterminated if it is found out because it is some sort of vermin, some sort of diseased creature. Along with a lot of other people at that time, I believed absolutely that I was a diseased creature.

That is pretty much how, right through the 20th century, I lived my life. And it was brought much more into focus when I joined *Coronation Street* as Alma Sedgwick, later to become Alma Baldwin. In the 80s and 90s, Corrie regularly pulled in 18 or 19 million viewers per show. More for a special episode. The show where Alma – and I – nearly drowned when she was driven into the murky waters of Salford Quays by deranged taxi driver, Don Brennan, attracted almost 20 million viewers. The Street still brings a degree of instant fame. Probably exceeded by certain reality shows now. In those days, from the moment you appeared on the cobbles, the level of attention was over-whelming. You were recognised everywhere you went. I have never minded that.

From the start, I considered it a privilege to be recognised and approached by people who had watched you on stage or screen and just wanted to meet you. It's what this business is about. But there is the other side to it.

As a Corrie regular, the tabloids were desperate to expose the most inconsequential details of your private life. In my case, there was always the little matter of my sexuality. And back then there was nothing inconsequential at all about a major character in the biggest soap in the world being revealed to be gay.

Previously the bulk of my work had been theatre. As a West End leading lady fortunate enough to appear in a succession of major productions in almost all of our great London theatres, I attracted considerable recognition. But that was like lying in a calm sea riding a flow of gentle waves, compared with the fight to stay afloat when faced with the tsunami of fame which came with the territory of Weatherfield. Nothing had prepared me for it. The fox was utterly terrified. Its head was bowed right down to the ground.

I was frightened of everything and everybody, fear of loss of work, fear of tabloid headlines, and, indeed, just fear of the opinions of others.

I always felt terrified and guilty, with no idea why sometimes, except that everything seemed against me and almost everyone seemed to be a predator of some sort. As a young woman, I developed serious mental health issues which lasted for many years, all whilst making a bit of a name for myself in West End theatre and films, notably *Carry On Cleo*. And, of course, becoming that well-known didn't help at all with my abiding fear of being found out for what I really was.

For me, it had always been much more about the intense emotional turmoil I was going through than anything else. And, in the unforgiving climate of that time, I have little doubt this was the primary cause of my mental health problems. I recently rewatched a TV show I featured in during the 1990s, which was a kind of mini *This is Your Life*, and I hardly recognised myself. This was a completely different Amanda Barrie.

Back then, I felt I had to treat every question, even those which appeared to be straightforward and innocent, with wariness. I was permanently on my guard. It was clear that I was editing every word I spoke. If you watched it now you might suspect I'd been created by AI.

In everyday life, you couldn't just talk to people about what you'd done at the weekend or who you'd been with. Everything was edited. Every story was edited. Where you'd been was edited. What you felt was edited. In fact, you were, basically, as a person, edited!

I was terrified when, during my Corrie days, I was first on *Loose Women,* because I was editing myself so much, I knew I must sound like a really boring bitch. I have since spoken to other people who experienced exactly the same thing. I had spent a very long time in the shadows. For 15 years, I shared my life with a woman who would not publicly acknowledge our relationship. To her family and the majority of those close to her, I was just a friend. I felt like saying: "It's not catching, you know."

Then I met and fell in love with the woman I was later to marry. I began to look to the future, to question the present, and to yearn to move on from my past. Rather, to the surprise of my former partner, I walked away, and never looked back. There is little doubt that I also somewhat surprised myself. The 'other woman', a writer called Hilary Bonner who is at this moment by my side helping me with this book, was also taken a little by surprise, I think.

Coming out was to become a necessary part in building a new life. Although I've always had trouble with the term. Was I 'in' before? If so, in what? It had to be done though.

Right through my time in Corrie people had been trying to out me, and it seemed like a pretty good idea to do it myself before someone beat me to it. The fox didn't have very much alternative, really, except to go for it and hope for the best. Even in the early noughties, it still seemed like a rather daring, frightening thing to do. But as the fox put its nose out through the door, it went, hey, wait a minute, the world is becoming a different place, maybe there's just a chance I will survive. Which I did. Indeed, I thrived.

Not only was I not stoned, but I got a lot of hugs. By and large, people were really nice to me.

There have, of course, been men as well as women in my life, notably a rather high-profile one, Billy Fury, and the man I married back in the sixties, the actor Robin Hunter. So technically, I must be bisexual, but I so hate labels. They're fine on luggage and packets of pasta, but not, in my opinion, on people. The truth is that I always leaned considerably further to the left than to the right. And, in the end, I toppled right over in that direction.

On TV, I came out on *Richard and Judy*, the Channel 4 early evening show which Richard Madeley and Judy Finnegan were presenting at the time. This proved to be quite a comforting place for it, and they were very kind to me, which I'll never forget. We had quite a lot of laughs. It was the most extraordinary feeling though. I thought, this is my mouth moving up and down, and I'm actually telling people about the real me. But out I came. And it was all so much easier than I expected. Some of the old prejudices remained, of course, still do, and always will.

Around the time that I came out I was asked to take part in no less than 20 episodes of a popular current affairs chat show, which was one of my favourites. I thought, great. That'd be lovely. And then, just as we were about to sign the contract, they said, well, it will actually only be 10. Then it went down to six, then three. Finally, the whole thing went away. I still think, at that time, somebody at the top said, we don't want a gay woman on here. I may be wrong, and maybe that was the fox in me again, but I strongly suspect that was the case.

Years later I did appear on that show, of course. The big change was happening. And fast. Nobody, except somebody who has been in my position, can explain what the last 25 years has been like in this country, the speed at which our lives have been transformed, the speed at which being gay has become very nearly totally acceptable.

Back in the day, I learned to be careful with my pronouns. And, long before 'woke' was invented, I would only very rarely use the second person. It was almost always 'they', and virtually never 'she'. Particularly when referring to someone I was having a relationship with.

Before I appeared on *Richard and Judy*, before I had actually revealed anything, I had to film a commercial for a book I had written in which I confessed my sexuality. It was filmed in a pub in the heart of the East End, God knows why.

I had to say: "Read about my love-life with men and with women." That was all.

Well, I have never been so scared in all my life. The place was entirely full of men, and most of them seemed to be rather large and rather loud. I was sweating down the back of my neck and I ended up more or less whispering.

The crew kept telling me to speak up. I thought, the fox is still very much here in the shadows. He's got no voice. He can't bark. He's in the wrong pub! I managed to do it, in the end, but I shook with fear, terror, sweat and horror. It still seemed such a momentous thing to do. But you know, life carries on as normal. You do what you usually do. You go to the supermarket, you go out for a drink or a meal, all those sorts of things. And that was the greatest gift of all. I became able to lead a perfectly ordinary and open life, or as much so as anyone can who has been in Corrie for 15 years.

In some ways, I barely noticed what was happening. I was

just being a normal person dealing with the everyday ups and downs of life, but in a way that I'd probably never been able to before when I was living with that underlying fear.

It was a gradual transition, though. The fox in me still lurked. It took a bit of time to get used to being able to walk about wherever I liked with whoever I liked without feeling threatened in some way. And I was quite astonished when I realised that people had read something, seen or heard something, and now knew about me, but they weren't pointing a finger at me at all. They were being rather nice, actually, and understanding, and I wasn't being questioned, or made to feel diseased.

I still found myself and, very occasionally to this day, I'm ashamed to say, still do catch myself diving back into the shadows. Little ordinary things happen. A taxi driver with whom I've been having a perfectly ordinary conversation might ask if I'm married, and when I answer that I am, go on to inquire what my husband does. And I can still find myself dodging – at the very least, probably using the 'they' pronoun again. I guess old habits die hard. I feel that I cannot go into the complexities of my life and that, in any case, the taxi driver doesn't want to know because he still thinks of me as Cleo or Alma. I've always loved taxi drivers and don't like to disappoint them.

In a strange way, one of the many reasons for my fox-like behaviour for so long was that I didn't want to let Alma down. Which is the way I thought about it in those days. There always seemed to be this fondness for her, which I was quite proud of, because I came to think of Alma as the better part of me.

I didn't want the audience to think I had cheated. But eventually, I went, oh shit, I've just got to get this out of the way. I can't live my life like this anymore. And what a relief it proved to be. Because of my past, because of all that I have experienced, and all that I have witnessed, including the suffering of homosexual people much less fortunate than me, I know just how lucky I am to exist in a place and at a time when I am able to be absolutely myself, to be honest. I'm not a fake anymore. If people like me, it is reasonable to assume they like me for who I really am, not as someone hiding behind a false image.

Of course, there was a considerable element of paying the price of celebrity in all this, because I was never dishonest with my family or my close friends. I was always out to them. It was just that I wasn't out in public, which was actually a big thing, and it did put this blight on my life. I did not have the privilege of being able to choose to tell who I wanted, when I wanted, and to live my life quietly. I was quite well known from an early age and I couldn't do that.

I was, however, so much better off than others. Back in the day there were vast numbers of homosexual people in this country who could never come out because they were frightened of their parents or frightened of the community they lived in, and not so very long ago, frightened of the law. But everything has changed to such an extraordinary extent that it is very hard now to tell younger gay people what it was like even 50 years ago, let alone 70 or 80, when I was beginning to question my sexuality.

You can't even explain what it was like not to have a washing machine or a television or a mobile phone. It's very hard to explain to anyone born in the last 25, or even 40 years or so, what it was like to have feelings for people of the same sex throughout the era I lived in for most of my life.

An era during which this awful conviction that I was some sort of diseased creature, abnormal, undeserving of the regard of others, a freak that, if found out, would be hunted down like the poor lurking fox it believed itself to be, came to dominate my entire being and continued to plague me for decades.

I suspect the present gay generation would not understand

that. I certainly hope that they wouldn't think any of it, thank God! I believe in the freedom of every individual to do and be exactly as they wish in life. To live their own way.

And I dream of a day when people's sexuality is regarded as so unimportant that nobody even bothers to remark on whether somebody is gay or straight, not even people in the public eye. It's probably a pipe dream, but I still like to dream it.

2

Bad Girls and Even Worse Decisions

The new millennium brought with it another big shock for me. I walked away from *Coronation Street* and, like every actor ever born, I naturally thought I would never work again. It is seriously scary when you finish a job as long running as my 15-year-plus stint in such an enormous show.

I was, of course, already signed up for the annual pantomime in Bradford, at the Alhambra Theatre, considered to be one of the best in the country. But to top the bill in a big panto was almost a right of passage after leaving Corrie.

I was the wicked queen in *Snow White*, alongside the wonderful comic Billy Pearce. I have always loved pantomime, and I was absolutely thrilled to be backstage again. It just felt like I'd walked into a very familiar family that I'd known all my life.

However, I didn't have a clue what was going to happen next. Or even what I wanted to happen. Part of me thought, oh well, that's probably it now, but never mind. I had no plan at all. There was nothing in my head that was clear. Which perhaps led to me making one of the most fantastically stupid decisions ever.

I did feel that I wanted to stagger back on stage in something other than panto. To really get my theatre boots back on. I had been in '*Noises Off*' in the West End, at the Savoy Theatre, in the 1980s, and was approached about resuming my part as Mrs Clackett in a new production. This was a show I loved and knew. And I have absolutely no idea, looking back, why I didn't jump at it.

Instead, for some Godforsaken reason, I decided for the first time in my life to do an end-of-pier show! In Bournemouth. It was *Absurd Person Singular* by Alan Ayckbourn, which I had also been in many years earlier in the West End. I'd played the lead at the Vaudeville Theatre opposite Paul Eddington. *Absurd Person* remains one of my favourite plays, but did not prove to be one of Bournemouth's. There I was for a summer season on the end of a pier, starring in a play that really did not go on the end of a pier.

It was not a happy experience. My first leading man, the lovely Gareth Hunt, had a major heart attack on stage, which was the only time in my life I've ever been in a theatre when the management actually went out front and asked, "Is there a doctor in the house?"

So then we got Leslie Grantham, best known as Dirty Den in *EastEnders,* who behaved as if he had been brought in to save us all, but in fact was the final nail in the coffin of the production. His online sexual shenanigans were yet to be revealed, but this was a man who, many years previously, had been convicted of murder. Now he was murdering Ayckbourn's rather wonderful play. Regardless of his past, I did not enjoy working with Leslie Grantham.

One of the first things he said was that Alan had written too long a play and he was going to cut it. I thought the next thing that was going to be cut was his throat. To me, the whole thing became a sort of awful nightmare; a play that I had cherished and loved in the West End nearly fell into the sea off Bournemouth.

It was possible that my head had been a bit turned by Alan allowing me to do *Absurd Person*, because no Ayckbourn play is ever put on without his approval, and he's always very fussy about who does his work. I doubt he'd ever agreed for it to be played on the end of a pier before, either! Also, I'd had such a wonderful experience doing the play with Paul and Milicent Martin. I'd enjoyed it so much, I thought, well, this is something I love; I'll do it just the once more. But you should always be wary of going backwards like that, because it can't ever be the same. Particularly not if you're playing the Pier Theatre, Bournemouth, opposite Leslie Grantham, instead of the Vaudeville Theatre, London, opposite Paul Eddington.

Bournemouth was not a step back – it was a bus ride back. And I really did wonder if I had finally ended my career. I honestly thought it might all be over. For good!

Then lo and behold, quick as a flash, following right behind Bournemouth, like some sort of spectacularly original and wonderfully captivating rescue pack, came *Bad Girls*, the ITV drama about a women's prison, which was already a huge hit. It was to be my first major television job after leaving Corrie, and was another shock to an old lurking fox like me, as *Bad Girls* was from top to bottom, full of gay women. It was written and run by them – and one gay man, my former *Coronation Street* producer Brian Park – and nearly every storyline in *Bad Girls* seemed to be a gay story. So, I had gone from one extreme to another.

It was Brian who invited me to meet him at a very nice club in Shaftesbury Avenue to discuss the possibility of me joining the cast of this already very successful show. He didn't order a glass of champagne, but instead called for the first bottle before we even sat down. So we drank, and we talked, and he didn't seem to very much mention anything to do with *Bad Girls* or what he actually wanted me to do until after, I think, about our third bottle of champagne. Then, just as I was making my way very carefully to the door, it was sort of mooted that I seemed to have got the job. Which was nice.

Particularly as this liquid interview with Brian may actually never have happened at all. I just couldn't get out of the door that day because,for some reason, I didn't know where anything was. I had what Hilary and I call a "where's my" moment. "Where are my keys?" I asked. "Where's my bag? Where are my glasses?"

Then, just as I was finally stepping outside, I turned to enquire, "Where am I going?"

There certainly wasn't much discussion about the pair of con artists who were to become known as the Costa Cons. I don't think I even knew I was going to be a Costa Con. Or indeed, what a Costa Con was. I certainly didn't know who I was going to be working with. I only learned later that my partner in crime was to be Stephanie Beacham.

We had met many years before but never worked together. Now, if you had deliberately wanted to put together two opposite ends of the scale, you could not have done better than choose the two of us. Stephanie was total *Dynasty*; I was total *Coronation Street*. And that was the way we expected to be looked after. To give an example, when it got very hot in the summer during our first season's filming, Stephanie summoned people around to the medium-sized cupboard which served as our dressing room and announced imperiously: "We have to have air conditioning."

Well, that was about as likely to happen as for Donald Trump to stop wearing orange makeup. I suggested we open the window. And at some point in between our two approaches, we did manage to get somewhere. A large fan arrived. It wasn't air conditioning, but it helped. And I think, in a way, that is how Stephanie and I operated throughout the series.

By the time Steph and I went into *Bad Girls*, filming took place almost entirely at 3 Mills Studios, this extraordinary building in East London that had once been a distillery. Part of it had been transformed into a truly incredible set, which was just like a real prison. The prison facilities were excellent. Everything was authentic. Once in there, you really did think you'd been put away for a few years. The facilities away from the set were a different matter. Our dressing room, for a start. Had our dressing room been a Chinese restaurant, it would probably have been condemned. It was very small. But Stephanie and I managed to squeeze ourselves into it reasonably well by stealing two mattresses off the beds in one of the cells and laying them on the floor side by side. There was just room for one upright chair, upon which we balanced a lamp and our little radio. We spent most of our off-time listening to Radio Four whilst lying flat on our backs. We made ourselves quite comfortable and, in fact, it became an enormous effort for us to move.

Working with Stephanie was quite an experience. Sometimes when we were rehearsing a scene with a lot of people, she would start saying to me, "Keep left, keep left." Like she was some sort of mad SatNav. Stephanie is an actress who is very experienced in camera work. I eventually realised that what she was trying to do was to keep us out of the background of what would be the next morning's first scene. So we wouldn't be in the back shot and wouldn't be called.

She probably managed to negotiate us out of half our parts, which I don't think made us very popular, to be quite honest. I'm not used to people trying to get out of a scene. I'm used to trying to get into one. But that was one of Stephanie's little foibles.

The other thing about working with Stephanie was that while the rest of us looked a wreck most of the time during filming of *Bad Girls*, Beacham was the only person I can imagine rehearsing for an outdoor jail scene in which, naturally, I was supposed to be full of drugs and leaning against a wall looking ghastly, whilst she was wearing a full-length mink coat and looking fabulous. I just thought, there is absolutely nothing Stephanie Beacham and I have in common. But, in fact, we got on rather well and are still good friends.

Ultimately, we found the set rather more comfortable than our dressing room and were sometimes discovered having crept back into our cell to have a bit of rest on our prison bunks.

The standard of our tiny dressing room dropped more and more the longer we were in it. We both smoked heavily then, so it was usually full of smoke for a start. It was pretty airless and the smoke never really cleared. I mean, you couldn't see when you came in there. People would open the door and peer around looking for us. When called for a scene, we were inclined to go, "Oh, darling, are you sure you need us right now? We're just finishing this thing on Radio 4."

I mean, the enthusiasm of actresses and the glamour of it. The two of us under clouds of smoke, lying on mattresses on the floor. It was pretty sordid. And when we walked into our cell, it seemed rather pleasant by comparison, which is why we ended up staying there as much as we could.

Another thing about Stephanie was that she could be extremely useful. She invariably had the cars and the drivers organised and would get them to stop off for coffee en route, or anything else she wanted. And she always managed to look wonderful, of course, even early in the morning, and every so often would sort me out too.

One morning we were motoring along in quite bright daylight, and I became aware that she was staring at me rather hard. Suddenly she said, "Just stay still a minute."

Then she dived into her bag, brought out her tweezers and leaned towards me, waving them at my chin.

"You've got a hair there!" she announced. And the offending hair, which seemed to have sprung up overnight, was promptly removed. So she really did have her uses in all sorts of ways.

What else can I say about Steph? In the end, after all the ups and downs and things that happen when you're making a major TV series, I became devoted to her. I found her extremely funny too. We once did a big TV interview and, I'm afraid, we behaved in a most unprofessional way. We just constantly made each other laugh. Hopefully we made the audience laugh too, but who knows?

When we were working, perhaps because of her Hollywood connection, she had the knack of turning all our English directors into malleable lumps of lard. Stephanie's every whim was answered. Whereas with me, it was rather different. They'd just walk past me, totally ignoring anything I might be trying to say, in order to get to Steph.

It could have been something to do with the way we both looked in *Bad Girls*, of course. Which leads me to another of my seriously bad decisions.

I have to say that I do not understand my capacity to so often turn myself into something that looks truly awful on television.

Bad Girls was the ultimate. I chose that horrendous red wig. That was me. I chose to look like that. I should have gone to Specsavers before I went near 3 Mills Studios, because there absolutely must have been something wrong with my eyesight. I had a chance to go back on TV in a major series and be anything I wanted, and that was what I chose to be! There is some flaw in me. I really do have a destructive app.

I thought, I've been on-screen for too long looking as I do, I need to look different. So when we went to discuss makeup and hair for *Bad Girls*, I said, "I really don't want to look like me. Not like Alma." Fair enough, I suppose. But I have no idea what possessed me to decide to look like some battered pre-Raphaelite version of Angela Rayner, the deputy prime minister, on a bad hair day.

It was all my own fault. I chose this unbelievably unflattering red wig, which took forever to get on in the morning, knowing that I would then be on camera standing next to the unbelievably beautiful Stephanie Beacham. I also thought I may have vaguely resembled a stray dog from Battersea. But never, never, was anybody going to adopt me.

So, I really did start off on the wrong foot, plus all my costumes were a total disaster. In fact, for quite a while I thought that I shouldn't have taken the job, that it wasn't turning out to my advantage at all. But strangely enough, the Costa Cons clicked with the viewers, and became hugely popular. Rather to the surprise of both Stephanie and me, I think. And, of course, it brought us quite a bit of street cred.

One way or another, going into *Bad Girls* turned out to be one of my rare good career decisions.

3

—

Out of the Frying Pan, Into the Fire

When I was trying to learn my trade, training to be a dancer, going to singing lessons, or watching West End actors at work. It had never occurred to me that really what I should have been doing was trying to learn how to swallow live animals and disgusting globules of gunk, how to jump out of a helicopter or stay underwater just about long enough to drown. And also, of course, how to withstand brutish psychological manipulation.

But the profession has changed. Drama schools should add classes on how to eat live frogs and not throw up, and how to learn to sleep with rodents and insects crawling all over you. Because, actually, if you make any sort of success of your career, and attain even a smidgen of celebrity, therein will lie your greatest hope of ever earning any real money – not performing Shakespeare.

Some pretty big-name thespians have succumbed over the years, like Nigel Havers, Stephanie Powers, Larry Lamb, George Hamilton, Britt Ekland, Linda Robson, and John

Barrymore, all of whom have been in *I'm a Celebrity Get Me Out Of Here*. And as I write, Stephen Fry and Celia Imrie have just gone into a celebrity version of *Traitors*. Indeed, I fear that in the not-too-distant future even our world-famous soaps, including *Coronation Street*, already devastated by nose-diving ratings as young people migrate away from TV towards the allure of the internet, will no longer be offering actors substantially attractive salaries, or at the very least some degree of financial security. Already all the soaps are drastically cutting both the size of their casts and the size of the pay packets of those remaining.

The age of the reality show was in its infancy when I left *Coronation Street* in 2001. The soaps were still flourishing, and in the early days I think there was a certain naivety about this precocious new television genus.

I was certainly guilty of naivety when I agreed to go into Gordon Ramsay's *Hell's Kitchen*. In the beginning, I was really delighted to be asked because, not being a very good cook, I thought, my goodness, I'm going to be taught how to cook by a top chef and I'm going to be paid for doing it. I was truly, truly pleased. However, it was going to turn out to be yet another of my extraordinarily bad career decisions. Although this time perhaps not entirely my fault.

I had no idea that I would be driven to the point where I would take a swipe at Ramsay on national television. Nor that, more than 20 years later, a clip of that footage would remain on YouTube and, as I write, has apparently attracted 16.2 million views. Unbelievable!

Back in 2004, *Big Brother* had already emerged, of course, and is often credited, probably correctly, with being the programme that changed TV forever. But it had originally been very much presented as a social experiment, without a celebrity element, and *Big Brother* is surprisingly honest. If you go into it, as I did many years later, you know exactly what you are getting into.

Hell's Kitchen was different. The whole thing was a pretence, except possibly the title – but I for one, assumed that was just a snappy way of drawing in potential audiences. I was taken totally by surprise by what actually happened. And I wasn't the only one.

I am quite certain that all the contestants tried to take *Hell's Kitchen* seriously at first, to take it absolutely at face value. We were each asked to prepare a signature dish, and I was determined to do my best. I knew I was never going to be a great cook at my age, but I thought at least I might be able to learn the fundamentals. I even got the young chef from our local pub to spend a couple of days with us to give me a bit of a crash course in the basics of restaurant cooking.

I found out later that Edwina Curry, the former Conservative government minister, had gone to the lengths of cooking in a pub to prepare for the show.

There's no doubt that when I accepted the job, I hadn't realised at all what was going to happen. I think all the participants were quite innocent of what is now pretty much accepted to be the purpose of an awful lot of reality shows. I didn't realise until the very last moment that we were going to be locked away from the world. I probably should have done but I didn't. I just thought I was going to go in every day, then there'd be cooking, and eventually, hopefully, we'd all manage to prepare something that might just be good enough to present on camera.

I had no idea that we were going to be shut up, removed from real life, and in effect punished at every opportunity. And by the time I did realise it, I'd signed the contract and was already committed. I am dyslexic and have always relied on someone else, mainly my agent, to read the small print. In any case, again looking back, I did not see the danger lurking ahead.

We all knew the show was a vehicle for Gordon Ramsay, but not that he was going to take every opportunity to insult and humiliate us. I don't think any of the participants, nor the viewers, expected it, which probably sounds crazy now, but this was 21 years ago.

Naturally, Ramsay indulged in a great deal of his trademark shouting throughout. There was a definite intent to raise the temperature of people's emotions to boiling point. And Ramsay himself often seemed to be out of control. Although I always suspected that might well have been just part of his act.

We participants had no idea what we were letting ourselves in for.

The hours in *Hell's Kitchen* were such that you quite simply worked the whole time. Even now, that is unlike most other reality shows, because it wasn't just a matter of being on camera; you really were working in that kitchen, working hard, for 15 or 16 hours a day, as well as doing interviews to camera and so on. You didn't have a minute to sit down and recuperate. Which, of course, was the intention.

Then there was the constant psychological warfare. There were some extremely disturbing incidents, notably when Ramsay was showing us how to kill a lobster. Now, I had no desire to do that, and why should I? I do believe we should all take responsibility for what we eat. I eat both meat and fish, and I'm not known for being faint-hearted. But neither was I a professional cook, and I didn't know how to kill a lobster. More than anything I was afraid of not doing the job properly.

The lovely Jennifer Ellison – who ultimately won the show, rather against the odds in my opinion – also refused. But Ramsay grabbed hold of my hand, pushed this horrible spike thing in it, and then forced my hand down so that the spike thrust into the head of the lobster. I will never forget the sound it made. I hadn't expected him to do anything like that. But it did give me a sort of whiff of what might be to come. And it's pretty much put me off eating lobsters ever since.

Ramsay was totally blasé and unfeeling about it. He told me I was being stupid. Actually, I'm pretty sure he told me I was being a stupid actress. He liked to call me a stupid actress.

"Don't be squeamish." he said. "This is what cooking is about."

Which was absolute hypocrisy, of course. If you hire a professional to clean your windows, surely you hire a professional to kill creatures that you're going to eat. I am not squeamish. The overriding reason I didn't want to kill that lobster was because I was afraid I'd balls it up.

Initially, all participants were divided into partnerships. I was with Olympian Dwain Chambers, one of the fastest European sprinters in the history of athletics.

Our first task was to cook a risotto at speed. So, as a sprinter and an actor used to soap schedules, we dashed at it big time. And we thought we'd cooked a rather good risotto when we presented it to Gordon. But he gave it one look, and then he just tipped it straight in the bin. Looking back, he was probably right, at that point. But then I expected to be shown where we had gone wrong. Isn't that how it should have worked? I'd expected that somebody would be coming to show us how to do these things properly. That never happened.

Instead, we were just given huge books with the recipes in them. Which seemed to be equally huge.

Now, I am dyslexic, so I was in serious trouble. I couldn't even begin to read these things, which came complete with complicated columns of weights and measurements. I'm afraid I started to panic, just as I had at school as a child with undiagnosed dyslexia when I'd realised I couldn't sort out words and numbers the way the other children could.

Dwain wasn't much better. We acted as if we were managing, but probably neither of us were coping. It all went from bad to worse. I would just stand around doing nothing because I couldn't begin to sort out these great long recipes. Meanwhile, something happened with Dwain, and I never knew quite what.

One morning we were informed that we had to go for a run very early, before we started work in the kitchen. Before dawn, it seemed to me! This was to be a proper run, of course, largely because of Dwain being on the show, and also because running was Ramsay's hobby. But ultimately, Dwain ran right out of the building never to be seen again, and the 'proper' run never happened.

Dwain didn't talk to me or anybody else as far as I know, about his feelings or whatever was going on. There is little doubt that he was unhappy with Ramsay's oppressive behaviour, because so were most of us. But I never knew in any detail what happened. Dwain just went. If only he'd told me he was going, I might have sought out some running shoes and gone with him...

Instead, I kept blundering on. Indeed, there was a period when Ramsay and I seemed to get on quite well. I'd sort of befriended him and talked to him about Wellington in Somerset, where Hilary and I have a house and where his brother lived.

Then he developed an awful cold and lost his voice, and I felt quite sorry for him. He had trouble calling out the orders, so I offered to do it for him. Of course, I wasn't much good at it, because of my dyslexia, but I think he did warm to me a little over that incident.

Gradually, however, I began to find more and more aspects of the show disturbing. We had loads and loads of washing up to do all the time and there were people there doing it with us. One of the first slightly off things I noticed were that these people, who were supposed be regular staff doing dishes and scrubbing pans, all had ear pieces in their ears and, I'm sure, were also fitted with mikes. Now, why would this be, I wondered?

Then Ramsay would start screaming for bread when everybody in the restaurant had finished eating. Just to make a scene, I suppose, because you don't scream for bread at the end of a meal, do you?

I reckoned they must almost certainly be coordinating something which would mean trouble for somebody. I'd done television for too long not to notice technical things, and that was when my ears began to prick up.

At first, Ramsay was always having rows with Abi Titmus, the former girlfriend of TV presenter John Leslie, once a nurse and then a glamour model. But it never seemed quite genuine to me. After a while, though, she seemed to become a favourite, along with the comedian Al Murray.

You couldn't talk about anything that was going on because everything was recorded. Belinda Carlisle, an extremely talented singer and songwriter, and I tried to write notes to each other. But the camera zoomed in.

I didn't help myself, of course, because I was foolish enough to stay up drinking with James Dreyfus, who is not only a very talented actor, primarily in comedy, but also great company. James and I got on rather too well. We tended not to be able to go to bed because it was all so fretful, and one night we sat up talking, laughing, and drinking until the birds were coughing at the window and dawn was breaking. This was a really stupid thing to do. From that point of view, I have to take responsibility for a certain degree of my own exhaustion. I did adore being with James though.

There were other moments of pure joy. I ended up sleeping

with Matt Goss, once the heart-throb lead singer of Bros and still a top international performer. Okay, not in the same bed, but right next to him. Amazing! We couldn't stop laughing. We were in a room which was a kind of dorm with partitions, then a partition was taken down and I found myself sleeping with Matt. Well, more or less…

Meanwhile, Edwina Curry and I became friends. I seem to specialise in unlikely friendships in reality TV shows. Years later, I would make friends with Ann Widdecombe in *Big Brother*.

For me, one of the worst moments in *Hell's Kitchen* was when Ramsey suddenly launched into an outburst against Edwina. He was vicious. He completely flew at her. It was really foul. She did something that annoyed him, just a cooking thing, but anything could set Ramsay off, when, referring to the affair she'd admitted having with John Major, Ramsay yelled: "One minute you're shagging the prime minister, and now you're trying to shag me from behind."

It was just unpleasant nonsense, of course, but quite upsetting at the time and within that environment.

My feelings for Gordon Ramsay are much the same as the ones I have towards Donald Trump. Neither of them behave like human beings, and they are both bullies. I can't stand bullies. And so, consequently, anybody who shouts and screams and swears and stamps their feet, is an Achilles' heel to me.

There was quite a sequence of incidents leading up to my taking a swipe at him. For example, the whole point of the show was supposed to be that you cooked what you were asked to cook, then you presented it to Ramsay who gave his verdict on it. We were asked to cook soufflés and, it has to be said, my first attempt was not brilliant.

So, when I went up to the pass – the area where food is passed out from the kitchen for waiters to serve in the restaurant – Ramsey was not best pleased. Mark Sergeant, this young chef who was working along with Angela Hartnett as a team leader and sort of second-in-command to Ramsay, led me off out of camera shot. Then he made my soufflé for me. He put it in the oven and, unsurprisingly, unlike my effort, it came up just like a soufflé. He then told me to take it to Gordon Ramsay at the pass, who praised me and told me how much better it was.

Obviously, Ramsay was implying that I had cooked the soufflé, more than implying in fact, and I didn't like that. There were people on the show who wanted one day to maybe get a restaurant and really cook and were all a great deal better than me. It wasn't fair, and I said so.

I said, "Look, I can't go on TV and have somebody cooking for me, for a dish being made to look as if I've cooked it when I haven't. I can't just let this happen and be seen to cheat. I can't do that."

The next thing I know, some sort of psychologist is seeking me out and seems to suggest that I am clearly having a kind of breakdown.

I said: "No, this is simple. This is not a mental breakdown. Nothing is impairing my judgment. Somebody cooked something for me and presented it as something that I had done. Do they intend to go on doing this? If they do, as a professional, and as I am under contract, I will do whatever they say, but somebody at producer level has to speak to me about it and formally instruct me to do it. I'm not just going to go along with cheating at the bequest of a cook."

Well, of course, this blew up – please forgive the pun – and became known as soufflé-gate.

I should point out that I was not alone in what was happening. Quite a lot of the people in the show were ill at ease and, in some cases, quite distressed. There were tranquilisers flying around all over the place. And there were a lot of people involved in psychological conversations.

As far as I was concerned, the interpretation of all the alleged mental health professionals involved in the show was that my saying 'I wasn't going to cheat on the say-so of a cook' was a clear indication that I was having a breakdown. I did tell them straight away that it might be better if I just left, but that didn't seem to be what they wanted. Not then, anyway.

I was still functioning okay, but it was the start of me putting my foot down a bit. Everybody was pissed off. Everybody had trouble of some sort. Everybody was exhausted. At the end of the live show, you had to clean the kitchens, then you were often called to do *Big Brothe*-style on-air interviews.

Another pretty nasty incident further pushed me towards breaking point. There was a cold room where all the vegetables were stored, and it was freezing. The vegetables were kept in big heavy crates, often on high shelves. And at one point there was a water leak in the room, so the floor had frozen over and turned to ice. We reported it several times, but nothing was done.

I'd been told to go and fetch the sprouts, and sure enough they were high up. And there were rather a lot of them. I stretched up for the crate, but as I tried to turn to go back into the kitchen, I just went flying on the icy floor – all of which must have been on camera, but they chose never to show it. I managed to struggle to my feet and went limping through the door into an adjoining room where Ramsay was doing interviews with people about their alleged special signature dish.

He didn't look best pleased to be interrupted, but then he called me over in his usual charming way. I was in pain and already angry because what had just happened had been so dangerous.

Ramsay had absolutely no idea just how angry I was. He started to be bloody rude to me. And I wasn't in the mood to take it. I wasn't even sure how badly I'd hurt myself.

I had a bit of a go back at him and he asked me if it made me feel better to show off.

"I'm not fucking showing off," I told him, growing even angrier.

And that's when I took a swipe at him.

"Don't be stupid," he said. But that didn't stop me.

And I have to say, I have never seen a face that was asking more to be slapped. Except perhaps Donald Trump's.

I hit out. And there was a lot more film that was never shown. Ramsay started yelling for security. Ridiculous, really, a fit young man over six foot tall and there was I, a 5ft 4ins tall woman of 69 years.

At first, I just carried on like everyone else and began to get ready for the show that night. We were supposed to do a Caesar salad. But I'm afraid my irritation and sense of injustice were beginning to overcome me. I grabbed hold of a bottle of tomato sauce and sprayed it all over the salad.

Angela and Mark had had enough of me, one way or another by then, I think.

And I did behave a bit crazily, but I was not going to be bullied like that by anybody. Which is how, more than half a century earlier, I got expelled from two schools – more on that later. I have never liked injustice, and I have never liked bullies.

Eventually, this very formally dressed man wearing a suit appeared, and said in a heavy French accent, "I am a doctor, and I want you to come with me."

I thought to myself, this is real; this is happening. I'm now being taken away by a doctor. Then I thought, oh no, I'm not.

So I shot off set and slammed the door in his face!

It had become obvious, though, that I wasn't going to be able to stay on the show for much longer. Not least because I obviously couldn't contain myself when I was in Gordon Ramsay's presence. I didn't trust myself. And ultimately, by mutual agreement, I left early the following day.

4

—

A Trip to India

Some years later I agreed to take part in an excellent and
quite important reality show, *The Real Marigold Hotel* –
inspired by the wonderful film, *The Best Exotic Marigold
Hotel*, which features a group of British pensioners, portrayed
by a star-studded cast led by Judi Dench and Maggie Smith,
who move to a somewhat dilapidated retirement hotel in India. *Real Marigold*, which in certain respects could reasonably
be regarded as a serious documentary series, took celebrities to
India to see if they would ever consider retiring there.

I was in the second season along with Lionel Blair – who I
had first worked with when I was a teenaged dancer – Sheila
Ferguson, Rustie Lee, Miriam Stoppard, Bill Oddie, Paul
Nicholas, and Denis Taylor. We were transported to Kerala,
in Southern India, and were taken on various excursions and
adventures, none of which appealed to me very much. Indeed,
I'm afraid I most certainly was not one of those who fell in love
with India.

From the beginning, everybody else seemed so excited to be
going there. I'm afraid it was just a job for me. But I thought,
come on, maybe you will love it too. However, I didn't. Not at all.

For a start, there was all this business about 'finding yourself' in India. I never got it. Did it mean that I hadn't found myself before? I seemed to be much the same person. And I am most certainly not going to be retiring there. In the unlikely event that I ever retire. I did not enjoy my Indian experience at all. I just didn't fit in it. I thought I was going to be all right there. And I did have a hell of a lot of laughs. But it wasn't for me.

As soon as we got to this big house we were staying in, there was a bit of a problem. Because, as anybody who was watching will know, we were all allocated rooms, but one bright person said, "No, let's draw them out of a hat."

So we did, and then a certain member of the cast, again anybody who has watched the show will know it was Sheila Ferguson, decided that she wasn't going to put up with that because she didn't like the room she'd drawn. She simply ignored the draw and took the room she wanted.

Now this caused a certain amount of resentment. It was, however, agreed that Lionel and I would remain on the ground floor, because we were the oldest. Which also came with its own problems. Streets in India are not like our streets. They are full of strange movement at night. I had an extremely large room with a lot of windows, all of which I absolutely had to keep shut with the blinds drawn. My ventilation was just one very noisy fan. Some of the rooms were rather lovely. Mine most certainly was not. And I found it quite scary. Even with the blinds drawn I could see all these moving shadows outside the windows. I had no idea what was going on.

Of course, Lionel and I went back a very long way, to the 1950s, and it was such a joy to have him there. Very comforting. He was so enthusiastic; at the drop of a hat he'd do almost anything that was asked of him. At one point, he was terribly disappointed because he'd ridden an elephant and they decided to cut the scene out. It had dawned on the production team that it's not the done thing to ride around on elephants anymore. But Lionel was really upset.

Neither did they show a moment that was probably the highlight of the whole trip for me. I went to this massive antique shop, a quite extraordinary place, where they had the most remarkable things. Great Indian carvings, all manner of treasures from China. It just had everything. The antiques were not only expensive but truly beautiful, only unfortunately almost all far too big to take on an airplane. However, I spied a relatively small blue and white vase, which I reckoned was at least a couple of centuries old and reminded me of old Delf china. I asked if it was for sale. The owner of the shop said it was, but it was damaged, the top of the vase having broken off. I said that was fine, it was just what I wanted. I seem to have a penchant for buying damaged goods, and from the moment I saw it I was determined that this vase should come to live with me. I could afford it too. It cost just a few pounds and now has a permanent home in the sitting room of our London flat.

Apart from Lionel, the person I bonded with most was probably Bill Oddie. I just loved his company. And he made me laugh too much. But he didn't find it easy either. Once they drove him, I don't know how many miles, to do this item on exotic birds, but it didn't quite work out. Not only did the exotic birds fail to turn up, but there were no birds at all. And the journey alone took about twelve hours, which seemed about par for the course on this trip. Understandably, Bill was not best pleased when he eventually returned.

There was another occasion when people went on an 18-hour train journey. These are among the joys of reality shows that viewers don't see.

Even in the evenings when we were having our dinner, we'd

still have our microphones on, so you're still working. Then when they were eventually taken off, somebody would tell us that we were to be collected at 4am the following morning.

Now that leads to the truth about reality shows – and in spite of its credible side, *Marigold* was still a reality show – which is that they never tell you what they're going to put you through. That's the real reality. It all sounds so wonderful, then when you get going, in the main, it isn't wonderful at all. Whatever they say, the hours that you work are always horrendous, and, in India, there were so many things that went wrong for me, as usual.

I managed to escape that train journey, thankfully, because apparently it was dreadful. I think I was in bed with Jenni Murray at the time. I had loaded podcasts of things like the Archers and Woman's Hour onto my iPad, and they came to my rescue throughout the trip, particularly on the occasions when I was unwell. Unfortunately, I was dogged by a variety of ailments during my stay in Kerala, including a perilous drop in blood pressure, my heart missing beats, the obligatory sub continental sickness bug, and a chest infection.

I was, however, still unable to escape all of the many interminable car journeys along quite terrifying roads, which for me were among the most ghastly aspects of India. To make matters worse we had a totally mad driver who drove at ridiculously high speeds, even by Indian standards. There seemed to be no form of traffic signals, speed regulation, or anything like that – or if there was he ignored them. Rusty Lee was usually in the same car as me and she shrieked the entire time.

I was ill for the first time within just a few days. We did something called laughing yoga every morning at seven o'clock, which didn't really turn me on. Actually, I couldn't find anything to laugh about. Bill Oddie refused to join in. Of course, he was quite right. He stood up on the balcony and taunted us. And I didn't blame him at all.

Unfortunately, I had completely forgotten that I suffer from a form of vertigo which can sometimes be triggered if I lie absolutely flat. I just didn't think and lay down flat on the floor.

Everything was all right at first, but when I tried to move, to get up off the floor to do the next exercise, I realised the whole of India was spinning at enormous speed. I couldn't stand up. I called out to the rest of our group, who seemed to be doing it very nicely, but they thought I was being funny. I wasn't being funny.

Eventually, everybody realised that I was in big trouble. I more or less passed out. I was then carried off to my room, doctors came rushing, and I ended up being taken to hospital to be checked over. The hospital was pretty primitive. I thought, if I'm not ill already, I'm sure to catch something in here. Actually, all was well, and I survived! But I was already learning that India is a country of extremes, the bad is very bad, and the good is very good.

Later in the proceedings, we were taken to this amazingly smart private clinic to be checked out on camera. It was a top-notch, seven-star place, with wonderful facilities. We each had everything examined: hearts, lungs, backs, teeth, noses, everything. Because of my vertigo problem it was decided that a doctor, who was something of an expert in it, would perform an Epley Manoeuvre on me. This is a procedure which involves quite dramatically twisting and suddenly flicking the head, in order to cause crystals, which can form in the inner ear and trigger vertigo, to dissolve.

I thought the doctor did a really good job, I could almost instantly feel something begin to happen inside my head. But the crew somehow missed getting it on camera. So they asked him to do it again. He protested that he really shouldn't, that it could be dangerous for me to have it done again. So they asked him to pretend to do it. Well, you can't pretend to do an Epley Manoeuvre.

But this was television. so I let the doctor do it again, and I can tell you, I felt like shit after he'd finished.

Talking of shit, one of my most embarrassing moments ever occurred shortly after this, in the same clinic. We were asked to give pee and poo samples. Well, I just about managed the pee sample okay. But then, and I think my poor whizzing head was still far from right, and I wasn't thinking straight, I looked at the container I'd been given to put poo in, and just couldn't work out what to do with it. Eventually, I decided I was probably supposed to put my poo on the top of the container, so I made what I can only describe as a little miniature sand pie. I smoothed it down neatly, and I was rather proud of it. Then I carried my sample back into the room where the medical staff were waiting, holding it out in front of me.

You have never seen so many doctors and nurses flee to the far corners of a room.

Finally, a thoroughly startled looking nurse grabbed me and showed me what I should have done, which involved using a little dipper thing to pick up a tiny bit of poo which you deposit in the container before putting the top on it. Not fill it to the top with poo. All of which should have been obvious to me in the first place, of course.

The rest of the cast fell apart. They couldn't stop laughing. But I really was embarrassed. Later, Rusty Lee sent me a picture of one of these containers as a memento. Thank you, Rusty.

A saving grace of Marigold was that there were some great people, whom I really liked and respected, on the show. Miriam Stoppard was very much one of those. She's a joy. She's funny, witty, delightful, and completely non-complaining. She just gets on with it.

Miriam and I went to an Indian wedding together, which was something of a mixed experience. I did enjoy going to buy fabric for a sari, but unfortunately, I am not sari-shaped, so I fear I looked like a Christmas cracker in mine. Then we had the embarrassment of going to the hairdressers with the bride. They shampooed my hair and massaged my head so many times I thought my ears were going to fall off. Maybe they thought this English person needed that. I certainly needed something, but possibly not the big hair the hairdresser fashioned for me. I ended up sitting next to the bride in front of the mirror. She was so beautiful, with this wonderful skin and gorgeous black shiny hair, and there was I, this red-faced creature looking like something out of Spitting Image.

Later, at the wedding, Miriam and I were asked, quite late in a long day, if we would do some Indian dancing quite late in a long day, and we said yes, because we both really thought we could do it. The cameras rolled, there we were dancing with these fit young men, and it was all extremely energetic. We just about managed to get to the end of it all, but then we pretty much collapsed. We could barely breathe.

Another outing not long after that was to an original old Indian wash house, which I was sure I would find extremely interesting – and I sort of did, but I was not prepared for what happened there. We were all told to take something with us that we wanted to wash. We didn't really have facilities to wash anything at our house, so I was pleased about that, and I had a couple of Armani shirts that needed washing so I took them. But what did they do with them? Why, they smashed them on this stone. Repeatedly. It's probably a tribute to Armani that my shirts survived – if only just.

An awful lot of health things went on in India, yet, on the other hand, with the hours we kept and everything else that was happening, it seemed they may be trying to kill us. So, for me, it just didn't all seem to go together. In more ways than one.

There is a form of medicine prevalent in India called Ayurveda, which claims to be one of the oldest healthcare systems in the world and allegedly focuses on maintaining a balance between the mind, body, and spirit. I'm afraid I just didn't take to it. It seemed to me that mostly what the Ayurveda therapists wanted to do was to sell you all their oils, potions, herbal medicines, and so on. And later, after returning home, I learned that several Ayurvedic preparations have been found to contain lead, mercury, and arsenic – substances which can be harmful to humans.

Therapy of one sort or another plays a big part in Indian life. On another occasion, we were taken to meet a sort of guru who seemed like 1,000 years old. He could allegedly see into the future, and we were told that all the Indian government people had appointments with him so that they could take instructions from him and be guided in the right direction.

He was supposed to be this man of great learning, and we had to sit down on the floor before him. He came to me and said, "I know what you do. I know what you do."

Then he said something I couldn't quite catch, but I thought I got the gist.

I said, "Yes, I'm an actress."

He said, "Yes, you are in *Blue Peter.*"

I said, "No, not *Blue Peter. Coronation Street? Bad Girls?* Not *Blue Peter.* "

He just repeated it, "You are in *Blue Peter.*"

This went on for some time until I realised he was saying, "You are in Jupiter." He meant Jupiter was my planet, it seemed.

It was a complete cock-up and I got the giggles, naturally. And then, amidst all this deep hallowed stuff, his mobile phone, which he'd been sitting on, rang. Upon which he began a long conversation, pretty obviously about money or business of some sort. I thought, I can't believe this is happening. We were there all afternoon. I can't describe it really. After the *Blue Peter* incident, I didn't follow a lot of what he said. But when we went outside, the crew had to interview us, and I was asked how I'd found this revered holy man.

I'm afraid I said, "Well, frankly, I'd rather go to Russell Grant." That didn't go down at all well.

I had a number of unfortunate misunderstandings of this sort. At the very beginning, travelling from the airport with Lionel, as an old betting woman, I got rather excited when I thought the driver had pointed out a betting shop to Lionel. However, when I made further enquiries about this, it seemed I'd got it completely wrong, and that Lionel had been asking about having some clothes made, which I hadn't heard, and the driver had been pointing out a tailor, and had said "get in shop, get in shop".

Packs of dogs roam the streets in India, of course, and another thing I didn't like is the way animals are treated there. But one of the nicest things that happened was finding the puppy we half-adopted.

We called him Goldie. I used to order chicken for my dinner every night and feed most of it to him. He was a lovely little creature. He was always trying to jump into my bag, which I found touching and possibly a bit symbolic. We all agreed we couldn't just leave him on the street when we went home. But even though it was talked about, we knew we couldn't take him back to the UK. The journey alone would probably have killed him.

We did do our best for him though. We took him to a vet where he was given all the necessary injections, and everything was done for him to stay as healthy as possible for as long as possible. Then we found a man who looked after street dogs and he agreed to take Goldie in. I stayed in touch with the man for quite a long time, and a year or so later he even sent me pictures of a healthy-looking, fully-grown Goldie.

God knows what happened in the end, but hopefully Goldie had a better chance of a reasonable doggie life than most street dogs.

All in all, although I thought I knew what to expect, India was a bit of a shock to me. Kerala is meant to be beautiful, but the piles of rubbish that are everywhere are not beautiful. I kept thinking, why doesn't somebody clear it up? Not that I'm a particularly tidy person, but the trouble is that India is very crowded and some parts of the country don't have the best infrastructure.

Regarding finding myself, I certainly did find myself constantly being ill. It wasn't the food. We had a brilliant chef. He was absolutely astonishing. Every morning he made these completely flat omelettes, probably just one egg, which were delicious. We had that and fruit for breakfast. All the meals were excellent, and very healthy. I don't remember ever having a curry. The good news was that I lost a lot of weight while I was there.

There were so many things about India I really didn't like. We were taken by one of our drivers to be fed at his home. A virtual banquet was laid out for us, but I was quite astonished and horrified that the women, the wives, grandmothers, and family, who had prepared all that food, were not allowed to sit down with us. Only the men sat with us at the table. The women had to stand outside in the corridor.

There were good things, of course. I was taken to this incredible retirement home where families buy an apartment within the complex, which is then there for all of them, and is passed on down the generations. Sometimes family members as young as 50, and still working, move in. It was a real community which had everything – swimming pools, restaurants, shops – and was very beautiful.

There was, however, a moment during our visit when I thought the crew might be planning to leave me there as some sort of terrible reality TV joke. Now, if I absolutely had to retire to India this would have been the one place I experienced that I could imagine just about tolerating. But not by choice. No way. I couldn't wait to get home!

5

—

Stockholm Syndrome

Being a glutton for punishment, in 2018, I agreed to take part in *Big Brother*, the mother and father of all reality shows. The huge amount of money on offer had absolutely nothing to do with my decision. Obviously.

My partner Hilary – known primarily as Hil going forward – issued a warning before I entered the house: don't mention Harvey Weinstein, don't lose your temper and, above all, don't misgender India Willoughby.

Yet, inadvertently, I fear I did all three.

As far as India is concerned, I scarcely understood what misgendering meant then. It may only have been seven years ago, but the whole trans debate was a long way from developing into what it is today. And even now I do struggle with misgendering people, especially when they've confided in you about their operations or their children, and if it's a woman you've known previously as a man. It's so easy to slip up – at my age, you can slip up over anything. And indeed I said "he" at one point, which caused an avalanche of emotional distress from India, as anybody watching would have witnessed. I meant no harm, There was never any intent to cause offence.

And I do believe that at the time the term "misgender" was nothing like as widely understood as it is now, I certainly didn't realise then why it was so consequential. Now, I understand better.

Although I do struggle still with "dead-naming." If people discuss their previous lives, when their gender was different and you inadvertently refer to that, it's easy to err.

I did not persist in misgendering India, that wasn't how it was at all, and I never intended to insult or even upset her.

She was, however, constantly temperamental and gave a prima donna performance throughout. She frequently appeared to be very overwrought.

One day, for reasons unbeknown to the rest of us, she spent hours crying under a faux fur rug in the garden. She likes attention and I think a lot of it was to get her camera time, which she certainly succeeded in doing. Although, later, it seemed that tactic may have backfired…

I did extend the hand of friendship. On camera, I told her, "Please, come back into the circle – none of us want this."

But the last thing India wanted was friendship.

Another housemate, Ashley James, previously best known for *Made In Chelsea*, brought her back into the kitchen and tried to be nice to her, but India was still being tricky.

So I'm afraid I said, "She's been playing the victim all day, It's probably a strategy, and I'm not going along with it."

However, I did feel sorry for India, and - even after she had screamed at me at the top of her voice: "I am a real woman".- I apologised for misgendering her. Quite genuinely because I hadn't done it intentionally and I told her so.

She said: "An apology's not enough."

So I said, 'What do you want me to do, cut my head off, then?"

People were actually very kind to India. And if her behaviour was some kind of a strategy, it certainly didn't work, as she was the first housemate to be voted off.

I would always support the right of any person, whatever their gender or sexuality, to be who they are and live how they want and need to live. With my background, it would be impossible for me to do or think anything otherwise. I know what it is like to feel as if you must live in the shadows. In my case, to believe deep inside that, because of who and what you are, you are somehow a shameful human being.

I would never ever be an enemy to the trans community. Rather, I would always be a friend. As I have been in the past. But that community can only be harmed by being publicly represented by someone like India Willoughby.

She may scream out at every opportunity that she is a real woman, but she sure ain't a real lady.

As for Harvey Weinstein, I fear that almost as soon as I walked into the house, I entered into a discussion about Weinstein. At the time, the story of his treatment of women, some very young women, was headline news, and everyone had an opinion. He is, of course, a dreadful man. And, don't misunderstand me, I think he absolutely deserves to be in jail and should remain there for a very long time. But I was a bit ambivalent about certain aspects of the case at the time. And I'm afraid I said so on television, within about five minutes of arriving in the *Big Brother* house.

Then we come to me losing my temper with Courtney Act, stage name of Shane Jenek, the Australian drag act and singer. This was later in the show. A little surprisingly, some would say, I lasted quite a long time before I lost my temper.

I rather liked Courtney to start with, but as time passed, I began to change my mind. He was actually an insidious bully and, as I've said before, I can't bear bullies. He enjoyed taking the piss out of people and making them feel uncomfortable.

My big row with Courtney stemmed from an incident with Ann Widdecombe, the former politician and TV pundit, who has very strong religious convictions. We'd been singing carols and Courtney had deliberately changed the words of one of them in a way that would be offensive to a lot of people, and certainly to Ann.

Now, in the past, mostly because of her religious convictions, Ann has repeatedly voted against gay rights legislation, something which clearly infuriated Courtney Act, and most certainly disappoints me. But I still felt that she and her views should be treated with respect. Unfortunately, I ended up in an angry confrontation with Courtney over it all. Wayne Sleep, my old friend and probably my favourite housemate, was involved and was supportive of me.

But I did ultimately lose my temper and shout at Courtney. I'd pointed out that I was married to a woman, and he turned this around to insinuate that I wasn't interested in the problems others faced. I think he said something like: "You're all right, so it doesn't matter about the rest of us.":

Then he started giving me a lecture on gay rights. This was a mistake. My shouting grew louder.

What I was trying to say, but I never got it out properly, was that considering how far we have all come, what you're complaining about now, Courtney, is not comparable. It certainly still is in some other countries, but not in this country. My God, if you'd been around in the early days like me, and seen so many gay men commit suicide and almost no homosexual people be able to live a life without fear, that is the comparison I always have in the back of my mind. I don't need anybody to inform me about homosexuality or what it means, or what it's like to live with, or what it's like to be afraid of being outed, or what it's like to be known and be afraid of being outed. I don't need teaching by a thirty-something man. You don't even know what everybody's been through to get us this far. Wayne and I were there when all that was happening 50-odd years ago and more. You weren't born, so who are you to be preaching to me about it?

Regrettably, I lost my temper, always a mistake, and failed dismally to articulate. I didn't say any of this the way I wanted to, and was subsequently trolled online.

Courtney, of course, went on to win *Big Brother* and, extraordinarily enough, Ann Widdecombe was runner up – which I think speaks a lot for this country.

Meanwhile, I made it to the penultimate episode before being voted off which, given the circumstances, I considered also to be rather extraordinary. Certainly, the experience was not a complete disaster.

I have, however, never been so terrified as during the two weeks or so before I went into *Big Brother*. I have talked to other housemates and they'd all felt much the same way. I've no idea whether it's because you fear you are going to be completely out of control of yourself, or because you simply don't know what's going to happen. I think it's possibly the unknown that is the most frightening. But one thing you do know is that as soon as you get in there, your phone is going to be taken off you.

To make things more difficult, I had developed an extremely heavy chest infection, something to which, as a child of the North, I have always been prone. Fellow Northerners will know it as Manchester Chest. I entered the *Big Brother* house in the rain with a terrible cough, and I'm sure, a temperature. I was feeling like death and, to tell the truth, I thought they would probably send me home. They didn't.

There followed several hours of each of us being locked away alone in a room, so you wouldn't know who else was there. Then they proceeded to stick bits of black tape on every branded item that you'd brought with you. Even a hairbrush or an eyebrow pencil. In fact, I'm still, to this day, picking bits of black tape off things.

I was teamed up for the opening task, in front of a studio audience mostly made up of friends, family, and associates of the housemates, with Jess Impiazzi, a young actress whom I really liked. We had to rearrange various bits and pieces of an electrical circuit and get them in the right order, so the whole thing lit up. And we turned out to be a bit of a dream team.

I'm quite good at working out mechanical things, which I think surprised a few people, and Jess, who's a very bright cookie, did all the running around and moving things about at speed. We won and got a free pass, which meant we couldn't be ousted at the first vote.

When later we were taken to our dormitories, I just couldn't stop coughing. I was sleeping next to Rachel Johnson, journalist and sister of Boris. She wasn't best pleased with me, and I can't say I blamed her. This was 2018, and pre-pandemic, of course, because I'm pretty sure that post-Covid they wouldn't have let me through the door in the state I was in.

My ghastly cough persisted and eventually, I think it was a couple of nights later, having coughed myself to sleep, I woke up with men in white coats all around me. I thought, my God, is this a dream? Am I having a terrible nightmare? The men said, "Come with us." I thought, oh, my God, it's real. I'm going to be taken away by men in white coats.

And I was taken away. To the sick bay, little more than a box with no window, where I stayed for two nights. But I have to say, the medical care within *Big Brother* was exceptional. They were so good. I was given steroids, antibiotics, inhalers, all sorts of things, and eventually I started to recover enough to rejoin the show.

Three times I've worked with people on reality shows who were politicians: Edwina in *Hell's Kitchen*, John Prescott in *Celebrity 5 Go Barging*, and Ann. All three, as it happens, had such nice sides to them.

On the night I came back to our dorm after my run-in with Courtney, Ann had put my two rabbits into bed for me and tucked them in. She knew how upset I was.

I did become unexpectedly fond of Ann. We were from entirely different backgrounds and at opposite ends of the political and religious spectrum. So we were far from a natural pairing, yet we became one of sorts. She made me laugh.

For example, when *Big Brother* turned out the lights, Ann would march across the room to turn them back on, only for them to be switched off again before she even got back to her bed. To the amusement of the rest of us, she would do that repeatedly, always with the same result.

Our dormitory was like something out of a silly girls' boarding school. Most of us hugged goodnight, and it was our absolute delight to tease Ann that she was going to be hugged and kissed by everyone. She would scream with terror and bury herself under the bed clothes.

We all had the most enormous sort of fondness for each other. We were so aware of each other's vulnerability. Everybody was very affectionate with everybody.

Ann and I often retreated to bed before the others, who were so much younger. We didn't have radios or any form of entertainment, but I quickly learned that I could ask Ann about almost anything, and she would always have plenty to say. I called it Radio Widdecombe.

One night the two of us spent some time discussing The Jacobite Rebellion. I'm not sure if this was ever broadcast, but it certainly wouldn't have done much for *Big Brother*'s viewing figures. They usually look for naked people jumping on each other. Instead they got two old ladies talking about The Jacobite Rebellion. In depth and at length.

On another occasion, we had a rather good debate about the Repeal of the Corn Laws, whilst sitting up in bed with our night-time drinks – which doubtless made it all the more bizarre.

I was rendered a tad askance, though, to discover that Ann had her own private place upstairs for showering and dressing. The rest of us shared four showers and two lavatories, as far as I remember. You couldn't lock the doors, and after the bell went off in the morning, you had just an hour of hot water and electricity. It was a manic scramble to get ready in the time, especially if you'd washed your hair and needed to dry it.

I have no idea how Ann managed to arrange this, but would assume her agent made it a condition. Of course, as an old chorus girl used to living in digs that made the standard *Big Brother* facilities look like something out of *Dynasty*, it had never occurred to me to try to negotiate any special privileges. Even though I was by far the oldest.

Another housemate I became fond of was singer Shane Lynch of Boyzone. We ended up performing a number together, definitely something to put in the CV, if I had one.

Then there was Rachel. She is the most amazing creature, able to stand on her hands just like that. She has a great figure, wonderful skin and, I might add, wonderful hair. Upon which, Ann, Rachel and I were having a bedtime chat one night, talking about this and that, and I was grumbling about my hair, as I often do, then said, "Most of your family seem to have wonderful hair, Rachel, but what happened to Boris?"

She said, "What do you mean?"

I said, "Well, you know, what happened to Boris' hair."

Rachel just looked blank. I persisted for a bit, then gave up.

Ann and I thought it was hilarious because Rachel clearly just didn't get it that there was anything remotely unusual about Boris' hair.

Apart from that considerable blind spot, she's quite an intellect is our Rachel, and has a great turn of phrase.

Maggie Oliver, the former police officer who blew the whistle on her own force over their handling of the Rochdale child abuse case, was the mother of the group. She even mothered me. When Jess and I arrived with only miniature bottles of shampoo and conditioner, convinced that BB would supply such things which they most certainly did not, Maggie came to our rescue, fully equipped with industrial-sized supplies, which she shared with us.

Wayne and I were teamed up to perform various tasks including racing a toy car, at which we'd thought we'd done rather well but ended up getting horribly beaten by Ann Widdecombe. I had great pleasure, however, in bathing Wayne with my sponge and washing his hair. He was very sweet, and I enjoyed doing it.

The most unpleasant thing was when we had to vote out another housemate because you may well have become friends with them, then you have to tell them to their face why they should go. It is the most unbelievably difficult thing to do. People really got upset doing it. Apart from Ann the politician, of course. She said, "Nonsense, just do it. Let's get on with it.'

Now, *Big Brother* was invented as a serious social experiment in Norway in 1999. Channel 4 took it up in the UK in 2000 with 10 housemates recruited from the public at large. Nobody ever really expected it to become what it did, and it was never planned for it to be any sort of vehicle for celebrities.

It was, of course, at least partially designed to make people behave badly. Much happens in the house that viewers never see, so they don't always understand the housemate's reactions.

But if you compare the way BB is run, and the way you are looked after, to the dreaded *Hell's Kitchen*, there is no comparison.

Big Brother is a wonderful set-up, and so professional. The scale of it backstage, the whole scenario that you never see, is absolutely massive, and everything runs like clockwork. Yes, the producers liked to have you making a fool of yourself and losing your temper, as I so obligingly did, but you always felt that care was being taken. In every respect. Again, totally unlike *Hell's Kitchen*, in 2004 anyway.

Another thing that was extraordinary about *Big Brother*, was what happened after it ended, when we all returned the next day to do a kind of show after the show. When we re-entered the house, we all shared the same experience, I think – a feeling of extreme fondness for the place. It was a weird thing. We were a bit like stray dogs going home again. When we returned to this place, which we had at times all thought so horrendous and terrifying, where we had been shut away from the world with nothing to distract from the constant psychological games being played on us, no television, no radio, no phones – we all felt this enormous affection for it.

I probably shouldn't say this as I am well aware that *Big Brother* is only a television show, but there was an element of Stockholm Syndrome about it – when people who have been taken hostage develop an emotional bond with their captors.

One way and another, *Big Brother* is certainly an extraordinary concept. And its viewing appeal has proved to be just as addictive nearly three decades later as it was back in 2000. I am sure there are many people out there who think that they absolutely don't want to watch it, but then they take a little peek. And once you've looked, it's just so hard to look away.

6

—

A Shock to the System

One way and another, throughout the new millennium I have engaged in more than my share of new experiences and unlikely adventures. I've never been mad about travelling, but in recent years my work has taken me abroad more times than ever before.

There were two quite long trips to places that, particularly at my age, I could not have imagined I would ever visit. There was over a month in India of course, in 2016, for Real Marigold Hotel, and, in 2018, almost a month in Israel, in Tel Aviv, making a TV sitcom called *The Bar Mitzvah*.

We were in Tel Aviv in the autumn. The people were great, the weather was lovely, and the hotel was excellent. I'd previously had no idea just how amazing the beach there was. Everything was beautiful. Indeed, it makes me so terribly sad to think about what is happening now in that part of the world. When we were there I could never have envisioned the death and destruction which lay ahead.

The show tells the story of a gay American couple who take their straight son to Israel for his Bar Mitzvah. It stars comedy actor and drag artist Ilan Peled, a huge star in Israel, with whom

I somewhat bonded. We share a love of antiquities and ancient history, and when I left for home, Ilan gave me a chunk of pavement from Caesarea, the Roman port city to the south of Tel Aviv. For reasons which now escape me – except that it was rather special and very old and supposed to bring good fortune if passed on as a gift – I gave Ilan an antique cross.

"You're giving a Jewish man a cross?" he remarked mildly before, bursting into shrieks of uncontrollable laughter.

The cross had, at my request, been collected from our flat and brought to Tel Aviv by our friend Chris Clarke, who had flown over from the UK for a few days to join me and Hil.

Actually, it should be said here that Chris is more than a friend, he has become family. A quite extraordinary thing happened when, fifteen years or so ago, we were introduced by a mutual friend. Chris almost immediately slotted into our lives as if tailor-made. When not acting as a fight courier, he is also a high-powered businessman running a successful international company, and we do sometimes wonder what he is doing spending so much time with two old ladies. But, my goodness, we have a lot of fun.

Hil and Chris seemed to spend most of his stay in Tel Aviv sitting on the beach together drinking a particularly palatable brand of pink Israeli fizz they'd discovered and getting gently sozzled, while I worked my little 80-something-year-old fingers to the bone.

As ever, there were a number of 4am calls to catch the light and a considerable amount of energetic physical activity including running up and down sand dunes and learning to ride a Segway – something at which, to the surprise of all, I turned out to be rather nifty.

Indeed, as I was to say later on *Lorraine*, only to be bleeped off, I was shit-hot on a Segway! Following that, I was even asked to ride one onto the set of *This Morning*, and did so, if you'll forgive the boast, with considerable aplomb.

To me – and I don't drive a car and was never very good at riding a bike – riding a Segway seems totally natural. It's a kind of electric scooter with no mechanical steering mechanism. You stand on it and steer by leaning. It goes the way your body goes. I clocked that from the minute I got on one, and I reckoned it was very like riding a horse, which I did a lot of as a child. You use your body to get a horse to change legs, and a horse will move the way you move. And that the way you lean, I found, is exactly the same way you navigate a Segway.

There is one scene in *The Bar Mitzvah* in which I appear to ride my Segway down a steep flight of steps. In fact, they brought in a stunt girl to do that, rather to my annoyance, as I was quite sure I could have gone down those steps on a Segway without any trouble at all. It would have been just like riding a horse down a dip. You lean back and let it take you. But they wouldn't let me. And, remembering an incident filming *Carry On Cleo*, when I very nearly did a stunt which ended in a bit of a catastrophe – more on this later – I decided not to argue.

I had a driver and minder assigned to me in Tel Aviv, who was very sweet and spoke very good English, but we did have a little misunderstanding, which still makes me laugh. Just as in India, I was listening to radio and podcasts online, which could be a tad frustrating because the Wi-Fi in our hotel was not the best. So I went down to the car one morning when it had been particularly temperamental, climbed in next to him, and said, "My God, my Wi-Fi is driving me mad today."

And he said, "Oh dear, how long have you been married?"

This may well not be that amusing in print, but nevertheless, it still makes me and the Wi-Fi giggle. Ever since I have taken to quite frequently referring to Hil as my Wi-Fi which we both think sounds suitably less respectable than wife, and rather more like us.

I also travelled to Spain – for *Bad Girls*, with my fellow Costa Con Stephanie Beacham – and later to the Costa Blanca when I joined the hit TV comedy drama *Benidorm* as Psychic Sue, the resident spiritualist. This led to me working again with Sherrie Hewson, another extremely close friend, and very much one of the stars of *Benidorm* in her role as hotel manager Joyce Temple-Savage.

It feels as if I have known Sherrie all my life. One of the first big shows we worked on together was a West End production of *Stepping Out* at the Duke of York Theatre in 1983. I topped the bill as dance teacher Mavis and Sherrie was one of my pupils.

Our paths have crossed professionally regularly over the years, most notably probably when we were in *Coronation Street* together, with Sherrie playing Maureen Holdsworth, wife of Bettabuys boss Reg Holdsworth. We are sometimes mistaken for sisters, regardless of my being old enough to be Sherrie's mother. Upon which I have been known to remark that Sherrie is my illegitimate love child and that Lionel Blair was the father. But that is a joke. Honestly!

We are also occasionally mistaken for each other. It is not unusual for us to be complimented on each other's performances. And we made a pact long ago just to accept the compliment and not to let on.

Après Corrie, and *Benidorm*, we have worked together a number of times, including filming a travel item in Ibiza for *This Morning*, when we were supposed to be investigating the merits of static caravan holidays. We also took over as disc jockeys at one of the island's hottest nightclubs. I'm afraid we were certainly the oldest DJs in town, but we had a ball. As we almost always do when we are together.

However, we were asked to do a similar job for *This Morning*, involving staying in a yurt in The Lake District, the prospect of which, upon arrival, filled us both with total horror. We had been promised a style of camping which was glamorous, luxurious and exotic. What we got was a flapping canvas monstrosity vaguely resembling a run-down Arabian tent, perched on the side of a hill, which was rather more like the side of a mountain, covered in boulders. And the tent was freezing cold.

We asked where the toilet was and were shown a bucket outside! We asked if there was a proper toilet and a shower and were told that there was a toilet block at the bottom of the hill – which could only be reached by staggering down the mountainside strewn with those boulders. Amongst which a large number of sheep lay in wait, looking as if they might ambush us.

So I'm afraid it is possible that we cheated a tad with that one, spending rather less time in our yurt than may have appeared to be the case. In no time at all Sherrie, one of the world's greatest organisers, had arranged for us to move to a gorgeous five-star hotel. If it had been left to me I would probably have stayed shivering in that yurt.

Sherrie is also one of the most generous people I have ever known in show business. And she always seems to know what's going on. Unlike me! I have often felt over the years that she is probably better than most agents. She has on several occasions passed on work to me. As, just once or twice, I have to her.

I love her to bits, and we are in touch nearly every day.

Sometimes, even on a relatively fleeting job, you meet someone with whom you instantly bond. One of those was Henry Blofeld, the former cricket commentator and broadcaster. In *The Baby Boomers' Guide to Growing Old*, a TV series which basically focused on celebrities of a certain age behaving inappropriately. Henry and I had a sort of partnership made in heaven. Unfortunately, or fortunately, we made each other laugh constantly.

On the very first day of filming, Henry was sitting alone on a garden bench, with his back to me, when I arrived. We had never met.

The director said, "Amanda, we don't want this show to be in any way ordinary. We want it to be quite daring. So, when you meet Henry, perhaps you could say something, you know, a bit unusual or challenging to him?"

Of course, I'm the last person you should ever say anything like that to because it leaves me rather too free. So I walked quietly up behind Henry and said, "I suppose a fuck's out of the question?" Upon which we both fell about laughing ridiculously, because we are of a somewhat childish nature, the pair of us.

Now, it has to be said that I'd believed this was a private joke, something to break down barriers. I had no idea that the cameras were rolling and that my somewhat unusual manner of greeting the venerable Henry was going to be seen on national television.

It certainly did set us off on a kind of theme. Every single thing that Henry and I said to one another became a double entendre of some sort. This is not something we were proud of. It just kept falling into place.

One day we were going off to do a gym session with The Green Goddess - Diana Moran - and Henry asked me, "What are we doing? What exactly are we doing, Amanda?'

I said, "We're doing Pilates, Henry."

"Pilates, Pilates. Pull? Pull? Pull who?" he replied.

Something similar, in terms of bonding, but not of quite the same nature, happened with *Celebrity 5 Go Barging*, which was filmed aboard narrow boats travelling along various English canals. This show was unusual in that it was a reality TV show which did not seem to be deliberately encouraging people to make idiots of themselves. One of the joys of this kind of TV is that if you get to spend time with people, many of whom you would not otherwise ever have met. And if you get along, if you bond, it's a real privilege.

My 'Barging' partners were Anita Harris, whom I did know quite well and had worked with before, Michael Buerk, Lord John Prescott, and Shaun Williamson.

We had an awful lot of laughs together. Dancing with John Prescott along a canal towpath was really something. As was listening to his words of wisdom. I remember him saying to me that he believed the trouble with modern politicians in the UK was that they had no history; they had rarely had previous jobs.

"They go off to university and learn to debate, and that's it," said John.

He, of course, had previously been a steward in the Merchant Navy and an amateur boxer not adverse, as we all know, to throwing a punch at anyone silly enough to offend him – most famously the man who threw an egg at him during the 2001 election campaign. Perhaps that was why John and I got on so well. He was quite a man, and I was so very sorry to hear of his death.

Anita Harris and I first met at the BBC in the late 1950s, both of us ambitious youngsters, and we chatted for a while about what our futures might bring. We were excited and full of hope. We never thought that when we eventually were to work together it would be aboard a canal barge!

Anita and I shared a narrow boat, called Elsie, and you couldn't wish for a sweeter shipmate. To begin with I did most of the steering. I took to it like a fish to water, and I really had not expected to, but I absolutely loved it and proved to be quite adept, even in difficult circumstances. Once or twice, we pulled other people's boats out of trouble. You couldn't knock the girls. The girls were doing rather well.

Then we were given a weekend off before starting the second part of our journey on a different canal.

Hil was hiding in Somerset at the time, desperately trying to meet the deadline for her latest book, and I went rushing back to our Covent Garden flat thinking what a joy it would be to get into my own bed, have a lovely rest, and return to Elsie fully refreshed a couple of days later.

Unfortunately, due to circumstances beyond my control, this was not to be. Upon entering the flat, when I tried to switch on the lamp by the front door, nothing happened. It appeared that I had no electricity. So with one hand still on the lamp to my right, I reached with the other into the fuse cupboard on my left, and began to push one of the switches which seemed to be in the wrong position.

The next moment, I was on my way to the ceiling. Or I would have been if I hadn't been stuck at both ends of my arms. I couldn't move my hands. One was attached to the fuse box, and one to the lamp - 240 volts of electricity were surging through me. I had received a huge electric shock.

Eventually, my hands released themselves, most of the skin from the left one remaining on the fuse box, and I fell in a heap on the floor. Amazingly, I was both alive and conscious, if only barely so. But I still couldn't move. Luckily, I had my phone on me. I called a neighbour who rushed to the rescue and promptly dialled 999.

I'm unsure whether or not my hair was standing on end, but it felt as if it was. I lost control of my bladder, a sure sign of the severity of what had happened. I was a total wreck.

Then five of the most gorgeous paramedics you've ever seen arrived. A shock of that magnitude can cause lasting damage, so they whisked me off to University College Hospital, just a few minutes away. Why so many of them I have no idea, but, wow, was I glad to see them! I was told repeatedly how lucky I was to be alive, but alive I was, and later that night I was allowed to leave the hospital.

Meanwhile, Hil had come hurtling up from Somerset, and together we fled back to the relative safety of our house in the country until the flat, and its near-lethal electrics, had been thoroughly checked out.

In spite of it all, I returned on schedule to resume filming of Barging. But, unfortunately, I was still something of a shaking mess, and I'd totally lost all my previous confidence. I suppose I was still in shock. Literally! I couldn't steer any more. I don't think I could have steered a child's pedal car, let alone a narrow boat. However, Anita came to my rescue. She took over and became even better at it than I'd been.

And I have to say that, regardless of my near-death experience, I had another rather pleasant surprise. I found cruising the canals of England a tremendous delight. It's like being in a sort of magic world, away from everything. It was just wonderful.

Something else that I found rather wonderful was discovering a new sort of acting, inclined only to come your way when you have reached a certain age. I did a couple of stints in two of our biggest hospital dramas, *Holby City* and *Casualty*, playing sick elderly people, and each time was filmed mostly lying in bed. Absolute bliss.

7

—

A Whole New World

Pantomime has featured a lot throughout my life. I topped the bill in two big ones straight after leaving Corrie. The Wicked Queen in *Snow White* at Bradford being the first, over Christmas 2001/2, followed by the Slave of the Ring in *Aladdin* at the Birmingham Hippodrome the following year, alongside two wonderful co-stars, Bobby Davro and John Challis.

I'm one of those people who really loves pantomime. When you look back over them, they all kind of merge into one wonderful great experience, but with different people, different friends that you make.

The theatre is a world of unreality to most people, but to me one of total reality. I find that the best form of social interaction is backstage. I love it, I would like built onto my own home a backstage area. And my dressing room – whether I was sharing with a whole bunch of chorus girls, or if it was number one, which I've been lucky enough to have for many years – has always been where the fox was most at home. The fox always felt quite safe in the dressing room. It liked the dressing room.

I've never been very pleased with my looks, but as soon

71

as I put on a full stage make-up, I'm fine. Particularly with pantomime make-up. There is no subtlety, which I really, really like. I also like pantomime costumes because they are extreme. I've always felt I could face anybody or do anything wearing those costumes.

The whole thing is so very English, and it's wonderful to be part of it. You have a very special Christmas, which not only gets you out and amongst friends, it also stops you having to see people that you really don't want to. You have an excuse to do exactly what you want to do.

My WiFi said, on the very first occasion she came with me for a pantomime season, that it was probably the most wonderful way to spend Christmas she'd experienced since she'd been a child. She has now accompanied me through a grand total of 10 pantomime seasons and, sounding like some dreadful Tory wife, has become inclined to use the phrase, "When we did pantomime at..." wherever it was…

It was not, however, Hil who had to sweat through 12 shows – minimum! – a week, as I have occasionally felt the necessity to point out. But she did throw herself enthusiastically into it all, making tea and pouring gin and tonics in the dressing room, getting food arranged, organising nights out – and nights in – with the cast, and ensuring our accommodation was suitably decorated for Christmas. All in between taking our dog Coco for long winter walks along the beach, of course. From the moment Coco came into our lives in 2008 I was obliged only to agree to pantomime venues by the seaside.

However, in spite of enjoying all the benefits of pantomime life, Coco was never a theatre dog. She was a very cute looking creature, half Patterdale Terrier and half poodle, and I was once asked to take her on stage.

I carried her on in my arms, and turned to face the audience.

I'M STILL HERE

Coco absorbed the lights and the noise in an instant. She was normally quite a bold little dog. She liked to leap and run over the hills, see off cats and rabbits in the garden, chase squirrels in the park, and swim in the sea. But this was not her territory. Her eyes widened in total terror. She jumped from my arms and raced into the wings, where she leapt into Hil's arms. It was not a successful debut. The dog was no trouper, to misquote W.C. Fields.

Pantomime life is, of course, just like any other sort of life; it does have its problems. At Bradford, I had to be squeezed into an enormous padded costume that made me look like a sumo wrestler. I couldn't say anything, though, because it had been designed and made by the producer's mother – who was quite a renowned and very experienced dressmaker – which was considered a great privilege. But for some reason, it was so heavy I could barely move, and there was an enormous headdress which added to my discomfort. Quick changes were quite a challenge and, on several occasions, I entered the stage with various pieces of my costume falling off me.

For *Aladdin* in Birmingham, I had to sing 'A Whole New World', a huge international hit written for the film *Aladdin* by the great Tim Rice – who is now a chum, adding to my terrible embarrassment at not having been able to sing it properly. The song was in totally the wrong key for me. A key I just couldn't handle. At rehearsals I fought endlessly to get the key changed, but I was totally ignored. And it still makes me cringe to think about my murdering that beautiful song on a daily basis. Twice a day actually. Eek!

Lovely John Challis was the villainous Abanazar. It was a delight to work with him for the first time and to get to know him, and his very special wife Carol, who was in charge of wardrobe. Years later, in 2015, it was a real pleasure to work with him again in a well-received short film called *Tea for Two*.

We were close friends by then and remained so until his death four years ago. The last time Hil and I saw John was when he and Carol had been working near our Somerset home, and, on a beautiful summer's evening, popped in for supper in the garden. We sat there until well after dark, chatting, eating and drinking. It was a real privilege, and I am so glad we had that night together.

Bad Girls put a stop to pantomimes for some years, but in 2005, a Christmas break in the schedules allowed me to go into a National Theatre Production of the *Wizard of Oz* at the New Theatre, Oxford. I was to play the Wicked Witch of the West, and, in spite of being required to be green throughout, I was rather looking forward to it.

However, things did not get off to a good start. Some time before we were to open, I was required to travel to Oxford for the usual in-costume press launch and photo call. I had, of course, been getting myself a bit more toned up and ready for this rather good, and extremely energetic production in which I had to spend a certain amount of time flying about on a witch's broomstick.

But as I tried to get out of bed that morning at our London flat, to my horror, and for no particular reason that I knew of, my back went into spasm. I could not move. This was clearly an emergency. Yelling for help, I immediately swallowed a handful of paracetamol and anything else I could stick down my throat.

I tried using a hair dryer on myself, the heat of which I have learned can help enormously with this sort of thing. Not on this occasion. Nothing did any good at all. I could still barely move. I was virtually frozen to the spot. The car sent by the production company was about to arrive downstairs to transport us to Oxford. The first problem was getting me down there. There is a lift, thank God, but I had to get to it, so I made my way in a crouched position, moving a bit like a rather large crab. The second problem was getting me into the car. Hil used a kind of shoehorn technique, and miraculously managed to somehow slide this stiff, bent creature, uttering frequent shrieks of pain, into the vehicle.

We were working on the principle that what goes in must come out. However, when we got to Oxford extracting me from the car proved even more difficult. And before us stood a welcoming committee of my prospective employers, the producer, the director, and other equally important persons, looking on in amazement as Hil tried to shove me out of the car onto the pavement.

There was a deathly hush as I finally stood, after a fashion, in front of them like some sort of crawling, grovelling gnome, bent almost double. Their faces were a picture. They were both shocked and horrified. Was I really going to be their leading lady? You could see quite clearly what they were thinking. "What in God's name have we employed?"

Nonetheless, I made my painful way to a dressing room, where I somehow or other managed to get into a witch costume and put on green make-up. But I was still bent double when they got me on stage where photographs were to be taken of me with a broomstick.

I had thought maybe the broomstick would be on the floor. But no, the broomstick was quite high up a bunch of ladders, and I was supposed to somehow get on it and look as if I was flying. It seemed to be impossible, but I just did what actors who were once chorus girls do. I got on with it. And as I crawled aboard my broomstick, I was aware of Doctor Footlights - as we call that strange theatrical magic which often makes it possible for previously stricken performers to somehow be able to strut their stuff as soon as the curtain rises - coming to my rescue.

Not entirely, but enough for me to somehow manage to pose for pictures looking as if I was flying that broomstick. It was a bit of a miracle.

The job itself turned out to be a really nice one. We had excellent accommodation too; a suite in the newly opened Malmaison Hotel, constructed out of the building which had once been Oxford Jail. And we were made particularly welcome because, before its transformation, the old jail had been the location used for much of the filming of *Bad Girls* ahead of the show moving entirely to 3 Mills.

After *Bad Girls* ended, I played the lead in eight more pantomimes, to the delight, at least, of Hil and Coco. The last one, in 2021/22, was *Cinderella* – produced by Matt Brinker, one of the UKs brightest young theatre producers, and written and directed by Lee Waddingham – at the Queen's Theatre, Barnstaple, just a stone's throw from all of North Devon's magnificent beaches. That will almost certainly be my final panto, which is somehow fitting, as it was at the Queen's that Hil's first play, *Dead Lies* – set in North Devon and also produced by Matt – premiered later in 2022 before going on a national tour.

8

—

A Road to Damascus Moment

S o, one way or another, I have continued to work in this new
millennium almost as much as I did in the last. Which has
rather surprised me.

A lot of it has been very different work, of course. The business
has changed so much. I have therefore changed with it, and I
don't have a problem with that. I am still working, and I want
to continue for as long as I am able. That means changing with
the times.

My personal life has changed too. I am living a life I could
never have dreamed would be possible. Not only did I leave
Coronation Street in 2001 after 15 years, but I also left the woman
I had been sharing my life with for 15 years. And I left to be with
the person I had asked to write my story of leaving Corrie, the
person whom I am now sitting next to, who, all this time later, is
helping me write this book. The person I was to marry.

If anyone had told me back then that I would actually get
married to a woman, that would have been astonishing enough.
And if they had said the woman I married would be a former

red-top journalist, albeit that she is now a novelist and also a playwright, I would have laughed in their face. But here I am. I did it. And I don't regret it.

We fell in love suddenly and unexpectedly. But looking back, I may not have let that happen if I hadn't become increasingly more and more distressed and humiliated by the behaviour of my former partner. Even though we were together for so long, she would never properly acknowledge my existence. For 15 years, she failed to be open about our relationship to her family, and most of her friends at home.

I would stay with her, but always as just 'a friend' because she was not prepared to be honest about me.

As time passed I found this increasingly more and more difficult to take. It was as if she was justifying my lurking feelings of shame, guilt, and most importantly, lack of worth. But I felt trapped. And I think I may have been subconsciously looking for an escape route.

However, what ultimately happened came as a total surprise.

Leading up to leaving *Coronation Street*, I went through a very difficult time on the show. It had been decided that Alma would die of cancer, and it soon became apparent that the writers and producers had managed to get virtually every single thing wrong about the whole process. For the first time, after the press office put out a story saying that I was "thrilled" to be playing a cancer sufferer, I had letters from the public that weren't absolutely sweet.

I had a letter from a man which said, "I'm glad you're thrilled, because I am watching with my wife and children and my wife will probably be dead with cancer before your storyline is completed."

Well, I wasn't thrilled. I had been content for Alma to die, I had wanted her to leave with a bang, but I'd expected and hoped that the story would be handled compassionately and, above all, accurately.

At 7:30 at night, when families are watching together, on a show like *Coronation Street* which is so important to people, or certainly was then, don't tell the audience horror stories that are totally incorrect.

For a start, they had Alma having a biopsy and getting the results the same day, which is not what happens. Or not then it wasn't, anyway. So many things were wrong that I became quite angry. I do believe soap operas have a responsibility to the public. Even more so back in 2001 when the viewing figures were gigantic and there was no social media. Corrie had enormous influence and was of considerable consequence to its audience.

Nobody at Granada would listen to me and I was really upset. I thought to myself; I'm leaving, I'm going to do something about this. I decided to leak the truth about it all. I couldn't yet go on the record because I was still under contract.

I had never leaked a story to the press in my life before, and I had no idea how to go about it. I tried to think of somebody I could trust to help me. And into my head came this journalist called Hilary Bonner whom I'd met many years earlier when she had been show-business editor of the *Daily Mirror*. Looking back, it is possible that I had thought of her occasionally, but I've no idea really why she came wiggling into my inner thoughts that day.

There had been quite a time-lapse since I'd last spoken to Hilary, who was by then a freelance.

Actually, we realised later, 10 years had somehow passed. We had got on well together from the start and had done that 'we must have lunch thing', but never carried it through. After all, I was in the biggest soap in the country and living in Manchester, whilst she was a tabloid journalist living in London.

However, guess whose phone number I had kept for all those 10 years? Now, I'm not a person who keeps phone numbers safe. Or I wasn't back then. It's different now with modern mobile phones. Back then my contacts directory was a tatty little diary with scribbled, often illegible, entries, and pages falling out. But there, still, was Hilary Bonner's home number.

And she duly placed an 'insider-said' piece, as journalists call it, in *The Sun*, which related my true feelings about the cancer storyline and how horrified I'd been by it. I really felt that placing this story was the right thing to do; indeed I felt I just had to do it, and the very positive reaction I had to it after it was published, from almost everyone I knew and met, seemed to uphold my decision.

From there on Hil and I began to work together in various directions. I'd been asked to do a photo spread for *Hello!* magazine. I needed a writer, and it seemed quite natural for me to ask Hil if she would do it.

A little later, after Alma had died on screen and when I was out of contract, I decided to go on the record with my feelings about the cancer storyline, plus certain other things happening inside Corrie at the time. Something I could do, but those under contract at Granada could not. And I did so in no uncertain terms. Again, there was a big spread in *The Sun*, which Hil had written for me. I felt I had done the right thing.

So, on the day the article was published, Hil and I went for dinner to Joe Allen, then my favourite restaurant in Covent Garden and a regular haunt, to celebrate.

We had a very nice meal, as I recall, and were having rather a good time together, until this obnoxious child, who was allegedly some sort of journalist working for a national newspaper, came and sat down uninvited at our table.

She was very drunk and proceeded to behave quite badly. Indeed, she was totally out of order.

Hil has always been quite sure of the insulting comment thrown at me by this apology for a journalist. A comment which might just have been responsible for changing both our lives forever.

"What are you going to do at your age, now that you've been chucked out of *Coronation Street*?" she asked.

I'd heard worse, and didn't take a great deal of notice to be honest. Maybe partly because she was so drunk and partly because what she said was simply not true. I had not been chucked out of Corrie. I left under my own steam. It was my decision and I had thought out very carefully when I should go.

But I later learned that my dinner companion had been instantly overwhelmed by a sensation of ice-cold fury. And this relatively mild-mannered creature that I'd been working with for some time on and off, suddenly stood up, more or less got hold of me by the back of my neck and said, "We're leaving!"

Then she frog-marched out of Joes. And I just went along with her. She always says it was both the first and last time that I ever did what she told me to! Frankly I had little choice. It was as if she was training a dog. I was picked up like some stray from Battersea and marched to the door. She yanked me out, and we proceeded to walk up Bow Street towards this rental flat I had in Broad Court, which was empty at the time, and where I'd allowed her to stay while she was working with me.

I don't remember much conversation as we walked. Apparently, Hil was concentrating on trying to control her anger at the way the young woman had spoken to me. She said she had to leave Joe's at once, as she was in danger of stabbing 'the bitch' with the cutlery. Something which, as she'd already become a crime novelist as well as a journalist, I had always thought she would probably have done rather well. However, by the time we got to The Opera House, Hil had started to ask herself what was the matter with her. Why was she getting in such a state about 'some old actress?' Her words, not mine!

Then came what she always calls her Road to Damascus moment. Ah ha, she thought. She says that she suddenly knew, absolutely and irrevocably, exactly why she was getting in such a state about 'some old actress.'

So when we got to the flat she asked me if I would like to come in for a drink. To come into my own flat, that is!

I had not had a Road to Damascus moment! Neither had I quite realised the relationship that my co-writer and myself seemed to have woven together. But I thought, well, it's been a funny sort of evening, I might as well. And it turned out that she had some champagne chilling. I was to later learn that the first thing she ever does when staying away from home – in a hotel room, a rented flat – anywhere that has a fridge, is to put a bottle of champagne in it.

She had by this time let go of the back of my neck, so I suppose I went in willingly enough.

We then had the most extraordinary night. I didn't go home. We literally talked, and talked and talked, nothing else, for seven or eight hours. I remember clearly that at one point she ended up sitting on the floor with her head on my knee.

I think we both realised without doing anything really, that something had happened. Something quite profound that took us both by surprise. Above all, something irrevocable.

In the morning she was going to Royal Ascot, of all places, and I finally went home. I think I did go to bed for a bit, but I didn't get much sleep. And then when my eyes opened properly,

I'M STILL HERE

I just thought, yes, something momentous has happened. It really has.

You can talk about falling in love, or you can say, as I like to put it, somebody's stolen my heart. Hil stole my heart that night.

Of course, I wondered if it had happened the other way around, too. I hoped so, but I simply didn't know.

PART TWO

My Beginning

9

—

Born to Perform

I was born in Ashton-Under-Lyne, Greater Manchester, on September 14,1935, four years before the outbreak of the Second World War. A war which was to dominate so much of my childhood.

The other dominant factor in my early life was my mother. She was never a professional performer, but she was one of the most theatrical people I have ever encountered, and she was very beautiful. She had lovely chestnut hair, soft brown eyes and always dressed as glamorously as possible. Every man she met seemed to fall for her, and she could always bend them to her will. She was a terrifyingly determined woman. You crossed Connie Broadbent at your peril.

Her ambition for me was extraordinary. And the nature of it was clearly indicated in the name she chose for me, I was christened Shirley Anne Broadbent after Shirley Temple.

One of my very first memories, still vivid, stemming back to when I was about two, I think, is of lying awake at night unable to sleep because I had rags tied into my hair and couldn't rest my head properly on the pillow. My mother, of course, had decided that I must have curly hair like my child-star namesake. So almost every night of my childhood, from when I was a toddler, it was Curly Top and rags for me.

My father, Hubert, an accountant, was a nice, gentle, quiet person who probably wanted nothing more than a nice, gentle, quiet sort of life, something he was never likely to get with my mother. Even my parents' wedding, orchestrated of course, by Connie, had been both unusual and extremely extravagant. The Broadbents and the Pikes considered themselves to be among the foremost families in the town, and my mother made sure that her wedding lived up to all expectations. She even arranged for a flock of doves to be released above Ashton parish church as the wedding party emerged after the ceremony. God knows what happened to those doves. Poor things, they probably developed a severe bout of bronchitis on the way over Oldham, I should think.

The local newspaper reported on the event.

At one o'clock, half an hour before the ceremony, the footpath along Stamford Street between Old Square and St Michael Square was crowded with people anxious to catch a glimpse of the bride and her bridesmaids, and of the guests as they arrived. Over 500 people crowded into the courtyard in front of the church, and a special detachment of police was necessary to control the crowds and regulate the traffic as the bride and groom left the church after the ceremony, the police had great difficulty in maintaining a passage for them in the street, and the bride was nearly swept off her feet.

There were no less than eight bridesmaids. If I'd been around to comment, I would definitely have said Connie went a bit too far.

My paternal grandfather was a very colourful character, an idiosyncratic entrepreneur. He too started life as an accountant, but he loved the theatre, and eventually came to run the Theatre Royal in Ashton, helping to start the show business careers of the Crazy Gang and Jack Hylton, among others.

Grandfather Broadbent was almost as ambitious for me to succeed in a show business career as my mother, and that was going some! Connie wanted me to dance, so I danced! Aided and abetted by Grandfather Broadbent, she sent me to dancing class when I was two and a half. It never occurred to me to say no. She made Gypsy Rose Lee seem like Mother Teresa, shy, modest, and retiring. Almost every night I would have to dance and sing for her. Then from the moment I started to appear in the theatre, she would be in the wings shouting, "Sing up baby, smile, smile."

My father thought the whole thing was ridiculous.

It was in Grandfather Broadbent's theatre that I made my professional stage debut at the age of three. I was introduced to theatre and thrown in the deep end, doing eight shows a week in *A Christmas Carol*. In the 1930s, no one controlled the hours small children worked in show business, and my mother certainly had no wish to do so.

I can clearly recall being carried around in my pink flowered dressing gown, which I hated. My mother might have wanted me to be Shirley Temple, but I was never the sort of child who liked ribbons and bows or anything of that ilk, any more than I liked having my hair curled. I was half asleep most of the time because I couldn't sleep at night. My mother was always saying, "Go to sleep; you've got two shows tomorrow."

Indeed, that remained my kind of schedule until I went into *Coronation Street*. But whatever the next day held, how could anybody with their head full of the most ridiculous pieces of old cloth tied tightly into knots and pulling the roots out of their skull be expected to sleep?

In so many ways, my childhood was taken over by this other world of show business, although I didn't think about it like that at the time. After all, I didn't know any better. But I did feel anxious about it. I also had a distinct feeling of déjà vu when I went on stage. From the first moment, I felt as if I had done it before. I guess that might have been why I took it all pretty much in my stride.

There was a scene when I appeared suddenly from the bottom of a Christmas tree. In order for this to happen I had to be shut in a box, curled up into a little ball, until the moment came. At some point, quite late into rehearsals, it was realised I would actually have to stay in this box through two long previous scenes. There was considerable panic about this. After all, I was only three, and most kids of my age would probably have been terrified. Indeed, the first time I had to do it, I could hear people going absolutely bananas.

My mother was on one side of the stage hissing, "Are you all right? Stay where you are. You'll be all right." And my dancing teacher was on the other side doing the same. But the extraordinary thing was that I didn't mind being put in the box. I just took the experience for granted, like everything else about performing in the theatre.

I crouched there in the dark, wishing they would all shut up. Then when I finally heard my music cue and I opened the little door, climbed up and saw the audience through a haze of cigarette and cigar smoke, I just thought, oh my God, I've done it again. I felt no fear, only a slight sense of tiredness. Of course, as I know well now, if you ask an actor going on stage what they feel, they will always reply 'tired'.

What made it work for me from the start was laughter. Laughter has always got me going. There was a very tall demon in the show who did a hands knees and Oops-a-Daisy routine with me. He found it extremely amusing to bump me so hard that I bounced straight off stage into the wings. I didn't like it, but as I went flying, I heard the audience laugh. Now that was different. I thought, I see, this is how you do it! And I learned fast from then on. I made a big performance of being knocked off stage. Mind you, could you imagine anybody being allowed to do that to a child nowadays?

At the end of the show, everyone was given flowers and a big tea chest full of toys and sweets was brought on stage for me. It was quite nauseating, really, but everyone had gone *ooh* and *ahh* about my performance, and this was my reward – which was indeed a huge treat, as the war had begun and these things were already getting to be in short supply. Then Grandfather Broadbent, an old trade union man and a former town mayor, who would make a speech at the opening of a fridge, led me forward and announced, "This is my granddaughter, who is going to be a star." I didn't know what he was talking about, but I do remember him saying it.

From the start, I was always anxious when I performed. Not surprising when you think about what went on, almost all the mothers were awful, relentlessly pushing their kids on in competitions and auditions.

My first theatrical tragedy was watching a little girl at some talent contest being zipped into a costume, and they zipped up her skin. Nobody seemed to notice until it was too late. I remember thinking, oh, dear, now it's got to be unzipped. Unsurprisingly, the poor girl screamed the place down. I still have such a strong memory of it.

Even family holidays were not allowed to be merely holidays. For me, the clue came when Connie packed. She always took my dance costumes, my tap shoes and my music. The bucket and spade came last. There was a crisis in Llandudno when she discovered that she'd forgotten to take my sheet music for 'I am just a little girl who's looking for a little boy to love', the Gershwin song which was my current party piece. She soon found a solution though. She simply walked into the middle of a full orchestra rehearsal on the pier and stopped it. There were hundreds of musicians there. I believe the orchestra was the Welsh Philharmonic. But that did not faze Connie one little bit. She strode up to the conductor and said, "Excuse me, I have a terrible problem, my daughter hasn't got her music. Could you help please?"

He was so astonished that he sat me on the piano on the stage and asked me to sing the song to him. Then he jotted the notes down on a piece of sheet music and instructed my mother to tell the pianist who would be accompanying me to play the chords which he wrote underneath. I won the competition. But I suspect that all concerned were probably afraid of what might happen if I lost!

Many years later, my mother gave me a scrapbook of childhood photographs, which included a snapshot of me that day, underneath which she had written in her big, sprawling handwriting, rather typically using gold ink, "You were wonderful, darling."

That holiday was a landmark in my early life for something of somewhat greater consequence than me freezing on the beach whilst struggling to win inconsequential talent competitions.

We were in Llandudno on September 3, 1939 when Britain declared war on Germany.

Although the outbreak of war was beyond my comprehension, I have never forgotten the day it happened, largely because that was when I was given Loppy, my beloved toy rabbit, who has been glued to my side ever since.

The whole family was there for that final holiday before the war, including my grandparents, Broadbent and Pike, and my

Uncle Graham, my mother's younger brother, who was joining the army. Uncle Graham wanted to buy me a present for my birthday 11 days later, and announced that as war had broken out, I could choose absolutely anything I wanted.

I was duly marched along to Lumley's, which I remember as a rather wonderful toy shop. The attrition of wartime had yet to bite, and the shelves of Lumley's were stocked with every possible toy a child could wish for. But I had eyes only for my Loppy. I spotted her almost at once in a huge glass case, along with a lot of other soft toys, and I just homed in on her. It was as if I had found my soulmate.

My mother, of course, was dismayed. Loppy was an extremely modest choice. The family was gathered in order for me to be bought a big, big present, but I only wanted Loppy. My mother took me to look at a rather advanced toy car you could sit in and drive with pedals, and she was particularly disappointed when I showed absolutely no interest whatsoever in a huge walking doll with curls, which may or may not have resembled Shirley Temple. I had fixed on Loppy: an ordinary, light brown, five inches or so tall, stuffed rabbit with no distinguishing features to recommend her. And it was as if my life depended on acquiring the creature.

I named her before she was mine. Connie had been reading Peter Rabbit to me, Flopsy, Mopsy, Cottontail and Peter were extremely dear to my heart, and Loppy was the nearest name to Flopsy that I could get my tongue around. I also thought it suited her because of her big floppy ears. So, Uncle Graham duly bought Loppy for me.

The family were all in a state about the war. And after we left the shop, I have this clear memory of Graham standing on the pier looking out to sea. I asked him what he was looking at.

He said, "Well, one day, if we don't win this war, ships full of bad people will come across the sea and take us over. That's why we have to fight."

It was an image that has always stayed with me.

That Christmas, my mother, who occasionally, albeit only occasionally, knew when even she was beaten, tucked into the top of my stocking another slightly smaller but equally plain rabbit whom I called Lena and grew to love every bit as much as Loppy. I have been devoted to both my rabbits from the moment I was given them.

To this day I cannot be separated from them. As a very small child, I went to hospital to have my tonsils removed and came around from the operation to find Loppy and Lena were no longer in my bed where I had left them. I immediately had a terrible panic attack. More than that, I became genuinely ill. My temperature shot through the roof, and apparently I came close to departing this life. It transpired that the nursing staff had taken my rabbits out of the ward to be fumigated because there was a scarlet fever scare. As soon as they were returned to me, I recovered.

The same thing happened again when Loppy and Lena were inadvertently shut in a trunk in our hotel room on holiday. Another time, when I was still a very little girl, my mother was unwise enough to use the removal of Loppy as some kind of threat when I misbehaved. I promptly threw a telephone directory, straight through a window. And yes, the window was closed at the time!

Many years later, when I was on tour with a revue and the suitcase containing my rabbits went missing on the train, my then agent Alec Graham travelled miles back from where we were in the North of England to Crewe to collect it because he realised I would simply not be able to go on without knowing that Loppy and Lena were safe.

I'm sorry if this sounds barking mad, but to this day, it would destroy me to lose them. They have been a constant factor through a life that for so many years had depressingly little continuity. They are bashed and battered and have lost most of their tufted wool and fur, and I periodically patch them up with bits of cotton wool and old nylon stockings. They look a bit like bank robbers. I clutched them in air raid shelters during the war. They were always with me whenever I performed as a child. Throughout my life, I have clung to them whenever I've been unhappy.

Among the wartime memories which have never left me was of the Manchester Blitz just before Christmas 1940 when my grandfather Pike took me up into the hills around Mottram to watch the city burn. He and my grandmother lived part of the time in a moorland bungalow, and the surrounding area gave a grandstand view. The bombing continued for two nights, tearing the heart out of Manchester and killing nearly 700 people.

Not long afterwards I saw a small plane crash into Mottram churchyard. I had been watching a number of these planes flying around in circles, when one of them started making a strange noise. I was so used to watching planes that even at my very young age I knew there was something wrong. Suddenly, the plane corkscrewed and nose-dived. Again, young as I was, it was obvious nobody aboard could have survived. Later I learned that the planes were piloted by young Polish men in training to fight in the RAF.

These were shocking and tragic events, but children were every bit as accepting of the realities of World War Two as were their elders. Also just as resilient. We just took it all for granted.

And it must be said that my main memory of the war is of spending one half of it in a bread bin with Loppy and Lena, and the other half performing to frequently bemused audiences. My mother had a great big tin bread bin, which she used to sit me in down in the cellar whenever there was an air raid. And in spite of the awful scenes I witnessed from the distance, the only time I remember my life being in peril was when two shelves carrying Connie's entire supply of black-market tins of Batchelor's peas collapsed on my head just as I was climbing out of my bin.

The performances, predictably enough, were usually my mother's idea. I think I was her war effort. It was thanks to her that during my *Coronation Street* years, I could never pass through Manchester's Piccadilly station without experiencing a vision of me singing 'Roll out the Barrel' by the ticket barrier, having been dragged there by Connie to see our boys off to war! I suspect they were far keener to get to Hitler once they'd witnessed the hideous sight of this Shirley Temple lookalike singing to them while being poked in the side by a mad woman issuing frenzied instructions.

"Sing louder. Smile, smile. Use your eyes."

I always hated the dresses my mother put me in. I can still remember them in every ghastly, frilly detail, as well as the bows she insisted on tying in my hair. The embarrassment of it makes me cringe to this day. Our poor boys didn't get to escape me even after they'd come back from war, at least not if they were wounded. Connie used to take me around the hospitals to sing to them. It was always the Brahms Lullaby, not a song you would associate with me, really, but presumably considered suitable for the sick.

I also used to perform in Grandfather Pike's air raid shelter beneath his tailor's shop in Ashton. Now that wasn't so bad. Both my grandfathers were true eccentrics and I absolutely adored them. My tailor grandfather, who looked very much like Charles Lawton, was very fussy about his appearance. By the time I was born, he had taken to wearing a hand-stitched white suit about the place, which was quite something in a northern industrial town in the 1930s. So naturally his air raid shelter was very different to most. He created an escape world in his basement. He turned it into a kind of South of France theatre set. There was this very pretty sort of trompe l'oeil seascape, complete with a sandpit for me to play in. He had tables laid up with umbrellas above them, and as soon as the air raid siren went off, he would dress up as a French waiter and pop a load of potatoes in the oven to bake. Then he would come downstairs, put a French singer's record on the gramophone and serve the baked potatoes to the entire family gathered in the basement.

One Christmas, he dressed up as a woman and pretended to be our long-lost aunt. I think that was my introduction to drag. He wore a huge and rather wonderful dress, which he had tailored himself. I remember thinking he looked fantastic, and it didn't seem at all odd to me for my grandfather to dress like that.

I continued to sing and dance, and after a bit, it began to occur to me that I might be able to turn this performing thing rather more to my advantage. I rounded up several of the neighbour-hood kids who played round the back, as we described it, and press-ganged them into becoming performers too. We used to climb up on the roof of our outside lavatory, in an alleyway a bit like the one behind *Coronation Street*, and put on a show, which, amazingly enough, people did come to watch. I was extremely precocious when it came to performing. I used to set the whole thing up and tell the others what to do. Then I'd go round with a box afterwards and collect money from our audience. So not only did our performances make a change from looking for German spies or collecting shrapnel, they earned us some extra pocket money. The grand sum of a halfpenny was the normal contribution, and the pretext was that the collection was going to the war effort. Actually, it was usually being spent on the comics *Dandy* and *Beano*, of which I was rather fond during the war. Indeed, during the whole of my early childhood.

I have a vivid memory also of VE Day, the day the war ended in Europe, as I suspect everyone who lived through the war does. The whole country was rejoicing. In Ashton we were all out on the streets. Clutching my rabbits, I ran from our house to my Grandparents Pike's house, through hordes of jubilant people, hugging and kissing each other. I had asked to wear my favourite dress, which I called my 'naughty girl' dress. because I used to wear it for competitions doing a number about a naughty girl. It was green with hand-stitched patches, and I loved it. I also remember that I was wearing red shoes. I almost always remember what I have worn for almost everything, but that was the most special and happiest of days.

Through the war and beyond, my mother remained my greatest supporter. She always treated me as a friend rather than as a daughter, and as a grown-up friend too. It would all be too easy to think of her merely as a typical stage mum, but she was much more complex than that, as was our relationship. It was just that she wanted the best for me. I don't think you can successfully push a child through a door it doesn't want to go through, but she spotted in me the one thing I was good at, which was dancing, and she nurtured it. Perhaps that is partly why there was such a special bond between us.

We remained close until her death, in spite of everything. And I do hope I have not made her sound like a monster, which she was not in any way. Those were different times, although I don't think stage mothers have ever really changed. Nor that they ever will. Indeed in some ways I suspect they may have gotten worse.

Nowadays the stakes are a lot higher. I suspect the ambition within the mothers has probably grown over the years, because now they doubtless believe that their children could be in a soap opera or win *Britain's Got Talent*.

I have to say I owe every single thing to my mother, because had it not been for what she thought I could do and then pushed me into, my life would have been so very different. Not least because meanwhile my father was considering the possibility of one day getting me a job in a local sweet shop. There was no comparison between his vision for my future and my mother's. I adored her.

10

First Love

Then she sent me to boarding school. Which was totally and utterly a betrayal. I had believed I was safe in my life, and suddenly it was all ripped away from me, I was only nine, and I thought I was going to die. My mother, of all people, was sending me away. I had become aware that she and my father were having problems of some sort, but nothing had remotely prepared me for this.

There have been many tough times in my life, but I have never since experienced absolute despair like I did then. It remains the ultimate betrayal. I couldn't believe that my mother, with whom I had this extraordinary close relationship, could be doing such a thing to me. My mother, who doted on me. My mother, who was obsessive about me, overly ambitious, overly protective. I felt that I was being abandoned, which I more or less was. And the whole experience turned out to be every bit as much of a nightmare as I anticipated.

In those days, nobody seemed to know anything about dyslexia. As a medical condition it had yet to be recognised in the UK. I was just a thick kid who couldn't read or write. I had gotten away with it pretty well at my primary school previously.

I think I was quite a bright child, actually. Certainly I always had an answer for people, and I was usually somehow or other in the top part of the class. I think a lot of small children aren't very good at writing. And when it came to reading, in the early stages there were usually illustrations, and I would get by with a kind of educated guesswork. I am a natural busker.

My fall from grace began when I started sitting boarding school entrance exams. The only one I managed to pass was for St Anne's College in St Anne's On Sea, the gentile near neighbour of Blackpool. Looking back, I should have ensured that I failed that one too. But it all seemed unreal to me. We met the headmistress – a dear little old lady with a bum, or she seemed old to me, but I, of course, was at an age when everybody over 25 was geriatric – and I was accepted, much to my parents' astonishment, I think.

When my mother delivered me there, some weeks later, the reality hit me like a punch in the gut. I begged, I pleaded, I howled, and I sobbed, but she still left me there. To make matters worse, the darling old lady was no longer headmistress. Instead, we were greeted by two spinsters, who were joint heads, Miss Foden and Miss Thompson. One was quite upper class Irish, and the other was quite upper class English. They were very much a pair. And the school they ran was a funny sort of place, to say the least. It was a private school full of supposedly nice middle-class girls whose parents all wanted them to have that sort of education. In fact, I got practically no education at all. My parents completely wasted their money. They almost certainly didn't get what they thought they had paid for. I have a photo of me in an alleged chemistry lesson at St. Anne's. It was mocked up for a school prospectus. I have no memory of ever having a real chemistry lesson there. There wasn't even a science laboratory.

I have no idea why people have children and then send them to boarding school. I was utterly miserable. I think there is a perceived wisdom that all those initiation ceremonies and stuff that you hear about just happen in boys' schools. Not true. Girls' schools are just as bad, at least St. Anne's College certainly was. Girls always seemed to have their heads stuck down lavatories.

The night I arrived, I was ordered by some of the older girls to open my tuck box. They wanted the contents for themselves and intended to get them. It was just at the end of the war, so food was of even greater importance than it usually would be to school kids. I didn't care. I didn't ever want to eat again. All I cared about were my beloved rabbits, Loppy and Lena. I was terrified someone might take them or harm them in some way.

Life was grim. I was continually in a mess. I couldn't properly recognise the words I was supposed to be able to read and write. And so I was confused and frustrated by my inability to do what everyone else seemed to do with ease.

I always had quite an imagination, though, and looking back, I think I was rather good at coming up with ideas for essays. We were once asked to write an essay about firework night – something which was not a feature of life in the Broadbent household – and by the time I was sent away to school we already had enough fireworks on a daily basis without any extra sparkles or twinkles. So I came up with the story of a worm that got chopped in half by a firework and then formed a rela-tionship with its other half because they were obviously very compatible, and they hid from the war in an air raid shelter. Nobody was impressed.

My dyslexia led to me frequently getting into trouble when I really didn't deserve it. Once I was sent out of the room during bible knowledge because I quite innocently asked what fornica-tion meant. The teacher thought I was being cheeky. Actually,

I had just seen the film *Bambi* about the adventures of a young deer, and I was trying to work out the connection between it and the passage in the Bible, because I didn't realise 'fawn' and 'forn' were spelled differently.

In order to cover up my deficiencies, I became the school clown. Every time class was stopped because I couldn't read, as it often was. I would put on my clown's hat and try to make everybody laugh. If that failed, I resorted to violence. Even before reaching school age, I'd always had a tendency to be aggressive when I, or anyone I cared about, came under threat. I once virtually beat to a pulp a far bigger boy who had thrown stones at our family dog. At boarding school, my aggression ran out of control and invariably manifested itself in the same way. I would launch myself at people, knock them over, and bang their heads on the floor. And I wouldn't stop until someone came and pulled me off.

I was quite dangerous, actually. And it occurs to me now that if Gordon Ramsey had known more about my past tendencies towards physical violence, he may have treated me with a little more respect.

The truth, of course, was that I was desperate. I was deeply distressed, both by the way I was being treated at St Anne's, and also by all that was going on at home. My parents' marriage was disintegrating and they had more or less parted. My home life no longer existed.

I was also confused by St Anne's. There was a particularly heady kind of atmosphere. I felt then that there was something different about a lot of the teachers. I later realised that the school had more than its fair share of gay teachers, a situation that could well have been manipulated from the top. There was also quite a lot of bonding going on among girls. As far as I know, it wasn't a question of real sexual relationships, just heavy crushes, which I think probably remains pretty much the norm in all-girl schools. In my first term, I think I behaved the same as everybody else.

But then something happened to me, which, because I was so young at the time, is difficult to explain and possibly even more difficult to understand. I fell in love.

It certainly wasn't a physical thing in the adult sense, but neither was it anything like the schoolgirl infatuations going on around us. It seemed good and pure, and was in stark contrast to all the mayhem that was going on at home with my parents. I even remember wishing that they were out of the way so that I could give my entire attention to this person.

Her name was Bernie; she was about five years older than me, and went on to become joint head girl, along with Thelma Holt, who was also a pupil, and was to go on to become a highly successful actress and producer. I was 11, and Bernie was 16, which some people might not feel comfortable with. I was very comfortable with it.

Bernie was beautiful and brilliant. She was everything I was convinced I was not. I don't think I knew at the time what the relationship was, but I knew how much it meant to me. And I do realise now that Bernie was partially a mother substitute for me, when I felt abandoned by my own mother. But that wasn't the way I thought about it then.

Bernie was quite tall, about 5ft 9ins, very slim, had mad dark hair and very dark eyes. I used to look at her and think, I must remember those eyes. I would do that over and over again. There was something about her that was androgynous. And I don't mean in any way butch. There are people who have a sort of charismatic dual sexuality. And I think everybody, including the two head mistresses, realised that I loved her to bits. It wasn't a crush, although, I suppose it started like that.

Other girls would say to me that it was different. Bernie was different.

Meanwhile, I was getting into more and more trouble at school. I continued to appear to be bright enough when I was talking to people. Then seem to be very stupid in class. I didn't work because I couldn't work. I was treated like an idiot, so I behaved like an idiot. Not only did nobody else understand what it was all about, I didn't myself. I didn't realise that I had these difficulties because I was physically and mentally unable to learn to read properly. So, at first, I would cheat, and then I would give up.

There was a plus side. The prefects and staff lived in a different house across the road. I behaved so appallingly badly that I was ultimately banished there so that they could all keep an eye on me. That meant I was living in the same house with Bernie, who had her own room. Now this was supposed to be punishment?

Sometimes I would go along to her room and just curl up with her. There wasn't any writhing around in bed or anything like that, just some kissing and an even greater amount of talking. It was a kind of exploration of life.

Bernie talked to me about everything. She also tried her best to keep me out of trouble, but I was already a lost cause. However, I think she was the one, even more than my mother, who planted in me the idea that I could go on stage professionally. Until then, it hadn't ever seeped into my consciousness that this was what I wanted to do with my life, permanently. It was just what my mother wanted me to do.

Bernie turned it into something real for me. Made it feel like my future. We also talked about death a lot. We both believed that she was going to die young. It might seem strange for two such young people, but we were both quite sure of it, and quite matter of fact about it. We used to talk about how it would be when she wasn't there anymore. That was when I became quite obsessed with remembering not just her eyes, but her hands, too. I've always been a very emotional person. Bernie had remarkably long, graceful hands. I used to look at them and think that I couldn't bear for her to be buried in the ground, for those hands to be allowed to rot. I know that might all seem hard to believe, for an 11-year-old, but it's the truth.

I think the way I felt about Bernie was the way most of us want to feel about people all our lives and hardly ever do. Indeed, it took me more than 50 years to feel that way again – with Hil.

Back then Bernie was all that mattered, and the only thing that kept me going; she was my support and my refuge. My home life was falling apart. I couldn't do my schoolwork, and didn't understand why. So my school life, such as it was, fell apart too. I became more and more aggressive. It was my defence mechanism.

I had the most terrible fights. I was always a bit of a bruiser. I might have been small, but, oh, could I fight! I would happily knock someone down an entire flight of stairs, jump down onto them and bang their head on the floor. I was constantly involved in fights that ended up that way. It didn't matter if it was a tarmac playground or a marble hallway.

The only time the staff wanted to know about me was when they were putting on a Shakespeare play or any other kind of show, and I'd be dragged out of my cupboard and told to behave. I never could. The fact that I looked different to the others didn't help either. That was down to my mother. She connived with my grandfather, who thought it was quite normal to make a few alterations to my clothes. My skirt was cut several inches shorter than the other girls, because Connie reckoned I had good legs and should show them off. Consequently, walking around St Anne's at that age, I must have been serious jailbait. In school,

I was teased mercilessly, but it stopped short of actual bullying, because I knew how to handle bullies. I beat them up. Indeed, I was lucky I didn't kill anybody.

There was a girl called Ann in my dormitory who nearly had it on more than one occasion. She took to running a steel comb down the side of her bed, which was also metal. The noise went on for hours. I asked Ann nicely not to do it several times, but she wouldn't stop. Eventually, I bashed her over the head with a suitcase. This was just after the war, so the case was made of cardboard, her head went straight through it, and she proceeded to run around the room screaming, with her head trapped inside the case.

I was in my usual awful trouble. But while the matron was still thinking up a punishment dreadful enough, something else happened, and Ann was the one to suffer again. The next day was a fire drill. It was a bit primitive at St Anne's, but I adored it. One by one, we were put on a kind of sling four storeys up, and had to sort of crawl down the wall while being lowered to safety. Being a dancer and a bit nimble in those days, I was rather good at it, and always went first. But on this occasion, as part of my punishment and as a reward for poor Ann, she was sent first.

However, because matron was so busy telling me off for my disgusting behaviour, how I shouldn't be allowed to live and should probably have been put down at birth and so on, she was somewhat diverted. Unfortunately, she harnessed Ann the wrong way, so that the poor girl was attached to the free end of the fire drill contraption. Instead of going bumpy-bump down the wall, she just dropped from four storeys. Well, matron grabbed the rope, and we all realised what was happening when we saw that her hands were burning-up and her skin was coming off in shreds. Most of the girls rushed to help. I'm afraid I didn't move. I thought it served them both right. I didn't really consider that a girl was being hurtled to probable death. I just thought it was all a kind of justice and there was a God after all.

A further result was that matron, who was having trouble finding her hands and was busily occupied trying to stick them together again, was no longer in a state to tell me off. And Ann did arrive just about in one piece at the bottom, with all those people grimly hanging on to the rope.

The Girl Guide troop was another area of school life into which I did not settle well. I hated the bloody Girl Guides, and I particularly hated their bloody badges. I never got any badges for anything. The only thing I liked were paper chases. I used to contrive to be the one leaving the trail. Then I would tell the other girls I'd meet them at the nearby riding stables, which was one of the few places where I did fit in.

In fact, I was so good at riding that I was once spotted at a show by people involved with international show-jumping, who offered to fund me at the famous Porlock Vale Riding Academy in Somerset – not far from the country house Hil and I now share. And as, in addition to dreaming of being a ballerina, I also dreamed of being National Velvet. I was furious when my father refused to let me be launched into a riding career on the grounds that I'd be on the scrap heap and miserable by the time I was 40.

I was therefore always welcome around horses. So instead of laying some silly trail, I would get a horse and go for a gallop on the beach. This arrangement suited the other girls too, because nobody in their right mind wanted to go chasing around after bits of paper. Anyway, it was such a waste of time. But inevitably, in the end, I was found out and, perhaps equally inevitably, I was expelled.

The final nail in my coffin came when the headmistresses claimed that I'd been spotted walking through St Anne's in my boater with chunks out of it – I had virtually destroyed the thing hurling it at people from five floors up – screaming repeatedly at the top of my voice, "St Anne's is a lousy bloody school, St Anne's is a lousy bloody school!"

As it happens, I don't remember actually doing that. But I did put on a limp when we were walking along in a crocodile while hissing at people as we passed by, "Don't send your daughter to our school, it's horrible."

I did feel that my end at St Anne's was dealt with in an overly dramatic fashion. First of all, my parents were summoned to the school. Then I was called to the headmistresses' office and made to kneel in the middle of the room. My parents had been living apart for some time by then. My mother was already pregnant with my sister Caroline, whose father was another man, and I don't think either Connie or Hubert knew the other would be there, so it must have been a bit of a shock. Nonetheless, looking back, I am a bit astounded that they allowed me to be left kneeling in the middle of a room like that.

There was then a procession of people, mostly prefects and teachers, including the drama teacher and the art teacher in whose classes I'd always done rather well, who came in to describe this monster-child who was rebellious, insolent, avoided work, hit people, and generally behaved atrociously. Matron was among the most vitriolic, but then she didn't have a lot to thank me for. To my intense satisfaction, although it had been a considerable time since the girl-on-the-end-of-the-rope incident, the skin on her hands had yet to heal.

As always, I didn't allow myself to care about what was happening. I just shut myself off from it all. I had only one fear. There was a window near to where I was kneeling, and I thought if Bernie comes in and speaks out against me, I shall throw myself through that window. I don't remember how many storeys up the headmistress' office was. I have no idea if jumping out of that window would have killed me, but it wouldn't have done me much good, that was for certain. I didn't care either way. If Bernie had joined in the demolition of that evil Shirley Broadbent, an 11-year-old-girl accused of bringing the entire idiot school to a standstill, there would have been nothing left for me at home or at school. Nobody I trusted anymore. I did think about my beloved rabbits and what would happen to them if I jumped, but even Loppy and Lena couldn't have stopped me. Bernie, however, did not take part in this ritual humiliation. Bless her, she should have done, because by then she was head girl. But I learned later that she had refused.

When it finally ended, and I was presumably considered to have been satisfactorily ripped to shreds, my parents took me to an elegant little tea shop nearby. It was totally bizarre. I was terribly upset, of course, but I had already learned not to let that show. Nobody could make me cry. I felt strongly that some strange injustice had been done, and I was full of defiance, so we sat in this tea shop, and my parents never even mentioned what happened. Indeed, I hardly remember them talking to me at all. I think I was already a great disappointment to my father, while my mother would never admit that I ever did anything wrong, never tell me off about anything. They were poles apart about me, and there they were in this dreadful state with each other, because my mother was having this big on-off affair, and I suspect my father was involved with someone too. I never really knew, because they wouldn't discuss it with me. But in that tea shop, to my astonishment, after what I had just gone through, I was pretty much ignored while they just went at it, at each other, hammer and tongs.

Years later, looking through some of my father's papers after he died, I found the letter one of the headmistresses had written him halfway through that final summer term at St Anne's. It was a letter I did not know existed. Nobody told me. It was such an extraordinary thing to be written about a child of that age that I cannot resist including it here in its entirety.

Dear Mr. Broadbent,

I am extremely sorry to have to write you this letter. As you were kind enough to say in your letter to me at the beginning of term, the relation (sic) between Miss Thompson and myself and you and Mrs. Broadbent has always been very cordial, and I should like to think it would remain so until Shirley left. But Shirley herself seems determined to ensure that there should be no regret on either side when she leaves. Since it was settled that she should leave here at the end of this term, her attitude has been that that day cannot come soon enough, and in the meantime, she will do as little work as possible and defy all school rules. The entire staff complains of her gratuitous rudeness, which at times borders on insolence. She makes no secret of the fact that she is glad to be leaving, and appears to hold this entire school in contempt. This is having a most disastrous effect among certain girls younger than Shirley. We have tried appealing to her sense of fair play with no effect at all. This weekend, we seem to have reached the climax. On Friday, she deliberately cut a special elocution lesson which Miss Knight had remained at school after her usual time to give to Shirley. As a result, Miss Knight has very properly, refused to allow Shirley to take the elocution exam to-day (sic), as she had not even learned the test piece by the end of last week. In addition, over the weekend, Shirley was extremely insolent to the staff on duty so much so that I received (sic) an official complaint about her from the staff. I have therefore refused to give permission for Shirley to dance at a Masonic party on Saturday, and have further warned her that if this continues it is doubtful whether Miss Thompson and I will feel able to permit her to remain until the end of term.

I cannot imagine what has come over her. Until last term, Shirley was a straightforward and very pleasant child who, though not over fond of work, was at least honest and pleasant to deal with during the last term and a half, a most disastrous change has taken place in her which is apparent to all of us. I feel quite powerless, as I can apparently make no appeal to her. I have to consider the good of a great number of girls, and if Shirley persists in using her influence to undermine authority, that influence must be removed. It is with the greatest reluctance that I write to you thus, and I feel sure that you will add your authority to mine in attempting to persuade Shirley that we should all prefer her last weeks here to be pleasant ones, rather than to part abruptly in such a way that her connection with this school will be broken permanently. Believe me, it is sheer desparation (sic) which causes me to write this letter to you.
Yours sincerely.
Joyce M. Foden

So there it is, my condemnation in writing from my headmistress, complete with spelling and grammatical errors, which of course, I as a dyslexic would still remain unaware of, had they not, to my considerable amusement, been pointed out to me by my co-writer. Who knows, maybe the staff of St Anne's College were ill-equipped to teach anybody to read and write properly, not just dyslexics like me.

Anyway, the letter seems to suggest that I knew I had been asked to leave at the end of that term. I have no memory of that, although threats of expulsion were a constant feature of my school life, and I certainly left ultimately with no regrets – except that I would be moving away from Bernie, the very thought of which shattered me.

The day my mother came to collect me, she refused to let me wear my school uniform for some reason, probably just her usual insistence on being different, and demanded I leave the school dressed in a completely inappropriate and very adult outfit she had brought.

I felt even more self-conscious than usual, and everything seemed to be so muddled and rushed that I didn't even get a chance to say a proper goodbye to Bernie. She was standing in the hallway with the two headmistresses when, clad in a grown-up, pale grey suit and teetering on high-heeled shoes, I was hurried past. All we did was look at each other. And I just somehow knew that this would be the last time I would see Bernie, which was a terrible feeling.

Otherwise, I didn't give a damn about being expelled. I was an awkward, blushing, 11-year-old with no home life left worth mentioning, unable to read or do anything else much except dance. I thought that I couldn't be more miserable. And looking back on that day almost 80 years later, I don't think I ever have been more miserable.

11

—

To Pantomime and Soho

Just a few months later, my worst premonition came true. Bernie died. I was living with my mother again at my grandparents' bungalow on the moors when I heard that she was very ill. She was at university in Dublin by then and she had collapsed while playing hockey. Apparently she was wet with sweat and had a massive temperature, so she was rushed to hospital. I didn't really know how ill she was, but I feared the worst.

One night I had a clear premonition that she had gone. I didn't tell anyone this for many years, including my mother, partly because I didn't think I would be believed, and partly because I was embarrassed.

There was no telephone at the bungalow, of course. So in the morning, I trudged down the hill to the nearest telephone box and called my old headmistress, Miss Thompson, who probably wasn't at all pleased to hear from the child she had written that awful letter about. But she confirmed what I already knew in my heart; Bernie was dead.

It turned out that she'd had polio, but had been wrongly

diagnosed with meningitis, and given the wrong treatment and medication. By the time this was discovered, it was too late. She was in an iron lung, a kind of ventilator which enclosed virtually the whole body and was used to treat polio cases in those days, but she did not survive.

I felt numb. I hadn't seen Bernie since leaving St Anne's. She had written to me, and I had scribbled notes back, but that had been the sum of our contact. Which somehow made things even worse. Now, suddenly, she had gone. And for a time I didn't think life was worth living without her.

The only person in the world who even began to understand the immensity of my loss was my mother. I don't remember ever discussing with her the details of my relationship with Bernie, but she seemed to know instinctively that there was something special between us. And being Connie, she just accepted it and did her absolute best to comfort me.

I don't know what the reality would have been if Bernie had lived and I'd met her again as an adult. But I do think probably the feelings you have at that age are so raw, they can even explain up to a point why dreadful things happen with children, even things like stabbings at schools. Emotions are so heightened at that age. You don't listen to anyone. You just believe your own truth.

I am fairly sure, and I can't explain why, that Bernie and I would never have had an adult relationship.

Nonetheless, her death was a loss that influenced everything that I was and did for many years to come. Certainly, I think my behaviour became even worse because of it and eventually led to my being expelled from a second school, The Arts Educational School at Tring, which should have been a great place for me, but turned out to be anything but.

My mother got me the audition for it and somewhat

remarkably, given my propensity for misbehaviour and my inability to read or write properly, I was accepted. It was supposed to be a very special place, and it was certainly housed in a very special building, an incredibly beautiful, magnificent mansion built by Sir Christopher Wren. But I didn't want to be there any more than I wanted to be at any other boarding school. All I wanted was a proper home, something I felt everyone else had except me. Then there was my northern accent. The other pupils at Tring spoke in well-modulated southern coast tones. I was deeply embarrassed.

One word I really couldn't say was envelope. I remember asking, "Has anybody got one of those things you put letters in?" They must have thought I was totally mad. I used to walk around looking at what other people did, and listening to the way they spoke. But I still couldn't work out how to do it right. I was convinced that my way was wrong. I just felt inferior in every possible sense – including, as always, the way I looked.

I still wanted desperately to be a dancer. I knew that I could dance, but as far as The Arts Educational School was concerned, I was just a little red-faced misfit.

At home, or what passed for it, the madness continued. My family had gone right up the spout. Don't ever let anyone tell you that children don't realise what's going on when their parents' marriage is falling apart, because they damn well do. My mother and father did the classic trick of each trying to turn me against the other.

The man my mother left home for, my sister's father, was a former army colonel called William Barrett, rather upper class and well-spoken, whom she considered a very romantic figure. Bill didn't like me because I reminded him of my father – as I would being his daughter. He developed a penchant for making me stand outside the house at night if he considered that I'd misbehaved in any way, which I found very frightening, particularly in view of the location involved. My father had remained in our family home in Ashton with my brother Chris, six years younger than me, while my mother had contrived to move into my grandparents' remote moorland bungalow – their main home still being above their Ashton tailors' shop – yet again displaying that avid romantic streak of hers. I think she saw herself as Cathy in Wuthering Heights, and was always attracted to isolated, remote places, even though she was the most gregarious person I ever met. I didn't find it romantic. I hated the place, and standing alone outside in the darkness was a dreadful punishment to me.

I have no idea why my mother let Bill do this, but I will say that she had already managed to reduce him to an emotional wreck, as she did so many of those around her. Divorce, of course, was a very big deal in those days. I was either 12 or 13 when my parents eventually divorced, but Bill took longer to properly leave his wife. Meanwhile, my brother and I were shuffled between our parents. We seemed to be constantly on buses between their two homes. We both found it quite frightening, particularly as to get to the bungalow, we had to walk about two miles up a lane with nothing except stone walls and sheep around us. And in the winter, it would be pitch black because there was no lighting. Then there was Bill's scary wife, Gladys, who would turn up outside yelling and brandishing a horsewhip. She would also lie on the ground in front of the garage. On countless occasions, Bill nearly ran over her in his car. As Chris and I walked back to the bungalow, I was always convinced that she would leap out of the darkness and attack us.

Once, when my mother had taken me shopping in Manchester, Gladys physically attacked her in Kendals, then Manchester's premier department store. True to form I flew at Gladys and absolutely flattened her. I did the usual, knocked her down and bashed her head on the floor. I was then picked up by the manager by the scruff of my neck and my backside and chucked out of the store onto the pavement outside.

That remains a vivid memory, and one I never failed to think of during my *Coronation Street* years, when I would walk through Kendals, usually with people calling out, "Hello Alma". I used to wonder what those Corrie fans would make of it if they knew that I had attacked my mother's lover's wife in that very store, bashing her head on the marble floor that was then still there.

I don't think my father ever knew about that incident. Certainly, on my mother's instructions, I never told him. I learned not to relate to either parent anything which happened while I was with the other. One of the worst things about the whole situation was that I never felt right wherever I was. If I left my father to go to my mother, that was wrong. And if I left my mother to go to my father, that was wrong. I was miserable at school too.

Salvation, albeit temporary, came in an unlikely package in view of my chronic insecurity. At Christmas, everybody at the Arts Educational School auditioned for a pantomime or some kind of show. And I was sent up to the London Palladium to do an audition for a panto at the Finsbury Park Empire.

By this time, I was in such a mess that I'd lost all desire to go on the stage. But I did have the idea that if I got into a pantomime, at least I wouldn't have to spend Christmas with either of my parents. Not only did I no longer have a home worthy of the name, but I didn't seem to have any of my things left either – except my rabbits, which I never let out of my sight.

I didn't hold out much hope of being picked up at the audition. Apart from anything else, who would want to dance with a little red-faced creature like me? However, a quite extraordinary thing happened.

To my total astonishment, once I walked onto that stage in the London Palladium, a wonderful theatre with such an amazing history of variety, I instantly changed into a person who didn't blush, a person who was, I suppose, a performer. Instead of being, as I'd expected, the one who couldn't do it, I was the one who could. You would have thought that with all my complexes and insecurities, I would have been completely overawed and gone to pieces. The opposite happened. I did it. I got hired for the chorus of *Babes in the Wood!*

In that moment, my life was transformed. I know it sounds like the most terrible cliché, but I felt, quite simply, as if I'd come home, as if I'd found a kind of family that would always be mine. Just looking up and around at the back of the scenery was the most unbelievably comforting sight. I felt absolutely at peace. And that has never changed.

Only anyone who has been lucky enough to find the one thing they can really do in life will understand what it means. Amongst all that I've done wrong over the years, going into the theatre, becoming a performer, this remains the one thing that I know I got right. I never yearned to be famous, to be a star. That wasn't it at all. I merely wanted to be taken into the world of theatre, to become a part of it.

It must be said, however, that my propensity for getting into trouble didn't entirely abandon me. I nearly got thrown out in the first week of *Babes in the Wood*. I was gazing at the principal boy – always a rather splendid girl in those days, of course – and I fell straight into the brass section. I was completely mesmerised. But the trombonist booted me out with one foot, so I was back in line pretty fast, and just about got away with it.

I so loved being in that panto. Going back to school at Tring after Christmas was a terrible let-down, and things went from bad to worse. The academic side totally disintegrated, and I virtually stopped going to lessons. If at the age of 12, I was going to be sent to join the five-year-olds, then, quite frankly, I didn't see the point.

All my old problems returned. My wonderful time in *Babes in the Wood* made no difference to all the blushing and terrible embarrassment I experienced when I was back in class. My paranoia about blushing became so extreme that I would smother my face with toothpaste to lighten it.

The school made matters worse by doing terrible things to me – on one occasion I was to dance before an extremely distinguished panel of patrons, including Dame Alicia Markova and Sir Anton Dolin, both famous dancers whom I hero-worshipped. It was a quite terrifying line-up, and in addition, the whole school was sitting on the floor. I knew that as soon as I opened the door to the ballet room, I would start to blush and that everybody would fall about laughing when they saw me, because that was what they usually did. I spent my whole ballet life at that school looking down so that people couldn't see my face. I may have appeared to be a headless dancer because my head was so far down. No wonder I couldn't do pirouettes! Anyway, I gritted my teeth and walked in. The principal, who had, after all, been trained by Anna Pavlova and had extremely high standards, turned on me straight away.

"You've got holes in your hairnet, return to your dormitory and make yourself tidy," she ordered.

Mortified, I duly set off to do her bidding, but the school was enormous and my dorm was miles away. You really needed a taxi! I had to run along endless corridors, and we were not allowed to use the main staircase, although I did on that occasion, and I went up and down it four at a time. I was in a fearful hurry, after all, the entire school was waiting.

By the time I came puffing back to the ballet room I wasn't

red in the face anymore. I was purple! I just wanted the ground to open and swallow me up. And I still don't understand the thinking of people who would do that to a child.

Ironically enough, the main cause of my ultimate expulsion was something for which you might have expected to win praise at a stage school. But then, initiative was not encouraged at either of the educational establishments which decided they could do without me.

The summer after my wonderful time in *Babes in the Wood*, I learned that the older pupils at Tring, the 16 and 17-year-olds, were being auditioned for a pantomime at the Theatre Royal, Drury Lane. I could think of nothing better than being part of this, but I was allegedly too young. Keen to escape both my school and my parents, I was determined to get in on the act. I decided I would sneak off to London on the train, and I pestered the older girls so much for details about the audition that a couple of the nicer ones smuggled me onto the school bus they were travelling in.

On the day, a momentous thing occurred. The producer, Freddie Carpenter, took a shine to me and kept calling me back to do a bit more and then another bit. I remember some of the others getting quite cross about it, while I just stood in the middle of the stage feeling completely at home again. I was so bewitched by it all that I didn't really take in what it meant when he suddenly said, "Okay, so where would you like to go? You can go to Newcastle, Glasgow, Bradford or Edinburgh."

Somehow, I managed to mumble that I'd like to go to Glasgow, in what was, for me, an unusual flash of practicality. I had a friend who lived there, so I thought that at least I'd have somewhere to stay.

After that, I settled down again to school life, or the nearest I could get to it, until the contract arrived. Then all hell broke loose.

I wasn't supposed to even be at the audition, and the school so liked to be in control. I'd broken the rules again. Nobody there was pleased that I'd got a job, not one little bit. The pantomime went on until the end of March, which meant that I would miss virtually the entire spring term. I was issued with an ultimatum: if I did the pantomime, I was out. My parents became involved at this point, and the row reached epic proportions. My father had virtually washed his hands of me by then, but my mother was over the moon, of course. Particularly when she found out that I was the only one from the school who'd been picked!

She and I decided that, of course, I was going to take the job. The prospect of my being expelled for the second time did not faze either of us. The school duly carried out its threats, and I was out on my ear once more. It was several months before I was due to start rehearsals, and I had no home worth mentioning to go to, or none that I wanted to go to anyway.

And that was how I ended up living and working in Soho at the age of 13 and a half, despite it being totally illegal, even then. Probably because my life was so chaotic at the time, my memory is a bit hazy about exactly how it happened. I do remember being allowed back to the school briefly, after lengthy negotiations between my parents and the head teacher, in order to sit certain compulsory examinations, and I also remember the only ones I passed were for drama and dance.

It was through the pantomime producers that I moved into the Theatre Girls' Club in Greek Street. The excuse was that I had to be in London for fittings and pre-rehearsal meetings. Whatever the reason, I grasped the opportunity with open hands.

The club was a wonderful place run by Miss Bell, a woman to whom I owe a great deal. It was a hostel for young women in theatre. Their ages varied a great deal, and in fact went up to people in their 40s or thereabouts, who were still struggling.

I was by far the youngest, and had to lie about my age to be allowed there at all. They charged just 30 bob a week (about £48 now). We slept several to a room, and the place was run like a boarding school, in that we took turns to wash in the morning, set tables and generally help out. But there all resemblance to boarding schools, certainly the ones I went to, ended. I felt I really belonged somewhere. Most of the girls were off auditioning all the time. I had a job to go to. I was just filling in until the pantomime rehearsals started.

When I eventually got to Glasgow, I found that theatre life for me was just the same as the first time in *Babes In the Wood*. Total bloody bliss!

At first, I stayed with my friends, and later I went into digs. The pantomime was *Cinderella*. It starred Stanley Baxter as Buttons, and a six-foot-tall ex Ziegfeld's Follies girl called Carol Eric was principal boy. I was extremely taken with both of them.

I was in the chorus, of course, but if anybody was chosen for a special spot to give Stanley or Carol a flower or something, and it wasn't me, I was furious.

Right from the beginning, one of the joys of theatre for me was stage make-up. Once I had on as many layers of it as possible, and as many eyelashes as I could muster, I just became a different person. There was no question of blushing. From the start, the theatre gave me a level of freedom I can't explain.

This was a top pantomime in a top venue, produced by Howard and Wyndham at the Theatre Royal, Glasgow. I had no qualms about that whatsoever. I thought the whole experience was sheer magic. There were about 24 of us in the chorus, but I got myself noticed because I kept trying to put little bits into my dance routine to make people laugh, just as I had in Grandfather's Broadbent's theatre when I was three, and as I'm inclined to still, whatever I'm doing in life, wherever I'm going. It could be a medical appointment. I still have to get a laugh. And to my delight, I got a little rave notice in *The Stage*. Of course, this put my mother in ecstasy.

I built up this life for myself within the confines of the company. In between shows, I would go to a café and sit there eating Scottish meat pie and chips, which were about as good as you could get, I reckoned, with a copy of *Reveille* propped up against the sauce bottle. I thought it was the height of sophistication.

I may have only been 13, but I decided that I wasn't going back – not to school, nor to my fragmented family. I was quite determined that I was never going to leave this wonderful new world I had found.

12

Life as a Theatre Girl

When *Cinderella* ended, my life in Soho really began. I persuaded Miss Bell to take me back into the Theatre Girls Club. She shouldn't have agreed – despite my fibs, I suspect she had a jolly good idea of how old I was – but I was very glad she did. Neither of my parents objected. My father because he was well past caring, and my mother because I was starting, however humbly, to live her dream. Connie phoned me every day and visited occasionally, which seemed enough for her at the time.

I don't think either of them worried about me, really, they both had enough worries of their own. It also has to be remembered that we'd all just survived a war, and once the bombs stopped falling, you didn't worry about the safety of those close to you, even girls of my age, in the same way that people do now.

In Soho, my life was transformed. Suddenly I found myself in step with everybody around me. Howard and Wyndham gave me a contract for pantomime and summer season which ran for several years. Between those, I lived in the Theatre Girls Club, and along with all the other girls, hawked myself around looking for work. We were in the heart of the red-light district in the late

1940s and 50s. Soho was something of a haven for gangsters, England's equivalent of Chicago in the 20s. I was totally caught up in the excitement of it all and completely oblivious to the danger, barely noticing the serious side.

I was already earning my own living as well as auditioning for all sorts of things that never materialised. I would do stints at the various Soho nightclubs that were big business at the time and always looking for new acts. You often didn't start work at the clubs until after midnight, and most of us used to be walking through Soho in the early hours. We couldn't afford taxis. There were no tourists in those days, just the people whose way of life was in that part of London. The resident prostitutes, who seemed really ancient to me, became my friends. I didn't regard them as being different to anyone else and I knew they would watch out for me. If any men were to approach me, one of them would call out, "Leave her alone, luv, she's a professional dancer, and she's just a kid." Thanks to them, I could walk the streets in safety, day and night.

Partly because of my fear of getting pregnant, I never had any sort of relationship with boys until I was much, much older. Even then, I wasn't particularly enthusiastic. I don't remember having any sexual urges of any sort. I was too deeply in love with the theatre. I read somewhere that Dan Leno, the Victorian musical star who is one of my great heroes, used to go to the Theatre Royal Drury Lane, when he first started working, and say his prayers on the steps. So I did the same. I made a bargain with God on the steps of The Lane.

"I don't mind if everything else goes wrong," I said. "I don't mind if I never have a relationship, I don't mind if I haven't got a proper family and I don't have anything much, but please, please, please, can I be in the theatre?"

When it came to auditioning, I was full of enthusiasm. There was a group of about eight or nine of us who used to buy one copy of *The Stage* between us. Then we'd all go to the Silver Grill in Leicester Square and squash up around a table over a single cup of tea or coffee, because it was all we could afford. Eventually, after five hours or so, the management would get fed up with us. Then we'd buy one order of Welsh rarebit or beans on toast and slice that up between the lot of us. We'd meticulously dissect *The Stage* and take it in turns to go rushing off for auditions. Later on, there was television too, but at the beginning the auditions were for pantomimes, summer season, cabaret, revue, dancers abroad and so on. I found it exciting just imagining what the jobs would be like. We used to share our make-up and all our rehearsal things. Our changing room was the loo in Leicester Square tube station. It was like a cattle market with 50 million people crawling all over you as you struggled into a leotard that was supposed to show off your shape and make some theatrical producer hire you. Amazingly enough, the mirror we used to use was still there in the Leicester Square ladies' loo until they rebuilt it only a few years ago. For me, that was a real slice of theatrical history.

There were some jobs I had my own reason not to bother with, particularly anything at the Windmill Club! My mother had been blessed with a rather large bosom, and as a small child I had prayed that I would not become similarly endowed. I hated the idea. And by this time, it was apparent that my prayers to God concerning my upper anatomy had paid off. I wasn't growing any boobs at all, and boobs in the 1940s and 50s were definitely in! It wasn't that I minded taking my clothes off. It was just that I thought if I went to the Windmill and they asked me to take them off, they would laugh. I was, after all, used to being laughed at. So I didn't go.

One year, I did a pantomime season at Southport with Tommy

Cooper, who made a big impression on me, but then Tommy made a big impression on everyone. He was larger than life in every way. He had the biggest feet I'd ever seen. He looked as if he was wearing Little Tich boots - the elongated footwear worn by that other famous comic from the 19th and early 20th century.

Tommy was always doing extraordinary, wonderful things. We were in a summer season in Southport when we were asked to attend a fireman's ball. They sent cars for everyone except the poor chorus, which was forgotten as usual. But Tommy wasn't having that. He dialled 999 and said, "There's a fire at the Garrick Theatre, for God's sake send the fire brigade!" Then when the engines arrived, he went out and told the men, "Right, now you lot can take the girls to the party."

It was a memorable season. Derek Roy was the lead comic. Tommy was yet to become a big star. And Eve Boswell, the singer also known as the 'forces' sweetheart', second only to Vera Lynn, topped the bill. I thought I'd died and gone to heaven, just being there with those three. Nothing, but nothing would have made me quit. Somebody once dropped me during a lift, and I broke two ribs, but I was so determined not to be off that I never mentioned the damage. I was doing cartwheels in the air with broken ribs.

I adored Eve, whom I understudied. She took me under her wing and was lovely to me, but she did have problems elsewhere. There was some kind of tension between her and another woman in the show. When something went missing from Eve's dressing room, the other woman was accused of stealing it. She promptly threatened legal action against Eve, simultaneously claiming, for some unknown reason, that our 'forces' sweetheart' was a lesbian. Eve's husband initiated a counter-action and came into the theatre one day with a huge sheaf of papers making various allegations.

Everybody was asked to read all this stuff, but only one person did. Tommy spent about 20 minutes in his dressing room in complete silence, studying the papers meticulously. At the end, he looked up and said, "It's no good, there's not a laugh in it." Everyone thought that was hilarious, apart from Eve's husband.

The following day, a notice in legalese appeared on the notice-board at the stage door. It began along the lines of: "I the under-stated Eve Boswell wishes to make it known that at no time have I ever had a lesbian relationship."

The day after that, another notice appeared beneath it. "I the understated Tommy Cooper wishes to make it known that at no time have I ever peed in the dressing room washbasin." How could you not love that man?

I did have my problems in Southport, however. There was a rather unpleasant series of incidents which, particularly as I was a 16-year-old virgin at the time, would nowadays probably be regarded as serious sexual harassment. Things were rather different in the 1950s. I was locked in the dressing room by our stage manager, who then tried to jump on me. I wouldn't play. He took his revenge. Firstly, he made me stand on stage from 10 in the morning until lunchtime because I had a hole in my fishnet tights. I just had to stand there – wearing only my leotard and tights and high-heeled shoes – with all the stage-hands around. They were divine to me, thankfully. But he was a right bastard, keeping this horrible punishment going for a week, all for that one crime of having a hole in my tights. He proceeded to get nastier and nastier, and threatened to stop me getting into the West End because of my terrible behaviour. I very much doubt whether he had that sort of power – with the benefit of hindsight, almost certainly not – but it seemed like a very big deal at the time.

Then one morning, he called me into his office, which was

on the top floor of the theatre. "You'll never work for Bernard Delfont again," he threatened, leering at me.. Delfont was already one of the most important theatrical impresarios in the country. And I knew exactly how I could have got on the right side of our awful stage manager, but I had no intention of doing so. Suddenly, I blew! I had a pair of brand-new pointe shoes with me, and I whacked him over the head with them, two direct blows right across his skull.

As he was reeling from that, I kicked him so hard that he fell and cracked his head on the washbasin. Without knowing what damage I'd done, I rushed out, locking the door behind me, and ran.

Much later in the day, I bumped into some of the George Mitchell singers and confessed. They guessed that he had probably been trying to get out of his office for several hours. They were right! He needed medical treatment too. Not surprisingly, he decided I had to go. I was out, sacked! But to my surprise, everybody stood by me, the stagehands and all the cast, including Tommy, stuck their necks out for me, bless them. They said I'd been victimised and if I was out, so were they. It seemed to me that for once in my life, I had experienced some justice. I think I loved the theatre and theatre people even more after that.

Soon afterwards, I started going out with my first real boyfriend, a journalist called John Law. There was no sex even then. In spite of, or maybe because of the world that I moved in. John was a really clever comedy writer who was responsible for me being rather better at auditions than some of my contemporaries, thanks to the pieces he wrote for me.

There is no doubt that he played a significant part in my eventual escape from the chorus line. Auditions were an absolute cattle market. Both Johnny Briggs, my screen husband Mike Baldwin in Corrie, and I were regulars at the big open auditions staged in London's Monmouth Street by Ronnie Curtis, who cast many of the Elstree and Pinewood movies at the time. Ronnie used to point at the people he wanted, but unfortunately, as one of his eyes was set at a jaunty angle, shall we say, he appeared to be looking in one direction while pointing in another. No one was ever quite sure whether they'd been chosen or not, and, without doubt, quite a lot of people were picked by mistake.

Precociously for a chorus girl, I also auditioned for the lead in *Where's Charley?*, a musical version of the play *Charley's Aunt*. I got down to the final two of the part playing opposite Norman Wisdom, already a huge name in the business, which gave me considerable encouragement.

Meanwhile, pantomime and summer season took me all over the country, and in between there were spots in Soho clubs like The Stork and The Ambassador, where Shirley Bassey starred for many years.

I was only 19, with all that work already behind me, when I was picked for a revue called *Five Past Eight*, which was a Howard and Wyndham production, in Scotland again. It was produced by Freddie Carpenter, who had taken a shine to me when he'd hired me for *Cinderella*, and I was thrilled when he again took me on. He then became responsible for a rather momentous moment in my life. I said goodbye to Shirley Broadbent forever. He insisted that I change my name.

"You'll never be taken seriously in this business with a name like that," he told me firmly. "You just couldn't succeed."

I did his bidding instantly, never dreaming for a moment that one day an actor called Jim Broadbent would win an Oscar. Almost everybody changed their names in those days, particularly if they were called Broadbent. However, finding a new name wasn't easy. I picked Barrie with a pin from the phone book, and I was pleased with my chance choice because of its connection with J.M Barrie, the writer of *Peter Pan*. Then I thought of Amanda because of my lifelong devotion to the actress Gertrude Lawrence, who'd always wanted to be called Amanda, as indeed she was in *Private Lives*, which was written especially for her by Noel Coward. But I decided that would be too pretentious, so I picked Lynn instead. Then Equity turned me down because there was already a Lynn Barrie listed, so I asked a friend to choose a book for me and open it at random. The book was *The Research Magnificent* by HG Wells, and it opened at two pages which were blank except for a one-word chapter heading: 'Amanda.'

I reckoned that was a message from Gertie, and Amanda Barrie I became. My mother, probably reacting differently to the way most mothers would, loved my name change. And from that date on, neither she nor any of my family called me anything but Amanda, except Mandy sometimes. For myself, I changed my name without giving it a thought, though occasionally nowadays, I do rather wish I'd stuck with the name I was born with.

13

The Winston's Dame

Five Past Eight played all over Scotland, and among the cast was the young and barely known Des O'Connor. He would come bounding down to breakfast, where the rest of us would be sitting like dead fish and say, "Right, point at something."

At first we thought he was barmy. Then we realised what he was trying to do. This was an exercise to make sure he always had a gag ready about anything and everything. Someone would point at the pepper pot, and Des would begin, "Well, I met this man wearing a pepper pot…" After a bit, as soon as he arrived, we'd all shout it once, "Salt cellar, sugar bowl, curtains…"

Also during *Five Past Eight*, I became good friends with a young woman called Jane Taylor, who was in the same digs. We had both worked on TV with Benny Hill, and we got into the habit of having long telephone conversations with him late at night when we returned to our digs. The only telephone was a pay phone in the hall to which we had restricted access. We weren't supposed to receive phone calls late at night, and we certainly couldn't afford to make many calls. So we used to crouch under the hall table until Benny phoned us, then grabbed the receiver and talked to him for hours.

I was thrilled to be in *Five Past Eight*, but as a mere chorus girl I had no billing, something which I decided to put right one night in Glasgow. As I left the theatre I scribbled my name at the bottom of a poster outside, and was promptly arrested by a passing policeman. Well, more or less! He pointed out that what I had done was against the law, took me to a nearby police station, supplied me with an eraser, and told me to return to the scene of my crime and remove the offending defacement. So that put me in my place.

Early in 1956, after my stint in *Five Past Eight* ended, I eventually became a regular dancer at one of the top London clubs, Winston's. I worked there for more than four years, while continuing with pantomime and summer season, punctuated by lots of TV, including commercials. I was also a regular dancer on the *Henry Hall Show*, when the celebrated bandleader moved from radio to TV. Henry's shows were immensely popular and attracted all the big stars of that era. I appeared alongside people who were heroes to me, like Harry Secombe, Spike Milligan, and Alma Cogan, who was then the highest paid British female entertainer, but died tragically of cancer aged only 34.

Winston's, where Danny LaRue made his name and Lionel Blair did the choreography, became a very important part of my life. It was where I first worked with Barbara Windsor, also Jill Gascoigne and the West End musical star, Maggie Fitzgibbon.

We were showgirls then at the start of our various careers. Like me, Barbara Windsor lived quite close to Winston's, and she and I were always bumping into each other in the middle of the night, as we toddled down Oxford Street in full make-up, mini-skirts, false eyelashes, the lot.

I met some extraordinary people in the club, including several of the gangsters who used to pretty much run Soho back then. These were the days of the Maltese mafia, when two legendary gang leaders, Jack 'Spot' Comer and Albert 'Big Alby' Dimes once fought each other with knives up and down Frith Street for almost an hour in the middle of the day. A huge crowd gathered to watch, but when the pair were arrested, the case was thrown out of court because of a lack of witnesses. Even a vicar allegedly accepted £14 to swear that the fight never happened. Mostly, these were rather frightening men, but they were inclined to be extremely gentlemanly to us girls. There were exceptions, however.

Our dressing room doubled as the meat store. There were two huge refrigerators, and we barely had space to move. The room was small and airless, and there used to be between six and eight of us girls squashed in there. Every few minutes, some commis waiter would come blundering through, lean across us and pull half a dozen bloody rump steaks out of a fridge. All too often, we'd end up with blood dripping all over us, which was particularly unpleasant as we were usually in a state of at least partial undress.

One night, this big, hefty man came into the dressing room and just wouldn't go away. He stood there alongside half a dead sheep, staring at us for what seemed like forever. The stage manager tried to get him to go, but he wouldn't budge. He just carried on staring. Eventually, I could stand it no longer. I had no idea who he was, and I didn't care. I hit him over the head with a chair, and he went reeling off, more than a little concussed.

Later I learned that he was Alby Dimes' minder, which was mildly disconcerting even to me, and that he had just come out of jail. Apparently, when he came round, he went quite mad, threatening to smash up the place and do me all sorts of damage. Alby was a regular at Winston's and we'd see him around and pass the time of day with him. So after I came off stage, I went to where he was sitting and said that I was sorry I'd hit his friend, but it was because he wouldn't leave our dressing room.

"He shouldn't have done it," I said. "It's not nice being stared at like that when you haven't got any clothes on."

I was very naive. Everybody else was horrified when they realised what I was doing, but Mr. Dimes pulled up a chair for me, sat me down, and agreed with me. Like most of his kind back then, he prided himself on treating women well and behaving properly in their presence. Indeed, if we had a bad audience who heckled a lot, it was usually Alby and his henchmen who would make them shut up and let us get on with the show. So it was quite in character for him to send me a huge bouquet of flowers the next day, which stunned a few people at Winston's.

Barbara Windsor was my contemporary at Winston's. She already seemed like a star to me. Her physical size never did anything to diminish her enormous presence. We were kindred spirits back in the day. And in many ways always remained so.

In 2017, my then agent, who was also Barbara Windsor's agent for 25 years, and I both attended an 80th birthday party for her, given by the Grand Order of Lady Ratlings, the showbiz charitable organisation.

He said to me, "Come quickly and have a picture with Barbara, look she's over there." He pointed across the room. She was standing with her back to us. I walked towards her, and, as I approached, said, "Hello darling, if I'd had a bet at Ladbrokes when we were working at Winston's that you'd be a dame, I'd be a rich woman now."

At first there was no response. Then she turned around and I realised at once that this was not Barbara Windsor, but a woman who had once been her stand in. The moral of this story, obviously, is never trust your agent...

Danny LaRue was in his heyday when Barbara and I worked with him at Winston's. You could say he made the drag scene respectable, but it was more than that. I was a great admirer, and saw how all kinds of audiences fell for him. He once advised me, "Just learn your ad libs, dear." One of the best lines I've ever heard in show business.

He was a true great. He wouldn't take any nonsense either. No audience ever got out of hand with Danny. He'd simply stop the show and say, "Right, I get paid for making a fool of myself; what's your excuse?"

You never knew who was going to be out front at Winston's, and some very impressive people would turn up. Ava Gardner was a regular visitor, and one night Judy Garland came along, which caused me great embarrassment, as I had the total humiliation of singing 'Swanee' with her about three feet away from me. I was so mortified that after a bit I muttered, "Oh sorry," crossed myself and ran off stage.

Nonetheless, her then-husband, Sid Luff, with whom, through our mutual love of horses and races, I had become quite friendly when he'd visited the club alone on previous occasions, insisted that I meet her. It was an astonishing experience. There she was, this legend, yet you couldn't believe anyone could be so small. She didn't appear to have a neck. I remember thinking that she wasn't built like other people. She was tiny, but she had a huge rib cage, which must have been why her voice was so extraordinary. She hardly spoke to me, or indeed, to anyone else.

Early on during my time at Winston's, I moved out of the Theatre Girls Club permanently. I still didn't have any money, but I was working all the time, so they wouldn't keep me at the club any longer. Television had started to become important and I was doing quite a lot of it during the day, as well as working at Winston's at night.

I'M STILL HERE

It was a somewhat hazy period of my life. I'm not quite sure where I was living half the time or in precisely what order I was appearing in each show or TV programme. It was inclined to all blend into one. I didn't have a permanent home to give my life any structure. Sometimes I used to stay with friends, and occasionally I'd visit my mother and my sister Caroline. They were by then living with Bill, who had finally left his wife, in a 15th century cottage in the village of Disley, just outside Manchester. I also stayed in Notting Hill with John Law, who had moved down to London from Scotland and had a flat there. We still didn't go to bed together, though. It was only the 1950s, contraception was medieval, and my absolute terror of pregnancy remained a great deterrent. I just did not want a child in or out of wedlock. And there was no way I could have had an abortion, as so many of my contemporaries did, as it would have seemed like murder to me.

John was a lovely man. He used to say he didn't mind if I didn't love him, as long as I stayed with him. He was just setting up as a professional comedy writer, and he continued to write material for me. We used to sit up all night with these wonderful people who came to his flat, and talk comedy. John wrote material for all of them. Marty Feldman, Barry Took and Michael Bentine were regulars, long before they became big names. Michael Bentine was always doing his act. He had a glove puppet he called Glovey, which got itself into all sorts of trouble, culminating in acquiring a gun and shooting itself. Most of this took place behind John's sofa.

During that period, I did a number of terrible gigs with Marty. I will never ever forget appearing at Tottenham Working Men's Club with him before going on to Winston's. We were a disaster. Marty was a comic genius, but at Tottenham Working Men's Club, nobody, but nobody, laughed at him. They didn't understand him at all. He just wasn't working men's club material. He was already quite off the wall. We did a cabaret act with little sketches, and I remember having to sing a terrible number: 'The Railroad Runs Through the Middle of the Track.' Then Marty would pick me up, I was very light in those days, and rush off with me through the tables. The members of Tottenham Working Men's Club remained singularly unamused.

After a while, I moved to my own flat in Romilly Street. I'm not quite sure how, or indeed why. Although John had said that he wanted to marry me, which was not what I wanted at all, and it did not seem fair to stay with him any longer. I was not alone for long. Soon my mother, Chris, and Caroline moved in. Bill had died suddenly and unexpectedly after a short illness, having never divorced his wife or left a will, so my mother ended up virtually penniless. She and my siblings came to sleep on my floor, and I became the major breadwinner.

Somewhere in the middle of all this, I finally surrendered my virginity at the age of 21. The first man I slept with was a choreographer. I can't explain why I chose him instead of poor John, except that he was extremely good looking and had a phenomenal physique, something I've always rather liked.

Ultimately, it was something of a relief to get it over with, but partly because I was still worrying about pregnancy, even while it was happening, I don't remember being particularly impressed with the experience. However, he was a nice, clever man whom I found very attractive. And I was beginning to have this thing which stayed with me for quite a while, about it being impolite to say no.

If somebody goes, I love you, I worship you, I adore you, I really want to be with you, and so on, you don't really want to say, 'well, I don't fancy you a bit', do you?

PART THREE

*The Road To
Coronation Street*

14

—

From Stage to Screen and Back to Stage Again

My work remained the closest thing to stability in my life. I was beginning to build quite a pedigree in television, working alongside people such as Peter Sellers and Spike Milligan again, who would go on to become major stars through.

There were countless television shows – many I have since forgotten, and of which there is now little record, as everything was broadcast live in those days.

I do, however, clearly remember appearing in the very first *Morecambe and Wise show*. It seems almost unbelievable now, but the show was a complete flop. I suspect this was because Morecambe and Wise were, at that time, modelled on another famous double act, Jewel and Warriss, and had yet to develop their own distinctive style. Nonetheless, they were already very funny and a delight to work with.

Unfortunately, I managed to disgrace myself during a dance

when my skirt fell off – live on air – giving the entire television audience a grandstand view of my knickers.

I was also chosen for a television show called *On the Bright Side*, with Stanley Baxter, Betty Marsden, Pip Hinton, and Ronnie Barker. The standard all round was exceptionally high, and the show won several awards. Other television work included *Cool for Cats* – a forerunner to Top of the Pops, which featured all the hit numbers of the week. Then there was the legendary *Sunday Night at the London Palladium, The Harry Secombe Show*, The *Dave King Show, Saturday Spectacular*, and *Seven Faces for Jim*, written by Frank Muir and Denis Norden for June Whitfield and Jimmy Edwards.

I worked on a host of other, less-remembered shows as well, not to mention television commercials. Every night, I continued to perform at Winston's Club. The most important qualification for anyone living that sort of life was not so much great talent as great endurance. I never had enough sleep; my biggest challenge was simply staying awake. I would work on some television show all day, from about nine in the morning until seven in the evening, then go home, snatch an hour or two's sleep, grab something to eat, and set off for Winston's Club, where I would work until about four in the morning.

The money was dreadful. I needed two jobs, especially as I was helping to support my mother and sister at the time. I used to book a telephone alarm call for 7am in order to catch the bus to the BBC rehearsal rooms at Shepherd's Bush, which meant I was lucky to get three hours in bed.

Being a chorus girl was certainly not as glamorous as it might sound. We were like an army in eyelashes – totally regimented, utterly anonymous, and there to be abused by anyone passing, from the lead comic who fancied a grope onwards. Our appearance was a total illusion. I am often told off nowadays for my lack of interest in exercise, but as far as I'm concerned, I had enough in my dancing days to last a lifetime. Indeed I probably covered more ground than Sherpa Tenzing and Paula Radcliffe put together.

The worst part was having to trust some half-awake camp boy dancer to catch you during early morning rehearsals. Some of them frightened the life out of you. You just knew they were going to let you go straight over their heads. There was one who did just that: when I was supposed to land around his neck, he missed me and ducked, so I went straight over his head and hit the wall – splat. I was spread-eagled like a starfish and scraped myself down six feet of wall. I lost two teeth in that escapade, but the choreographer simply called, "Okay, from the top…"

"I think I've broken my back teeth…"

There wasn't even a pause.

"And a five, six, seven, eight!"

You just got on with it. Indeed, I suspect I would probably rise from my grave if someone called after me, "And a five, six, seven, eight!"

As a chorus line dancer you were thrown about, held up, and dropped. You never had a name; you were "them" or "the kids", regardless of age. And some chorus dancers could be quite advanced in years.

"When are they coming in? Well, they can start first."

We were creatures of little consequence, expected to obey orders instantly and without question, and barely noticed unless we did something wrong.

We got through it thanks to a mixture of herd instinct and terror. We were always either struggling to stay awake or battling pain because something had been pulled, bruised, or broken, while some unfeeling director or choreographer shouted, "Come on, kids, come on!" By the time I was 15, I already felt like a very old horse. One thing you do not experience in the chorus is any sense of ego. In fact, I defy anyone who has spent as long in choruses as I did ever to develop one.

There is a saying: you can get a girl out of the chorus, but you can't get the chorus out of the girl. I know that's true of me. I'm still inclined to take food parcels with me wherever I go, just in case nobody feeds me. I'm surprised if I'm treated well by people I work with. And I never, ever walk when I can stand, stand when I can sit, or sit when I can lie down.

In 1959, my career briefly changed direction when I was asked to be a hostess on *Double Your Money* with Hughie Green. Apparently, Hughie picked me out of the chorus during one of my many TV dancing appearances because he thought I was funny – whether or not I was supposed to have been funny, I have no idea. I was delighted as people became recognised on those shows, and I thought *Double Your Money* might provide a route out of the chorus line before I became so bruised, battered, and worn out that I would be incapable of moving on to anything else. This did not prove to be the case.

For a start, I was not the hostess type. Hostesses were supposed to have either immense bosoms or endearing Cockney person-alities, like little Monica Rose, who got it so right she turned the whole thing into an art form. I was supposed to provide my own clothes, and I simply didn't possess anything suitable. I didn't go to cocktail parties, and even if I'd had the time, I doubt I would have attended the sort of events that required the kind of clothes expected on *Double Your Money*.

"Bring three or four gowns," they would say. Gowns! I owned absolutely nothing that could remotely pass as a gown, except perhaps a candlewick dressing gown with Bovril stains down the front. I ended up buying a collection of dreadful little frocks.

Unsurprisingly, I looked extremely peculiar on stage and

realised I had absolutely no idea what I was supposed to do. It was a complete mystery to me. I was supposed to deal with the money handed out to contestants and keep track of their progress. I was, of course, hopeless at it.

But *Double Your Money* was an immensely popular and highly professional show, and Hughie Green was almost certainly the most professional TV presenter of his kind at the time. He had come to the UK with similar experience in Canada and was unlike anyone we had seen before on British television. By God, he was slick. He had the whole thing worked out down to the last eyelash flick. He knew exactly how to handle his audience, and, boy, could he turn on the charm. "Sincerely, folks," was his catchphrase, but anything less sincere than Hughie Green at work on an audience is hard to imagine. It was all just an act – he was mechanical – but an extremely good act.

Later in 1959, I made my West End debut at the Phoenix Theatre in the stage revue *On the Brighter Side*, which had evolved from the television show On the Bright Side. I found myself working with much the same cast as before, with Stanley Baxter and Betty Marsden starring, and Ronnie Barker once again among us. This was early in Ronnie's career, and he served as Stanley's understudy. At the time, he bore little resemblance to the comic genius he would later become; he looked more like a bank clerk than a future star. Yet even then, one could sense the dry wit constantly bubbling up in him. He was also the person everyone turned to in a crisis.

These were the days when the Lord Chamberlain's censorship of theatre was at its height,. Until 1968, when theatre censorship was abolished, he had the single-handed power to ban performances, demand cuts, or even cancel plays altogether, for alleged moral or political reasons. And nothing could be performed without his approval. It was an era so ludicrous that even lines such as "we had fairies at the bottom of our garden" could be banned. The whole thing was absurd, particularly for a revue, the very purpose of which was to skirt the boundaries of propriety. I recall one number entitled 'Little Nell', in which the Old Curiosity Shop was reimagined as a brothel. There was a line, "all this knocking and banging must stop in our Old Curiosity Shop," which the Lord Chamberlain promptly forbade.

It was Ronnie, with his quick comedic mind, who saved the day, suggesting we bring in a donkey and change the line to, "I will not have that noisy clip-clop through my Old Curiosity Shop." We managed to sneak that one past the censor, even though, in truth, it was just as suggestive as the original. The audience, of course, picked up on the innuendo immediately, but fortunately, His Lordship did not.

Ronnie always had a remarkable head for comedy. When we were on tour, we would sit up for hours at night writing "quickies" – those brief sketches in which someone would enter from one side of the stage, deliver a single line, and exit on the other. They were mere one-liners, but vital to the rhythm of the revue.

Silly things, such as, "Doesn't the boss dress nicely?"

"Yes, and so quickly."

The secret was always in the speed of the delivery. Ronnie and I were fascinated by these, and we would spend endless hours trying to devise new ones, all while desperately searching for more funny ideas – something that has always rather obsessed me. We would play cards and drink wine, which at the time felt terribly avant-garde.

During that show, Ronnie and I became especially close friends, and it was he who introduced me to antiques – a passion that has remained with me ever since. We would spend hours rummaging through antique and junk shops together, and he taught me all about Victorian postcards. Of course, Ronnie eventually retired from show business and established his own antiques business – a way of life I have always thought would suit me admirably, and in which I have dabbled from time to time.

Judy Khan, Una Stubbs, and Greta Hamby were also in the show. Una was a petite doll-like figure who was always immaculate and in control, in stark contrast to me. My bit of the dressing room was invariably in a terrible state. That hasn't changed. You can ask anyone who has ever worked with me.

So, imagine my humiliation when we were on tour, and I went into the dressing room one night to find that Una had not only cleared up my corner but had also turned out my entire suitcase and tidied that up too.

15

———

A West End Trio

My personal life at that time was equally chaotic. All too often, I found myself hopelessly attracted to the leading lady in a show, only to plunge into denial and attempt to balance things by going to bed with the leading man instead.

That is precisely what happened during the 1960 tour of *The Merry Widow*, starring Vanessa Lee. I ended up having an affair with Richard Curnock, the actor playing opposite me, while harbouring a tremendous crush on Vanessa, of which she was entirely unaware. I did confess to her years later and she laughed, apologising for all the trouble she had unwittingly caused me – not to mention poor Richard. At the time, though, it was no laughing matter. There was a moment when Vanessa had to sing to me on stage, and I blushed so fiercely I must have turned purple. In retrospect, I should have thrown myself at Vanessa's feet, rather than those of a married man like Richard.

The affair developed into a relationship. Richard ultimately left his wife and acquired a flat in Endell Street, Covent Garden, not far from where I still live, and I moved in. There is little doubt, though, that Richard wanted more from our liaison than me, and my being rather in demand at the time and working non-stop didn't really suit him, though we did muddle along for some years. I even used to go fishing with him, in spite of never really liking it.

Following *On the Brighter Side* and *The Merry Widow*, I switched from theatre to film, securing a small role in *Doctor in Distress* – a production with a distinguished cast, including Dirk Bogarde, James Robertson Justice, Samantha Eggar, Barbara Murray, Donald Houston, Leo McKern, and Dennis Price.

In the autumn of 1962, I returned to the theatre with the revue *See You Inside,* alongside Jon Pertwee, Moira Lister, and Harold Lang. The show toured the country for ages before finally reaching the West End. Although written by the clever Barry Cryer, it was not as well received by the critics as it might have been. Nevertheless, I was fortunate enough to enjoy a considerable personal success, and a notice in *The Times* did me no harm at all: "One good reason for seeing the show is the presence of Amanda Barrie, a doll-like figure with huge fluttering eyelashes, a slack jaw and clockwork movements, who is that rare creature – a female clown, a role in which she dances one of the best routines of the evening."

Indeed, I believe the impression I appeared to make in *See You Inside* was a major factor in establishing me in West End theatre. I was soon engaged for the revue *Six of One* at the Adelphi Theatre, based on the life of Dora Bryan – already something of a legend. Dora and I became great friends and remained so until her death. Her real surname was also Broadbent, though as far as we knew, we were not related. Dora led the show, of course, which also starred the distinguished leading man of the time, Richard Wattis – known to us all as Dickie.

While on tour before moving into the West End, the three of us became extremely close – perhaps a little too close. In

Leeds, there was a mix-up over rehearsal rooms, and we found ourselves one wet Monday morning rehearsing outside a church hall because we couldn't get in. We tried not to tread on too many graves while going over a rather twee little number called 'A Versatile Trio', and soon succumbed to fits of giggles. That was only the beginning.

By the time we reached the West End, our corpsing had reached epic proportions. I know stories of actors making each other laugh on stage can be tedious, but the scale and sheer idiocy of our behaviour makes it impossible for me to overlook it.

All hope was lost a few performances into the run; during a number for which I was dressed as a daffodil, Dickie was a bluebell, Dora was a primrose, and our hands were supposed to have been made to look like leaves, but actually just looked like long prongs. I had to do the first part of the routine alone, and I was waiting for Dora and Dickie to join me when I realised that they were behind a mound on the stage in uncontrollable giggles. I was left in the middle of the stage doing the whole number, singing not only "I'm a daffodil", but also "I'm a bluebell, I'm a primrose."

This was the era of "purple hearts" – amphetamines which, at that time, we all thought were marvellous. Dora and I believed they might even cure our corpsing. They did not.

They did most other things though. They made you love the world, and you could keep going for hours after you would otherwise be exhausted. They were a kind of tranquilizer and an amphetamine together. All you had to do was take half a purple heart and you could learn an entire play at a sitting. But most people took about 16 rather than a half of one, and they were very addictive, which is why they ended up being banned.

They were no big deal in 1962. This was the beginning of the decade when almost all young people experimented wildly with every mind-changing substance available, and a lot of older people too. For my sins, I was even a pusher for a while. I knew a lovely man who had a chemist shop in the Charing Cross Road. He was a mad-keen theatre-goer with a daughter he desperately wanted to get on the stage, and he just used to give me the things by the box load.

Of course, it quickly became known in the business that I had a regular supply, and dressers were always arriving at the stage door from other theatres asking me for them. I didn't charge anybody. I just used to hand the pills out and say, have a good show! Though I must admit, to my shame, that if people whom I did not regard as my greatest friends came asking for purple hearts, it was not unknown for me to slip them a laxative instead.

During the run of *Six of One*, almost every night Dora, Dickie, and I used to nip out of the back door of the Adelphi and straight into Rules, the famous old restaurant in Maiden Lane.

One night the three of us were sitting at a table rather towards the back of the restaurant, and Dora was in full flow when I noticed something which looked like grey mud starting to run down the wall. I tried to alert the others but they weren't listening. Dora was mostly concerned about the non arrival of her fish.

Finally the Maître D' came to say he was sorry about the fish, but Rules was on fire. We then noticed that we were the only customers left. At which point the fire brigade arrived, as we looked on with interest. Still nobody asked us to leave. So we just carried on drinking. It seemed the fire was somewhere upstairs and after the gallant fire fighters succeeded in putting it out, they came and joined us for a drink. Or several. The staff joined us too.

The whole thing turned into a party. And by the time Rules

eventually closed its doors in the early hours we three thought it was a jolly good idea to go back to Dickie's flat and carry on drinking. Which we did pretty much all night. I've no idea what time I got home, but I do remember waking rather late the next morning feeling as if I had three heads, when Dora phoned to share with me the horror of having realised that we had a 2.30pm matinee. Which we'd all totally forgotten! I staggered to the theatre a couple of hours later and just had to lean against the wall outside for a bit before entering. I became aware of someone else also leaning against the wall, looked around, and it was Dora doing the same thing.

We went on like three zombies. I feel sure we were still drunk. And God knows what it looked like from the front. I had never done anything like this before, and certainly never have since.

16

—

Can-Can in Cannes

A s *Six of One* drew to its close in the summer of 1963, something occurred that would change my life forever. At the time, I wasn't entirely sure whether it made me happy or not. It certainly thrilled me, but it also frightened me. From that moment on, my entire existence would be shaped by what happened next.

I was to have a gap of three weeks before joining the already acclaimed musical *She Loves Me* at the Lyric Theatre, taking over from Rita Moreno. I had also been hired to play Cleo in the film *Carry On Cleo*, which, as it turned out, became a real landmark in my career. I had already played a much smaller role in *Carry On Cabby*, but apparently, I caught the producer's eye. Unfortunately, my agent made a ghastly mistake: filming for *Cleo* was scheduled to start on the very same day I was due to begin *She Loves Me* at the Lyric. By the time he realised, it was already too late to extricate me from either commitment, even if I'd wanted to be extricated. So, lucky me, not just eight shows a week, but two productions at once.

Faced with this prospect, and having worked non-stop for what felt like forever, everyone in my life urged me to take a holiday – something I hadn't done since those early, thoroughly uncomfortable experiences at Llandudno. Richard had been in America for almost a year, appearing in a series of plays being produced by Joan Littlewood, including *Oh, What a Lovely War!* and I had remained alone in the Endell Street flat with him returning briefly only a couple of times.

Coincidentally, during the final week of *Six of One*, I was told that two people were waiting at the stage door after the show, wanting to give me a drawing. One of them was Kay Ambrose, a ballet artist who had written books on famous dancers, and the well-known manual Ballet for Beginners. The other was a marvellous, wild Canadian dancer named Ian Robinson, who had once danced with the Kirov Ballet and was Rudolf Nureyev's boyfriend.

Kay handed me a drawing of me which she had completed during the show. We went to Rules for dinner and struck up an instant, ridiculous friendship. So much so, in fact, that when Kay and Ian told me they were going to Paris at the weekend and asked if I'd like to join them, it seemed the most natural thing in the world to say yes. I had never done anything like that before, and it turned out to be much more than a holiday; it became one of the most momentous experiences of my life.

The very day after we finished *Six of One*, Kay, Ian and I set off for Paris – at the last moment, travelling by train instead of plane due to an airstrike. Originally, I had agreed to go for a week, but they persuaded me to make it two. I was armed with both my *Carry On Cleo* and my *She Loves Me* scripts, and Kay and Ian assured me there would be plenty of time to work on them. Of course, that did not turn out to be the case.

After just a few days in Paris, Kay suddenly suggested we go to Cannes. We were on a roll. The next day, we boarded the legendary Train Bleu and set off for the South of France. I still had my scripts in my basket – a very fashionable accessory at the time – alongside the remnants of a considerable number of Purple Hearts. The journey itself was wonderful: the Train Bleu was an experience in itself. We were given beautifully embossed playing cards to help pass the time, while elegant waiters served us raspberries, strawberries, and drinks in crystal glasses.

But the greatest experience of all for me was waking up as we arrived in Cannes and seeing the South of France for the first time. The streets of Cannes were bright and bustling, the sea was truly blue, and everything was bathed in sunshine. It all seemed so amazingly colourful, and I loved the warmth – my only previous experiences of the seaside having involved freezing to death on British beaches. I had never been abroad before, which was not at all unusual then, and suddenly I was being introduced to the extraordinary world of Cannes in the 60s.

We were instantly swept up in a nightlife I hadn't known existed. It was all wonderfully adventurous and daring. Being with Kay and Ian, and feeling so relaxed and at ease with myself – a feeling I was wholly unaccustomed to – led to the cracking open of a shell I didn't even realise I had.

The nightlife was like some kind of underwater world, with people floating around in an apparently aimless fashion, never making formal arrangements, yet all turning up at the same club as if by instinct. Then they would all drift off somewhere else. There were extraordinary cabaret acts, many dating back to the 30s, still performed by old men who had once been quite famous. Many of the clubs were gay haunts, and Ian was in his element because there was plenty of opportunity for trolling – something I had never encountered before.

One of the places we started to frequent was a gay club called the Can Can. It had a smoky, hazy, intimate atmosphere, and people danced with partners of either sex – something I had never seen before. Although there was still a law in France against same-sex dancing, the club simply posted someone at the door to raise the alarm if the police were about, at which point everyone would quickly switch partners.

On our first night there, after sitting and observing for a while, Ian and I decided to dance together. We knew all the music – it was just as the Beatles were starting to emerge, and most of the songs were English, a lot of them of the kind now associated with Dusty Springfield, Cilla Black, and the other big names of that era.

Ian was from the Kirov, and not at all above a little serious showing off, and I was a very good dancer. Almost before we knew it, Ian was lifting me and throwing me over his head. We stopped the entire club; we made quite a couple in those surroundings. Ian was extremely good-looking, his hair bleached white by the sun, while I was so thin and brown that some people weren't even sure what sex I was.

Eventually, we sat down, having danced until about three in the morning. A very attractive dark lady with two enormous wolfhounds came prowling around, surveying the crowd. She smiled at me and ambled off. This, it turned out, was Ginette, the owner of the club. Kay said, "You've made quite an impression, Amanda. I want you to realise that if any of the women ask you to dance, it would be very rude to say no."

That was a remarkable thing to hear. You have to remember that neither Kay nor Ian had any idea that I'd ever had any feelings that had been other than strictly heterosexual. Since Bernie died, I had not allowed anyone in my life to know that there was even a hint of anything else inside me. I had completely shut down my leanings in that direction. I knew I was attracted to women but at the time it was in a more emotional than sexual way; sexually, I went to bed with men, but emotionally, I was always drawn to older women. It never occurred to me to seriously consider sleeping with them though. There was a block inside me – a barrier between a lurking sexuality I had yet to recognise and my strange, almost otherworldly relationship with Bernie. I never allowed any of it to surface.

So, when Ginette came over and asked me to dance, I had never been so scared in my life. My heart felt as though it would burst from my chest. I was terrified of that kind of physical contact with a woman. If Kay hadn't given me my instructions, I think I would have refused, but I didn't. I got to my feet, and Ginette and I danced together for the rest of the night. Instantly, something clicked inside me. I was still scared – really scared – but my poor heart was pounding. I realised I was feeling things I hadn't felt since Bernie. It was like opening Pandora's box. Suddenly, so much in my life made sense.

In that moment, I understood why I suffered from a constant feeling of discomfort, why I never seemed to fit in, and why I blushed so easily. I had always been trying to hide something fundamental to my nature, living in constant fear of being found out – though I hadn't even known quite what I was afraid of being found out about. But when I danced with Ginette, I knew I would never be the same again, and I was acutely aware that she could be a threat to me.

The next day, I tried to dismiss it all, to tell myself that nothing momentous had happened. I spent the day on the beach, trying not to think about Ginette, trying to deny the feelings that were rising within me. Yet, I couldn't wait to return to the club that night. My heart was pounding; I was still terrified, but I couldn't have stayed away. When we arrived, Ginette came straight up to me and asked me to dance. I spoke only English and virtually no French, but we danced all night again.

After the club closed, she took me to a funny all-night café. There, in a secluded corner, she asked if she could kiss me.

"Oui," I replied – one of the few French words I knew! She did, and I melted. We didn't take things any further; she didn't suggest we go to bed, for which I was grateful, as I would have been quite incapable of coping. Instead, she went home, and I returned with Kay and Ian. There is little doubt, though, that in that instant, I fell head over heels in love with Ginette. It was the first crack in my defences. I had never let myself go before. I had kept all my emotions tightly reined in, convincing myself I didn't care what happened with my parents, didn't care about being alone, didn't care about unsuccessful relationships, didn't care about anything except my work. But that moment when Ginette kissed me changed everything. I cracked open, and I dissolved.

As soon as I returned to our hotel room, I started to cry – and I couldn't stop. I must have cried for 24 hours. Ian was a great support, talking to me endlessly. Somehow, through the tears, we carried on with this extraordinary holiday, all mixed up with my sobbing and realising I didn't know what I was or what to do about it, and being wildly excited at the same time.

I am well aware that most young people today simply accept their own sexuality and that of others, but it wasn't like that in 1963 – not at all. You must remember that it would be another four years before male homosexuality was legalised, and the only reason female homosexuality was not illegal was that when Queen Victoria passed the law on sexual practices, she had not imagined such a thing possible between two women. Silly queen.

I was confused, frightened, and yet ecstatic – for a while, anyway. In the South of France, for the first time in my life, I seemed to fit in. Whether in the clubs or on the beaches, people were lovely to me. I was at ease, whether we spoke the same language or not. It was all right to be bonkers and barmy.

We fell into a routine. Evenings were spent at the Can-Can, where I danced all night with Ginette. I came alive at night. During the day, I was tired, exhausted, completely out of it. I didn't bother with the sea – I couldn't swim – but Ian was an excellent swimmer. Our habit was to visit a very stylish beach beside the Carlton Hotel.

The South of France in the 60s boasted a remarkable mix of people, in spite of the war they were still tinged with the decadence of the 20s. There was plenty of cabaret to watch through half-closed eyes as we lay baking in the sun, trying to summon the energy for another night of excess.

There were all these faded bits of ex-royalty, deposed from various places, and ancient queens of another kind, in their white pyjama trousers with gold piping, looking like Dirk Bogarde in *Death in Venice*, sitting around in corners waiting for their toyboys. It was mad, and it was magic. People would come up and ask, "Do you prefer women or men?" as casually as if they were offering tea or coffee. It was totally matter-of-fact. Nobody cared what anyone else was doing. Nobody judged you. In a way, it was extremely sophisticated. Nothing was forced upon you, yet everything was available.

There also seemed to be quite a lot of French men who'd run away from farming communities to have sex change operations. This was probably my first experience of transsexual people. One of the most beautiful was known as The Duchess. She looked like the most gorgeous film star. She was grand too. She put your ordinary film star to shame.

We were also aware of the tragedies. We could see all the beautiful people who were no longer beautiful, yet still trying so hard. I realised that in this community, desperately living out its swan song to the wildest extremes, looks and appearance counted for everything. What an eye-opener for a girl from Ashton-under-Lyne, straight out of the chorus.

People didn't jet off around the world then, seeing how the other half lived. I felt immensely privileged to be in Cannes and to experience that way of life, even briefly. It was sheer bliss. And then there was Ginette, whom I came to adore. I was completely under her spell. I refused to go to bed with her, though. I really didn't know how to go about it. Understandably, things became a little frustrating and strange between us.

Eventually, I had to leave – the two-week holiday had stretched to three, and I was right up against my deadline for returning to London. I had work to return to: eight shows a week, plus a film. And, for once, I wasn't all that keen. I had begun to discover myself. I suppose I had certainly discovered that it was possible, even for me, to be myself. I would have liked a little more time to explore the possibilities, but as ever in my life, that was not possible. I just had to get on with it and go back to work.

17

—

Back to Reality

My return to London – and the looming mountain of work awaiting me – brought me crashing back to reality. Suddenly, I was once again in the real world, and not, it seemed, popular with everyone. In less than three weeks away, I had become thinner than ever, and deeply sun-tanned.

The producers of *Carry On Cleo* didn't seem to mind, although in those days anyone playing a role like Cleo in a *Carry On* film would have been expected to have ample curves. In my case, any curves at all would have been a miracle. The irony is, just a few years later, after Twiggy arrived on the scene, I might have been considered quite fashionable.

However, I shall never forget the mortification of my costume fittings for Cleo – not for as long as I live. The costumier, Mr. Schneider, fancied himself an artist and had the temperament to match. At that time, almost everyone wore padded bras, and I was no exception. As I stood before him, fully clothed, he more than likely assumed I was the same shape as all the other *Carry On* actresses. Showing me the costume designs, he explained, "Now, we want the bra to expose the breast – only the nipple will be covered, and the breast will be pushed up."

I kept insisting, "But Mr. Schneider, I don't think I can push anything up. I haven't anything to push up."

"No, no, no," he replied. "Everybody has a little to push up. The straps will be there, the nipple covered, and the breast exposed."

He went on and on, refusing to listen. He was an artist, after all – he knew best. In the end, exasperated, I unzipped my dress, removed my padded bra, and simply stood there, topless. Mr. Schneider stopped mid-sentence and was silent for a full 30 seconds. I believe he was in shock.

"Oh my God!" he finally shouted, before running to the telephone, leaving me standing there, naked to the waist, weighing under seven stone, deeply tanned from head to toe, and utterly flat-chested. I could hear him on the phone to the *Cleo* producers at Pinewood Studios – not so much talking as screaming, "What are we going to do? She has no breasts! I cannot make costumes for this! I am not a miracle worker. We have to do something..."

I very nearly burst into tears. You must remember, I was pre-occupied with not being like other people, and already thought of myself as a monster, a freak. Now, it seemed, this had been confirmed. I had undressed in front of someone, and he had been utterly horrified by the sight of me.

Eventually, Mr. Schneider returned. "You will have to see a doctor," he ordered.

"What for?" I asked nervously.

"We're going to get you some injections," he said.

I knew about those sorts of procedures from the South of France. Now it was my turn to go into shock. There was no way I was going to have those injections. *Cleo* and I seemed destined to part company before we had even begun.

However, I think Mr Schneider overreacted. After all, I hadn't had any boobs worth mentioning when I'd been chosen for the role in the first place. And thankfully, doctors and injections were never mentioned again by Mr Schneider, or by anyone else at all involved in the production.

My shape was just one of the anxieties I faced as I prepared to launch myself into *Cleo* and *She Loves Me*. Though I was already an experienced performer in many ways, and always at home on stage, I had done little acting. My experience was mostly as a dancer or in short sketches in revues. It had never really occurred to me that I would do anything other than dance and make people laugh. I would have loved to have been a mime artist. This was the first time I had to learn scripts properly, and at that stage in my life, it was a Herculean task. My dyslexia kicked in, of course; I simply couldn't get my head around it. Over the years, I have developed various techniques for dealing with the thoroughly daunting task of reading, understanding, and then memorising a new script. But back then, it was an absolute nightmare and, a little later, would be a major factor in my having a breakdown.

In fact, I was just becoming rather ill. My stay in the South of France – chewing all those Purple Hearts, drinking everything in sight, and eating virtually nothing, not to mention the emotional turmoil – had certainly not helped. I didn't realise it then, but I had already developed an eating disorder. Some years earlier, I had learned how to make myself sick when I was nervous. It seemed to help me conquer my nerves and function again.

Something physical was happening to me which didn't show, but it was as though I had a sort of internal tremor. By the time the filming of *Cleo* began, with my first night in *She Loves Me* coincidently on the same day, I was in quite a state.

I had to be up at 4am for filming and arrived on set to find myself surrounded by all these beautiful girls with thick, billowing hair and beauty queen figures while I, in the middle of it all, this oddity with a little red face, put on my make-up and poked at myself as usual. I felt decidedly inferior. When they took my wig off at the end of the day, I thought I looked like an earthworm. Then I had to rush to the Lyric Theatre for *She Loves Me*. It was utter madness.

The truly astonishing thing, however, was that I received excellent notices for *She Loves Me*, and for *Cleo*, which, of course, became a huge hit. Variety, the prestigious Hollywood weekly, declared: "Best discovery is Amanda Barrie as a poor man's Cleopatra; her take-off of the Queen of the Nile gets nearer to the tongue-in-cheek sense of what the filmmakers were aiming at than any of her more experienced colleagues."

I was also sent a review from America which referred to my "brilliant pastiche of Elizabeth Taylor". Well, I hadn't even realised I was doing one, though our film was meant to be a parody of the famous Hollywood blockbuster, *Cleopatra*, starring Taylor and Richard Burton, which had just been released, and our Pinewood set was the same one that had been used for *Cleopatra*.

But none of us realised at the time that the *Carry On* films were anything special. In fact, quite the opposite. It wasn't only the critics who were dismissive – really big-name actors wanted nothing to do with them. People looked down on the *Carry On*s, particularly agents, producers, and casting directors. Years later, when I was up for a part in the TV play *Early Struggles* with Tom Conti, directed by Stephen Frears, he suddenly realised I'd done *Cleo* and said, "Oh God, I'm going to have to think overnight. I've never employed a *Carry On* actor before." He did employ me, though, and I adored working with him. Actors would pay to work with Stephen Frears, and I still consider *Early Struggles* one of the best things I've ever done.

There were definitely these prejudices, however, which were quite unfair, because I don't think there has ever been a more professional bunch on a movie than the *Carry On* team. A roll call of just some of the regular stars of the 31 *Carry On* films – Sid James, Kenneth Williams, Barbara Windsor, Charles Hawtrey, Kenneth Connor, Hattie Jacques, Frankie Howerd, Leslie Phillips, and Joan Sims – speaks for itself. They were all immensely experienced leading artists, top-notch at what they did. They were lovely to work with, too – with just one or two exceptions, most notably Kenneth Williams.

Charles Hawtrey was a real favourite of mine, both on screen and off. Twice a week, he would bring me a piece of Finnan haddock – because he thought I was too thin and wasn't eating enough, about both of which, of course, he was quite right, though I didn't realise it at the time.

"I've got you a nice bit of fish for your supper; don't forget to eat it," he'd say. It was very sweet of him, but unfortunately, I don't think the Finnan haddock ever quite survived the day's filming and the long trip home, via the small matter of a show at the Lyric, in an edible condition.

The *Carry On* scripts were pretty good too, which is why, of course, the films have stood the test of time and are now regarded as classics of their kind. It wasn't like that then, we just got on with it. The pay was dreadful, about £250 a picture. In view of their lasting popularity, it still rankles that we received only one-off fees, with no residual deals for TV or video exposure – which, of course, didn't even exist at the time.

The schedules were relentless too. It was probably the fastest filming ever: seven minutes a day, a staggering amount for a major feature film. As soon as we finished one scene, we were straight on to the next, because the next set would already be lit and ready. And the highest standards were demanded. It was a hanging offence to be late or to arrive on set not knowing your lines – you simply didn't do it. An entire *Carry On* was shot in six weeks, and the budget for *Cleo* was £160,000; seriously tiny for any film, even in the 60s. *Cleopatra*, on the other hand, ran up a budget of millions and took almost two years to make. It was a joke to even attempt a comparison, but in terms of professionalism, *Carry On Cleo* would not have fallen short.

To keep to that kind of schedule and budget, everything had to work like clockwork. However, there were occasional hiccups, and, as ever, if anything was going to go wrong, I was usually involved. Everyone, it seems, remembers the scenes of me in the film bathing in asses' milk. The milk was genuine – well, not asses' milk, but certainly cow's; 200 gallons of watered-down, semi-skimmed. It would go off from time to time and had to be replaced. The bath had to be kept at a certain temperature, and on one occasion, something went wrong with the thermostat, and it became so hot it nearly killed me. My stand-in refused to go in because it was too hot but, like a fool, in I went.

"I'll do it, no problem. It's not that hot."

As I climbed down the four steps into the bath – which was really more like a small swimming pool – the water seemed to press against me. The cameraman said, "Just go in quickly, let me get one shot, then straight out."

I did my best, but as the water passed my heart, something went bang and I passed out. Fortunately, one of the stagehands had stayed nearby, even though it was supposed to be a closed set, and he grabbed me by the wig, so I didn't go right under. I think if I'd gone under in that heat, it could have been the end of me.

I remember reading at the time that when Elizabeth Taylor finished the bath scenes for *Cleopatra*, she was given a week's holiday. I was given a cup of Pinewood Studios coffee, then on to the next scene. Though tastefully shot from the back, apart from bits of plaster over my nipples which looked rather silly, I really was naked in that bath. This was very unusual in the early 60s, but it seemed perfectly normal to me. Of course, I was an old chorus girl, more used to being undressed than dressed, but it was considered quite outrageous at the time.

Because of it, I was offered a *Playboy* centrefold, which I turned down. This was not out of modesty, it was simply that I was, as ever, paranoid about my body – particularly my breasts, or lack thereof. The Mr. Schneider incident was still making me cringe. If I'd had an inch more bust, I'd have said yes to *Playboy* straight away, jumped back into my bath of milk, and done the backstroke for them. I now regret turning *Playboy* down. As you get older, you're inclined to realise that once upon a time, your body may not have been quite as bad as you thought. I recently watched *Cleo* all the way through for the first time. And, I know actors always say this, but I really do have a horror of seeing myself on screen, yet I must admit that I watched myself climbing out of the bath and thought, "Why on earth did I say no to *Playboy*?"

A couple of years later, I made the first colour front cover of the extremely upmarket *Tatler* magazine, which both impressed and astonished me, but I would still rather have been in *Playboy*.

On another occasion, while filming *Cleo*, I had to be rolled up in a carpet and a table was supposed to collapse on me. Again, a stunt girl had been employed, but she was late, so, not having learned my lesson from the hot bath episode, I promptly offered to do the stunt myself. Fortunately for me, if not for her, the stunt girl turned up at the last moment. They rolled her up in the carpet, but the table, a huge, long trestle affair, collapsed far more dramatically than intended, breaking several of her teeth.

Had that been me, I would have been out of the film and out of *She Loves Me*.

By and large, it was a privilege to work with the *Carry On* cast. They were so good, and there was never any nonsense with them. One exception to the latter, though certainly not the former, was Kenneth Williams. He was a genius, of course, and so witty, but his wit was usually cutting, and often cruelly directed at someone else.

Like many who worked with him I suspect, I was, quite frankly, terrified of Ken. You never knew what he might say or do, and he had a dreadful sourness about him. He was also prone to bouts of quite fanatical professional jealousy, and there was considerable unspoken rivalry between him and Sid James. In fact, there is little doubt – and Kenneth certainly made his feelings clear enough in his diaries – that they thoroughly disliked each other.

I was too preoccupied with surviving a day filming and a night performing to worry much about who hated whom, but I do recall one day when Kenny was at his trickiest, and I was involved in a rather unpleasant incident with him. We had a caravan by the asses' milk swimming pool, and in it hung about a dozen dressing gowns for anyone who had to go into the milk to use. Someone would throw a dressing gown over me as soon as I got out of the water. On this particular day, I was sitting in the caravan, desperately learning my lines, because they had just informed Sid and me that we were to do an extra scene of about five pages, when I was suddenly called on set. I was practically naked, apart from the sticking plaster over my nipples, so I just grabbed the nearest dressing gown, which was hanging right by me, and walked out.

As I approached the set, I suddenly felt something behind me -someone was ripping my dressing gown off. I ended up stark naked. Then came the unmistakable nasal tones of Kenneth Williams, "That's my dressing gown, dear, I think."

I half-turned towards him. He was in a white rage, trembling, his lips pulled back in a kind of snarl, and there was real menace in his voice. Kenneth had a well-known thing about personal hygiene, of course, but there was no question of my having put on his dressing gown. The dressing gowns were there for all of us. Typically, it was Sid who came to my rescue. As soon as he realised what had happened, he grabbed another dressing gown and threw it over me.

His swift action shielded me from further embarrassment. Kenneth, meanwhile, stalked off, still muttering about hygiene and the sanctity of his personal effects. I laughed about it later, but at the time, I was mortified.

Sid was a true gentleman, always quick to step in and diffuse an awkward situation. I adored him, and I was saddened after his death to read or hear stories of how miserable he was. I am sure he went through periods of his life, as perhaps most of us do, when he was depressed, but I find it hard to believe Sid was like that most of the time. I worked with him a lot over the years. And I always found him the easiest, most likeable, and funniest of men. I defy any sad, tortured man to have the amount of humour in his eyes that Sid James had. I don't think he could have come across the way he did if he really was depressed.

I became especially close to Sid while filming *Cleo*. However, unlike Barbara Windsor my relationship with him was never more than a close friendship, enhanced by a shared love of horse racing. It was very much Sid who was responsible for the growth of my abiding passion for the sport. These were the days before betting shops, and many many decades before the internet and online gambling. I became Sid's runner, placing bets for him with unofficial private bookies, and checking on our winners in between shots. If I wasn't on set with Sid, I'd be tic-tacking (the bookies' secret sign language) him across the studio.

Despite these occasional dramas, the camaraderie among the bulk of the *Cleo* cast was genuine. The *Carry On* family, for all its quirks and rivalries, was bound together by a shared professionalism and an unspoken understanding of the demands we all faced. We worked at a relentless pace, often under less-than-ideal conditions, but there was a sense of pride in what we accomplished – though none of us could have foreseen the enduring legacy of these films.

The *Carry On*s do remain a testament to a particular kind of British humour – irreverent and bawdy, but human. And I remain quite proud to have been a part of them. Though at the time I never thought I was any good in *Cleo*, and it really surprises me that I still receive so many letters about the film.

Meanwhile, I did enjoy *She Loves Me*, in spite of the various pressures from outside, not least filming *Cleo* at the same time, but also still being in a state of great confusion because of my unfulfilled South of France liaison with Ginette. However, despite being critically acclaimed, *She Loves Me* did not last that long, partly, I have always thought, because people were inclined to get the show confused with the latest Beatles hit, *She Loves Me*, and were half expecting to be entertained by the Fab Four.

On the show's last night the lovely Ian, whom I believe was having a particularly bad time in his relationship with Nureyev, turned up in my dressing room, and suddenly said, as we downed copious quantities of alcohol, "Oh God, wouldn't it be wonderful if we were back in the South of France?"

I was without a job, Richard was still in America, and Ian was without Rudi. So we just went. Straight away. We caught a night plane to Nice and arrived at the Can Can club just as everyone was having breakfast the next morning.

There was still a kind of magic about Cannes for me, and about Ginette, who once more made her feelings for me very clear. I adored her too, and found her extremely attractive, but I still could not bring myself to do anything about it. We clearly did not have a future, and it was all my fault.

After a few days, emotionally drained, I returned to England, and I was never to see Ginette again. Nonetheless she did change my life.

18

———

Lodger to Lover

S hortly after I got back from France, Richard returned from America. I decided to tell him about Ginette and the feelings she had awakened in me. I thought this was the right thing to do. It proved to be a mistake. He reacted as if I'd grown horns and become some sort of sick animal.

I became very upset. I'd had a few drinks, but I was already in an extremely fragile state. After all, I had repeated my previous performance in Cannes – no sleep, too much sun, not enough food, too many Purple Hearts. And I was absolutely miserable over losing Ginette. Even though I was full of guilt and fear, it didn't take much to push me into a confession.

Richard's reaction devastated me.

I already felt that I was peculiar, and although my feelings for Ginette had seemed so absolutely right, I suppose I also half believed – probably still the prevailing view in the 60s – that my sexual leanings meant there was something wrong with me, that I was unnatural. The way Richard reacted merely confirmed what I already believed: that I was some kind of freak. I needed to get away from him.

Work came to my rescue yet again in the form of the film *I've*

Gotta Horse, starring Billy Fury playing a fictionalised version of himself. I was to play Billy's girlfriend. I left quietly, and with a considerable sense of relief, for filming in Yarmouth, and what would turn out to be a whole new episode in my life.

I'm not quite sure at what point I started to fall for Billy, or he for me. I was still trying, albeit without much success, to convince myself that the thing with Ginette had been just a phase.

Billy and I quickly became very friendly, mainly because we were both such great animal lovers. Indeed, the film was loosely based on Billy's real life love of animals. In his dressing room and everywhere he went, Billy was surrounded by large travel bags. In one, there would be several Chihuahuas; in another, some stray creature he had rescued. He also had an Alsatian called Sheba and a Great Dane named Rusty. I thought it was rather wonderful that all his animals were strays or rescues.

The film had been set up by Larry Parnes, Billy's manager, who also co-wrote it. For some reason, Larry asked me to look after Billy. That was no hardship. Billy was incredibly charismatic, and strikingly good-looking – just a thoroughly beautiful creature. Men sometimes go through that stage in adolescence, I think, when they are neither men nor boys, but some kind of unique creature. Billy had that quality, even though he was well past adolescence. Perhaps it had something to do with the fact that he was already quite ill and knew it; I'm not sure. But he was an absolute sweetheart, and I adored him.

During our three weeks or so on location in Yarmouth, nothing actually happened between us, but I think a little flame was lit.

Work on the film started off much like with any other. We had quite a nice little family set-up. I knew most of the other dancers quite well, particularly Sheila O'Neill, who had been in *Six of One*, and my friend Doreen Cran; Michael Medwin, and Jon Pertwee also starred. The director, Ken Hulme – Shirley Bassey's first husband and one of the funniest men ever born – had a great way of talking as if nothing ever went right for him.

He'd say, "Should it be that I got up this morning? Should it be that I come here on set and find I have no actors?" Almost every remark he made started with, "Should it be?" He was also one of those directors who would think rather dramatically on his feet. If someone pointed out that we were behind schedule, he would simply tear up a few pages of the script. So, if anyone found the continuity hard to follow in *I've Gotta Horse*, that's why.

There was another reason as well. About two and a half weeks into the location shoot, Kenny discovered that he had been using the wrong film stock, which was also much more costly than what we were supposed to be using. So we ended up literally re-shooting two and a half weeks of filming in about two days. Strangely, I don't remember any tension. It was mostly very funny. Kenny proceeded to shoot at speed. Of course, all this put the whole filming schedule out of kilter. We had permission to film at Epsom, and the footage was to be cut with newsreel footage showing Anselmo – the horse Billy really did own – coming fourth in the 1964 Derby at 100/1. But we ended up going on the wrong day. It was the day of a big race, and the stewards, quite rightly, wouldn't let us through to the paddock.

"Take no notice," ordered Kenny. "Should it be that anyone tries to stop you, just walk, push your way through. Take no notice."

Michael Medwin, who was a racing man, tried to explain that you don't push your way into a paddock full of horses worth millions of pounds. Kenny wouldn't have it. Owners and trainers were complaining about us. In the end, the police were called, but we managed to escape without being arrested – and, miraculously, with a few inches of film too. People should watch *I've Gotta Horse* to spot the mistakes. The weather changed, the film itself changed. Anselmo was a riding-school hack, and the Epsom scenes were chaos. Never mind *Summer Holiday* and Cliff Richard – *I've Gotta Horse* was so terrible it should be the cult-film of all time.

But somewhere along the line, Billy and I laughed together. It always does something to my heart when I laugh with someone, and when Billy and I started laughing, my heart went thump. Because I'd been so upset and desolate after Cannes, I was both surprised and relieved at the same time to have these feelings for a man again. It was a bit confusing, true, but at least I knew what to do with a man. I did have a basic understanding of how it all worked.

We returned to the London area for more filming, mostly at Shepperton Studios, and it seemed perfectly natural that when Billy sold his house in Richmond and had yet to acquire another property, he should move in with me. I had moved back to Endell Street, whilst Richard had moved back to America. Billy brought with him his various animals, and a rather hysterical suitcase full of socks and a gun. Now, Billy was the gentlest creature in the world, and what he was doing with a gun in his suitcase, I have, to this day, absolutely no idea. I just accepted it. I never asked him why he had a gun, nor did I ever ask if it was loaded. I did, however, handle it with great care when I was looking for his socks to wash.

People are sometimes surprised, but I've always happily done chores like this for those I've lived with. With Billy, it was mostly me who got the surprises. Larry Parnes was the old-fashioned kind of pop star manager who looked after everything for his boy. He used to invest most of Billy's earnings for him, pay all his bills, and give him about £60 or so in cash every week, which was a lot of money in those days. Billy had a habit of crinkling up the banknotes and stuffing them in his socks. I discovered this the first time I washed his socks in the bath, which served as a washing machine as well as everything else. I realised the socks were full of paper, and I thought it was probably tissue. I'm so messy myself that it would seem perfectly natural to find a stash of paper handkerchiefs in someone's socks. But to my horror, I discovered Billy's socks contained those big £5 notes we used to have, all scrunched up and sodden. So I ironed them and set them out to dry as best I could. When Billy came home, all his money was hung up around the kitchen with clothes pegs. He didn't seem to mind. He was always easy-going, and I think he quite liked having someone washing his socks.

He also had a shoebox full of marijuana, which lived under the bed alongside the suitcase with the socks and his gun in it. Billy liked to smoke dope a lot. Once he forgot to take any with him when we were filming at Shepperton Studios, so I ended up ringing my mother, who was staying with us at the time, to ask if she could come out to Shepperton and bring the shoebox with her. Typically, she took this request entirely in her stride.

"It looks like it's got the contents of a Hoover in it. Just wrap the whole box up in something and get a taxi, OK darling? And don't go in the suitcase next to it, because it's got a gun in it, all right?"

"All right, darling, is it loaded?"

"I don't know. Just don't touch it."

"All right. Do you want anything else?"

"No, thank you."

She duly arrived with fresh supplies of marijuana for Billy, and she never batted an eyelid.

Billy also liked to drink rum and Coke. We used to rush back to Covent Garden after filming, don these identical denim caps we both had, and go on a pub crawl drinking rum and Coke. Everybody around the Garden was really fond of Billy. My mother adored him, and he was divine with her. He was, without a doubt, the sort of son anyone would have wanted.

I don't quite remember when Billy the lodger became Billy the lover, but I suspect it was pretty soon. I moved effortlessly from carrying maggots around whilst fishing with Richard to rum, Coke, and jokes with Billy. I was, as ever, playing the chameleon, trying to fit in with my partners. At first, we kept our affair a secret. I knew vaguely that Billy had a girlfriend, although I think he might have stopped seeing her during the time we were together. We just didn't talk about it. Eventually, though, it did become public knowledge that Billy and I were together.

At one stage, my sister was staying with us, as well as my mother, and we all piled into this tiny flat. My mother was, as usual, completely unfazed by anything I did or was involved in – the dope incident being a very good example – and she used to bring Billy and me tea and toast in bed in the mornings, get us up for filming, and feed us when we returned. In fact, we struggled a bit when she went back to Manchester. Left to our own devices, we never seemed to get around to eating much. Our principal sustenance was rum and Coke and, as a result, we were both like skeletons.

Quite early in our relationship, there was a frightening incident, which probably hadn't been helped by our lifestyle. Billy collapsed in the studio during filming. He just went out cold. After a couple of minutes, he came around, very pale but otherwise apparently okay. Nonetheless, a doctor was called, and after examining Billy, he expressed a desire to speak to whoever Billy was with. A number of people were aware that we were an item, so I was sent for.

"Do you know that Billy smokes marijuana?" the doctor asked. I was a bit nervous, because possession was a serious offence in those days – nobody got off with a caution in 1964. If Billy had ever been arrested on a drugs charge, he would almost certainly have gone to prison, and I could just imagine the headlines. It would have been disastrous. So I avoided making a reply.

The doctor then told me just how ill Billy was. He had TB, kidney problems, and a serious heart condition, which, of course, was ultimately to cause him to die so young, at the age of 43. I was shocked because I had no idea about any of this, and I was absolutely astonished by what the doctor said next.

"You make sure he keeps on the marijuana," he instructed me. "It's probably what's keeping him alive."

Now, extraordinarily enough, I had never smoked dope with Billy at that stage. Indeed, I'd never smoked it at all. I was a bit nervous of it. However, mindful of the doctor's instructions, I proceeded to play my part in ensuring Billy had plenty of supplies.

Shortly after this incident, Billy suddenly remembered that he'd left behind a number of marijuana plants in the garden of his Richmond house, which by then had new owners. So one night after filming, we borrowed a van and drove across London to surreptitiously repossess his precious plants. The house was surrounded by a huge security wall, and there were no prizes for guessing who had to climb over it. It wasn't a problem for me, though. You can always knock an old dancer over a wall. There was one minor difficulty, however. Innocent as I was, I didn't even know what a marijuana plant looked like. Billy had to describe them to me, then call out directions over the wall as I stumbled around the garden in the dark. Eventually, I located the blessed things and handed them back to him over the wall to load into the van.

We then drove miles to the country mansion he'd just bought, where we replanted them. Billy seemed to spend very little time there, and this was my first visit, but from then on, we used to go there occasionally for weekends. The place had a deserted feel to it, and we'd sit around surrounded by all his animals, drinking rum and Coke while Billy played music and sang some of his own material, much of which I don't think has ever been published.

I also used to go down to Brixton with Billy, where we'd meet up with wonderful West Indians who were in fact drug dealers, but I thought they were rather splendid. It was all quite secretive. We would sit around a great big round table, and they'd get all the stuff out, and the deals would be struck over endless cans of Coke. Most of them were musicians of one sort or another, and they adored Billy, who moved a bit like a black performer and was, without doubt, far better at what he did than he's ever really been given credit for. I didn't realise until later that he was never able to sing quite to his full potential because of his health.

Ultimately, while we were staying at a hotel in Shepperton because the filming schedule had been stepped up to such a level that we seemed to be on set about 20 hours a day, I was persuaded to try dope myself. Unfortunately, I reacted badly and had a massive panic attack. I thought I was dying, my heart was beating so loudly and so hard. I remember ending up face down on the carpet. I understand it's pretty much unheard of to have such an awful attack of the horrors on perfectly ordinary joints, but of course, I didn't weigh anything, I drank a lot of brandy and rum, goodness knows when I'd last eaten and I was, as usual, in a state of exhaustion. I know that I very nearly went under. Eventually, I managed to drag myself into the shower, turned it to ice cold, and sat slumped under it until I recovered.

Billy took it quite lightly. I don't think he realised how bad I had been. It put me off smoking dope with a vengeance. I was afraid of the stuff for years. Fortunately, Billy was quite happy smoking alone, and never put pressure on me to join him.

We were together for almost a year and we became very close – so much so that, rather to my surprise, he proposed to me. He asked if I would marry him as we were driving past the Star and Garter home for disabled servicemen on Richmond Hill, right by the entrance to the park. I was stunned and I remember that my first thought was, "Oh my God, what a romantic place to propose." But I don't remember what I said. I know I didn't give him a proper answer – not ever. I just couldn't.

Billy was really precious to me. And I really did consider marrying him. But Ginette and, indeed, the whole scene in the South of France had changed everything for me. I wouldn't have dreamed of marrying Billy without telling him about that side of me, and Billy was one of those people I just could never tell. It wasn't that he would have been judgmental; it was just that he was so completely immersed in his own world of music and animals. In many ways, he was like a child, and I just couldn't have burdened him with my worries and anxieties. He wouldn't have had a clue how to deal with someone else's troubles.

So I just dodged the issue of marriage. And for a while, things carried on much the same between us. Then one night, when we were actually going to eat together for a change, and I was preparing a meal, Billy went out to buy some cigarettes, and he never came back. Maybe it was my cooking. I never found out where he went that night or why he just went. Of course, at first I was worried, had he had an accident? I called the police and the hospitals, to no avail. Then the next day, I called Larry Parne's office, and somebody there said to me, "Just leave it, Amanda, he's had to go back." By which I gleaned that he'd probably gone back to whoever he'd been with when we got together. I never knew for certain what happened. I'd always thought, partly because of the gun, although I made jokes about it, that there was this other side to Billy, and that he might have been involved in a more heavy drug scene. But I knew nothing really.

There was, however, something about the way in which that message was relayed to me that made me do exactly as I was told. It was rather as if I'd been warned off. And I never saw nor heard from Billy Fury again.

19

——

Playing it Straight

Work came to the rescue yet again. Shortly after Billy left, I was offered a season at the Bristol Old Vic. The first production there was the revue *See You Inside*, which I had already performed in the West End. I was also asked to appear in two other productions: *Hobson's Choice* and *The Beggar's Opera*.

I liked the idea of doing a straight play such as *Hobson's Choice*, but the reality terrified me. It was a huge leap forward, and my nerves went into overdrive. I was nearly 30 years old by now and had been in the theatre since I was three, yet I had never been on stage when the curtain rose without music. I shall never forget the horror of that experience – the curtain rising to complete silence. It never ceased to be a shock.

My mother, of course, loved the whole thing. She swiftly made the trek to Bristol to see me perform, as she did almost everywhere I appeared, regardless of her own circumstances.

Years later, when she presented me with a scrapbook she had kept of the highlights of my career, I saw that she had pasted in the *Hobson's Choice* programme from the Bristol Old Vic and written underneath it: "Congratulations, darling, legit at last," which was copied from the telegram Noel Coward sent to Gertrude Lawrence when she did her first straight play.

I have always had two great heroines in the theatre: one is Gertrude Lawrence, and the other Kay Hammond, whom I still believe was the finest British light comedy actress ever. Noel Coward wrote *Blithe Spirit* for Kay. I'd seen her on stage in the West End and couldn't believe that anyone could be so funny while appearing to do absolutely nothing. She was married to Sir John Clements, the very distinguished actor-manager who, after she suffered a chronic stroke in her early 50s which destroyed her as a performer, nursed Kay for the rest of her life.

At about the same time, Alec, my agent, told me that Val May, the Old Vic's artistic director, wanted to talk to me about a new play he was putting on. We all had dinner together in Bristol, and it turned out the play was *The Killing of Sister George* with Beryl Reid. This could have been considered quite appropriate in view of my own experiences, but Sister George was a brand-new play then, and neither Alec nor I had a clue what it was about until Val started to explain – very hesitantly – that he wanted me for the role of Charlie, Sister George's young female lover.

It took him some time to say the word; obviously I found this rather amusing. Alec, who was one of the few people who knew about my sexual confusion, kicked me hard under the table, and I just managed to hold myself together even when Val remarked apologetically, "Charlie is the sort of person who still has cuddly toys at home." I could see my rabbits, Loppy and Lena, sitting up in bed going, "Ha ha!"

As you can imagine, I was intrigued by the prospect of playing Charlie, but my agent was heavily against it, thinking the role was too controversial. However, while Sister George was still under discussion, I received a telephone call just before curtain-up one evening that changed everything. The caller was Kay Hammond. Although I had never spoken to her before, I recognised her distinctive voice immediately. Kay Hammond calling me at the Bristol Old Vic – it was unbelievable.

"Amanda, darling," she said. "They're putting on a play in the West End called *A Public Mischief*, and there's a part in it I once played. I think you should play it."

This was like a summons from God. Nobody said no to Kay Hammond. It turned out that her husband, Sir John, was one of the play's backers, and the couple's influence was such that because they thought I should have the role, I was promptly offered it – without even an audition.

It was, however, then that my troubles began. I was to play the lead in *A Public Mischief* opposite George Cole. I still had very little proper acting experience, and there was the small problem of my reading difficulties. I had never had to deal with so many words before, and the prospect overwhelmed me. To make everything just perfect, I didn't even have anywhere to live. Richard was finally coming home from America for good, and, quite understandably, had sent word to Bristol that he wanted me out of his flat. Given the circumstances, I couldn't complain.

Meanwhile, my mother found me a flat of my own in my beloved Covent Garden by following a group of building workers. She saved the day. She had to fight hard to acquire it, but that was something she was rather good at. She spotted a group of workmen going into a building in Bow Street and decided, with her own particular logic, that they must be working on a flat. She discovered there were two flats in the same property and found out the name of the letting agency. However, this was during an era when landlords around Soho were reluctant to rent to women, fearing they might be prostitutes. But my mother wore them down, as she was inclined to wear down almost everyone, with an avalanche of letters, phone calls, and personal visits.

Harold French, director of *A Public Mischief*, was naturally anxious to hear the play come alive at a read-through in the St Martin's Theatre. Adding another dimension to my terror, Sir John Clements and Kay Hammond were also to be there. Harold knew nothing about me, and based on my performance at the read-through, I could not blame him for murmuring to Kay, "Has she ever done anything, dear?" I overheard him clearly, and my despair was total. I just wanted to hide.

Instead, I was taken to lunch at Sheekey's, the very smart theatre-land fish restaurant. Kay came too, and I already felt I'd let her down. I was numb from the effort of spending the morning trying to read the play, and by the time I returned to my mother, I was almost rigid with fear. I had a terrible ringing sensation in my head and felt as if all my nerve endings were gathered in my nose.

I simply couldn't get to grips with the play at all. Throughout rehearsals, I struggled. Halfway through the second week, with two and a half weeks to opening night, I started to get really ill. I didn't know what was happening – whether I'd missed a costume fitting, or a meal, or sleep. Or all three. My mother kept saying, as she always did, "You can do it. You can do it. Come on, come on. Just sit and work." But I couldn't. I didn't know where to begin. Every so often, Kay Hammond would come to rehearsals, so I'd become even worse, and I have always regretted being in that state when I had the chance to spend time with her and get to know her.

George Cole barely spoke to me, for which I forgive him entirely. He must have been horrified. He pretended I didn't exist, which was fair enough when you were expected to work with someone as bad as I was. The kindest to me was the actor

Robin Hunter, Harold French's godson, who was also in the play. Robin was extremely charming and handsome in those days, and his support meant a great deal. I felt all the other actors were laughing at me, but Robin sent me up gently and laughed with me.

The crisis came about five days before we were due to open in Newcastle, where the pre West End run was to begin. Harold French suddenly said, "You've got a very common voice, dear. Get rid of it before we open."

In the context of the time, he was absolutely right. I only had a slight Northern accent, which I did get rid of, though I reacquired it a bit during *Coronation Street*, I think. But at that time, West End actors really didn't talk that way. This was the era of *Diddy, Diddy, there's been a frightful 'iccident. Hippy birthday, Diddy.* Actors tried to put on an air of theatrical grandeur, to quote Noel Coward. They wore their smartest clothes to rehearsals, which led many impecunious thespians to trim their shirt cuffs and struggle for hours to remove the shine from well-ironed lapels and pockets. I've always thought there was nothing worse than theatre grand, and I never had any part of that. Hence, the way I spoke. I hadn't even been to acting school.

However, to be told such a thing so bluntly by my director was the final blow. I went totally to pieces and collapsed in a sobbing heap. My mother could do nothing to help. In a panic, she called Alec and asked him to come over immediately. She should probably have called a doctor, but that might have meant me being ordered out of the show for medical reasons, so for her it would have been absolutely the last resort.

Alec came straight away and was brilliant.

"It's no good," I wailed. "I just can't go on. There's no way I can do it."

"OK," he said. "But why? Is it because you can't learn it? Is it something else? Let's work out exactly what's wrong."

"I'm not sure," I replied at first, then gave him, and myself, the key to it.

"I keep thinking I know the play," I said, "But I don't."

Which in a way, is lesson one for a dyslexic.

Alec sat with me and helped me learn. He promised that if it didn't work and I felt the same the next morning, he would hand in my notice if that was what I wanted. We stayed up all night, going through it again and again. He made me say the lines out loud repeatedly.

The next morning, he and my mother persuaded me to give it one more go. So, with my common voice and all my other handicaps, I gritted my teeth and got on with it. It was one of those moments in life that could have gone either way. I had to put all my effort into something impossible or give up. I have never been a quitter, but *A Public Mischief* was a very close call.

Although I was far from perfect at rehearsals, I got through that day's run-through much better than before.

Afterwards, Alec said, "You're doing it again."

So we worked most of that night too, reciting every page three times. If I made one mistake, I'd go back to the start and do it again. We did this for three weeks, three nights a week, and by the time we travelled to Newcastle the day before opening, I'd finally got it.

Opening night was a miracle. Something happened that became a pattern throughout my career – although with *A Public Mischief*, the contrast was far greater than it was ever to be again. Thank God! I had been a total disaster throughout rehearsals, but on opening night, I was fine. In fact, I was told I'd been rather good.

20

The Inevitable

We toured with *A Public Mischief* for six weeks before going into the West End, by which time I had almost started to enjoy it and to relax a little. It was in Blackpool that what was probably the inevitable happened. I had quite seriously fallen for Robin, and in the Clifton Hotel, Blackpool, having drunk a fair amount, and despite him being married and me thinking I was probably gay, we went to bed together for the first time.

I had never drunk as much as we did on this tour, not even in the South of France. I was trying to play with the big boys, and I had been to bed with somebody again, which always came as an emotional shock to me. I felt awful.

That night, I suddenly had an extraordinary experience. It sounds stupid, but every time Robin came on stage, I began to heave. I didn't know then, but it was the start of big trouble for me. The beginning of a period of illness that was to blight my life for many years. I felt as if I couldn't speak and on one occasion was in such a state that I passed out, collapsing in a heap behind the sofa. Robin, ever the pro, just stepped over me and went on ad-libbing with George Cole. George froze; he'd never seen anyone fall over on stage before the curtain dropped. Robin picked me up, shook me, sat me down, and on I went again. In fact, I have hardly been off stage during my entire career which, considering all that has happened, is something of a miracle.

Later, they called a doctor who said I had a kidney infection. In hindsight, I had become bulimic, though I didn't know it at the time. I was famously secretive. I'd get ready before a show, put on my make-up, and then go straight to the lavatory. I was in danger of ruining my voice. I knew that, but it didn't stop me. I was obsessed with emptying my stomach before I went on. I told nobody. As far as management and the rest of the cast were concerned, everything was fine. In fact, I seemed to be doing rather well. I was getting good reviews everywhere, and the only indication that something might be amiss was the night I passed out in Blackpool. However, I appeared to make a swift recovery, and there were no further incidents during performances.

The first night at the St Martin's Theatre was a bit of a triumph. I got great notices, including one that described me as second only to Maggie Smith as a comedy actress. There's probably been a stewards' inquiry on that since then, and I may well have been placed last, but I shall always treasure that notice, particularly considering what was going on off stage.

I could do nothing except perform. As always, I became someone else on stage. Otherwise, I was a total disaster. I was anorexic, bulimic, generally neurotic and frightened. I needed a minder. I needed my mother, but she had disappeared, as she was inclined to do. I knew she'd be back, of course – she never stayed away for long – but I needed her right then.

What I didn't need was Robin, the new man in my life, saying, "I think if we have a good drink, you'll be fine." That was not what I needed. I needed some structure in my life. I needed a home, and somebody there to look after me, to sort me out.

Somehow, I kept going through the West End run of *A Public Mischief*, but as it ended, I completely cracked up. The breakdown that had been threatening for months, if not years, took me by the throat and shook me rigid. It was 60 years ago now, but I remember it so clearly, and ever since, I have felt an affinity with people suffering from mental health problems.

Once, I had a panic attack so bad that I lay on the floor all night, curled up in a ball. I couldn't stand, couldn't breathe, couldn't see properly – I just lay there frozen. Alec and Robin did their best to help me, though they didn't really know what to do.

To make matters worse, in the middle of all this, out of the blue, I was invited to play the lead in the American comedy *Any Wednesday*. The play was a big deal at the time – its New York star, Sandy Dennis, had won the Tony Award for Best Actress on Broadway. Apparently, a team of 13 or so producers had to approve the choice of lead, and they all approved me. Mind you, they might have reconsidered if they had seen the state I was in.

I went on my knees to Alec, sobbing and begging him to say no. To this day, I have no idea how I was persuaded to let him say yes, but he did. So I had to cope with my breakdown and the prospect of another daunting West End lead.

However, when rehearsals began for *Any Wednesday*, nobody I was working with had a clue what I was going through. And somehow, against the odds, I managed to survive rehearsals, which I have always found difficult, and completed the run. After *Any Wednesday* ended in 1966, I did a lot more TV work and continued to struggle on. There were regular visits from Robin, who was still living with his wife, and from my mother, who came and went between Manchester and my Covent Garden flat.

Then one day, up the stairs came Robin with a suitcase, much to my mother's horror. He'd arrived! He'd left his wife. I don't remember ever being asked if I wanted him to move in. I think he just took it for granted. In some ways he did help me with my mental problems, although his methods were unorthodox. There was a pub game at the time called Shut the Box, which was a bit like a cross between checkers and Shove Ha'penny. Whenever I had a panic attack, Robin would say, "Right, shut the box," and drag me across the road to the pub, where he'd make me play while he poured a couple of large gin and tonics down me. Another thing he did was to make me run on the spot, which I can, in fact, recommend as a cure for panic attacks.

Robin came from an amazing theatrical family to whom I was duly introduced. His father was Ian Hunter, who played Richard the Lionheart in the 1938 Errol Flynn blockbuster *The Adventures of Robin Hood*. The Hunters had lived half their lives in Hollywood, but when the Second World War started, Ian had done the right thing, like the English gentleman he was, and returned to Blighty to join the Navy. When I met Robin, his parents lived in rather grand style in Jermyn Street, St James, surrounded by well-known and fascinating people, including some of the greatest show business stars of the era. Which, to me, was magic.

However, Robin's mother, Casha, did not like me. I simply was not good enough for her son. Neither, though, did my mother like Robin. It was the clash of the titans. After all, my mother had still been in the habit of sharing my bed when she came to Bow Street, and I only had one bedroom. Also, there was, from the start, a much greater sense of permanence about Robin's arrival in my life and home than that of either Richard or Billy. I think Connie felt as if she had finally been usurped.

Robin and I were very much a couple in the beginning and enjoyed each other's company enormously, so much so that we wanted to work together as much as possible. I think I probably behaved rather stupidly because rather than pursue my own career, which deserved looking after at the time, I chose to work mostly with Robin. I still had plenty of TV work, such as the Jimmy Tarbuck show. I was Jimmy's first Tatty Head, and I used to dance and sing on his show, songs like 'Kinky Boots' and 'Chim Chim Cher-ee'. This was an absolute delight for me, because it was before *Mary Poppins* opened, and was the first time the song had been performed. I sang it with two kids sitting on top of chimneys.

My personal life remained in turmoil. I succeeded in getting named in two divorce cases on the same day. Both Richard and Robin's wives sued them for divorce on the grounds of adultery and cited me. The story of Robin and I made all the front pages, but I was spared from even more lurid headlines because I was named as Shirley Broadbent in Richard's divorce proceedings, and the press fortunately failed to put two and two together. Otherwise, it could have been a professional disaster for me!

A little later, during the 1966 World Cup final, which England men so famously won, Robin proposed to me - just as Gordon Banks saved a goal. I always thought it was a funny moment to choose. First Robin shouted at Gordon Banks on the TV screen, "I love you." Then he said to me, "Will you marry me?"

"Do you mean me or Banks?" I asked, just to be sure.

I rather surprised myself by accepting his proposal straight away. However, I did think that this was the moment when I should tell Robin about Bernie, and my experiences in the South of France with Ginette. His reaction was rather different to Richard's. As I might have known it would be.

He said, "Oh goodie, I've been looking all my life for a small, fuckable chap who drinks."

I took that as a compliment, which, coming from Robin, it

most definitely was. Certainly, I used to quite frequently go to the Nags Head at six o'clock in the morning with Robin, when the Covent Garden pubs were open for the porters; I'd stuff my hair into a large cap and do my best to look like a small chap, because women weren't allowed in pubs at that hour. I even had a false moustache, which I sometimes stuck on. It was all a bit of a joke, really. Of course, everybody knew exactly who I was. We were just paying lip service to the law, whilst we tucked into a Covent Garden breakfast of black coffee, toast and dripping, and brandy.

Once again, it seemed, I was doing my chameleon trick and had indeed turned into this small, fuckable chap who drank at dawn and was a total racing fanatic, spending every spare minute running around Covent Garden chalking up bets. Once when racing was cancelled for a particularly long spell because of bad weather, we even had a book going on the condensation on the windows of the Nag's Head. You had to pick a drop of water and follow it down to the bottom of the glass. First to the bottom won.

Even in bed at night, racing was much more of a passion for Robin and me than sex. He used to set racing quizzes for me. "Okay, what is a spring double?" he'd ask. "Which Grand National winner was accused of only going around the course once?" And so on.

My mother was not overly delighted with the news of my pending nuptials. Robin had already invaded Bow Street, spoiling her dear little bijou residence with its delicate antique furniture and silk walls. There was now a dartboard over the kitchen table and holes all over the wall where'd we missed when playing darts while slightly pissed.

Although I'd accepted Robin's proposal, we did not actually do the deed until the following year. And the main reason we

Far left: Early Photoshop. Heather Chasen and her childhood bear with a pic of me as a child, superimposed by actor and writer of bear books Peter Bull

Top right: I can still remember the smell of that pram

Left: Me with Grandma Pike

Right: Me on Llandudno pier. Of course! I should have shares in that pier

Bottom right: With brother Chris. A rare moment when we weren't trying to kill each other

Below: Ashton's wedding of the year 1933. Hubert and Connie Broadbent

My first stage appearance aged three, sitting on Santa's knee

The chemistry class that never was

Left: Me at Winston's looking very fifties

Below: Me and Barbara Windsor together at Winston's. I still have the programme

WINSTON'S CLUB
NEW YEAR'S EVE
GALA 1957

A special Gala with Augmented Cabaret, Novelties Etc.

From 9 p.m. until 5 a.m.

£1 Including Breakfast

Winston's Club

Announce...

'ALADDIN AND HIS WONDERFUL LAMP'!

AMANDA BARRIE

BARBARA WINDSOR

Below: Connie and me at Babbacombe, South Devon

Above: That's not a smile. The chimp hated me. With Billy Fury on the set of *I've Gotta Horse* in 1964

Above: Up to my neck in milk. In Cleopatra's bath at Pinewood

Left: Artist's model. Me in fishnets and not much else. Drawing by Maggi Hambling

Above: Me and my asp, with Sid James in *Carry on Cleo*

From the play *Any Wednesday*, at The Apollo Theatre. The great Dennis Price presenting me with a birthday cake

My wedding to Robin Hunter at Caxton Hall. You'd never guess it was the sixties, would you?

Left: Our tribute to the Beatles in Liverpool in 1963. Me on the right next to Dora Bryan, standing

Left: With Connie on the first night of Oh Kay!, at the Westminster Theatre in 1974. I think she might have been quite proud of me...

Above: Rehearsing for *Oh Kay!* with Ann Hamilton, for many years feed to Morecambe and Wise

Above: With Milicent Martin, in *Absurd Person Singular* at the Vaudevile in 1974

Saving Covent Garden. Me and the potato sacks

Me looking coy, on the set of *Hickory House* in 1973

Below: Early Alma. Outside Granada in 1989

Above: In Blackpool with *Public Mischief* – en route to the West End and my first leading role

Left: With that naughty Mike Baldwin

Below: Brought together by Rummy. Only we didn't know it at the time

Above: With Hil and Red Rum. I only had eyes for Rummy...

REVEALED Red Rum...the real love of Street scarlet woman Alma

Eat your heart out, Mike

By HILARY BONNER

Left: Fenner doesn't stand a chance with us *Bad Girls* - particularly Steph and me, the Costa Cons

Below: A selfie taken in the dressing room. About to go on for my very last pantomime performance

Left: Going into *Hell's Kitchen* – little did I know what I was in for...

Above: Me and my paramedic heroes. Well worth getting electrocuted for...

Left: With Emma Willis. On my way into the *Big Brother* house

Above: On the steps of the Drury Lane Theatre before my wedding to Hil

Top right: Looking cool in Paris – or so I'm told...

Right: The deed is done. Happiest of days

Above: Hil and me with our much loved and much missed Coco.

Right: On holiday in The Maldives the year after our wedding

Hatty days in our garden...

went ahead then was because there had been an unpleasant story in the press about us living together, which in those days, was really not very good news.

We married at London's Caxton Hall on 19 June, 1967. As a 'small fuckable chap' I wore a trouser suit and one of those little jockey caps we all wore in the 60s. Inside my cap were two miniature bottles of whisky, which Robin had joked he would need to get through the ceremony. At least I think he was joking...

Covent Garden really became my life during this period. I live there to this day, and cannot imagine ever moving away, but it was a very different place in the 1960s, when the market was still operating. It really was an extraordinary part of London. Porters, writers, artists, the press, the police, opera singers and dancers from the opera house, all used to come into The Garden and mix. In the mid to late afternoon and at night the streets were empty because the place was full of warehouses, which had closed down by then. Most of the people disappeared until the early hours.

There were certain idiosyncrasies. Porters passed around very badly spelled pornography in brown envelopes. It was so bad, it was hysterical, even to a dyslexic like me. Pornography, of a very amateurish type, featured quite largely in the Covent Garden lifestyle back then. A group of us once had this great wheeze of showing a blue movie on the side of the Opera House, which Garden people are not inclined to treat with quite the same reverence as the rest of the British population. Unfortunately, we put the film in the projector upside down, making an already bad bit of porn completely incomprehensible.

From Friday night until Sunday night, The Garden belonged to us. No traffic, no people, no shops. Everything seemed closed. Everything was closed. Except a pub or two. It seems hard to imagine now.

The porters used to bring their wives in on Sundays for a drink. They were like different people to how they were in the week, when they'd be shouting obscenities at each other and screaming their bets across the bar. On Sundays, butter wouldn't have melted. They'd be all dressed up, in their best suits and would be horrified if we swore in front of their wives.

21

The Odd Threesome

For the first few years of our marriage, Robin and I were exceedingly happy, in spite of, or maybe because of, some of the crazy escapades we were involved in. People used to say that we were made for each other, and it really did feel like that.

I had started to be offered really good work again, a production of Shakespeare's *A Midsummer Night's Dream* for the BBC prestigious Play of the Month spot came first. I played Hermia opposite Lynn Redgrave's Helena. Edward Fox, Robert Stevens, Michael Gambon, Eleanor Brown and Eileen Atkins also starred. For the first time, I realised that I didn't feel totally out of place in such a company. Indeed, I felt quite comfortable.

I also appeared in another play of the month, William Wycherley's *A Country Wife* with Bernard Cribbins and Helen Mirren. In 1971 I went into Noel Coward's *Hay Fever* with Judy Campbell, and we became lifelong friends. I used to stand in the wings with Jonathan Kent, who went on to run the Almeida Theatre in Islington, and we couldn't take our eyes off Judy. We knew we were watching a great star, and listening to her rendition every night of 'Hearts and Flowers' was a theatrical privilege. It was no wonder Eric Maschwitz wrote 'A Nightingale Sang In Berkeley Square' for her for the revue *New Faces*. Not only was that another really good production, but off stage, the three of us had the most enchanting time. It was probably one of the best times I've ever had on tour. And Judy remained my friend until her death in 2004.

Another production I was proud to be part of in the early 1970s was Joyce Rayburn's play, *Come When You Like*, at the Shaw Theatre, with Raymond Francis of *No Hiding Place* fame. During this play, Robin's parents, Ian and Casha, returned in a very bad state from where they had been living in Spain. Robin and I went to pick them up at Heathrow. Casha was carried off the plane on a stretcher, and Ian walked straight past Robin without recognizing him. It is no secret that most of their problems had tragically been caused by alcohol.

This had a great emotional effect on Robin, and I began to worry that he might be going the same way. I also had reason to believe that he was having an affair. Without question, we were beginning to grow apart.

However, just as I was thinking that our marriage was becoming dangerously rocky, it was propped up in a most unusual way, when a woman whom I shall call Sally, came into our lives. She was gay and used to get teased a lot, sometimes quite unpleasantly. There was, of course, quite extreme prejudice against homosexuals of both sexes then, but I've always believed that women suffered particularly. Robin liked Sally a great deal. He made friends easily and was always quick to befriend people who needed support. Robin didn't have any prejudice against anyone, and he was inclined to be very protective towards people who might be suffering from it. He had a lot of gay friends and, at first, Sally was just another one.

I suppose I was probably attracted to her from the start, but because I'd been trying to bury that side of me for so long, I didn't let myself think about it. She was just a friend until one night when everything changed and Sally became the first woman I ever slept with.

I have changed her name because her personal situation is such that to do otherwise could cause her embarrassment in her present life. I was alone in Bow Street. I'd just washed my hair and was drinking a glass of Alka-Seltzer – we got through a lot of that stuff back then – when the edge of the glass broke in my mouth and I swallowed a big chunk, harpooning my throat. I managed to cough really hard, and the glass popped out, but it cut the back of my throat quite badly. I was pretty shaken up, and just as I was recovering from the shock, Sally phoned to ask if Robin and I would like to go out for a drink. I told her that Robin was already out, and I'd just had a near-death experience. She simply said she would come up. And maybe because I was still in shock, I finally threw off my inhibitions and started a relationship with Sally. It happened quite suddenly. It was about the first time we'd been properly alone together, and there I was, with wet hair and no make-up, having just nearly choked to death. If anyone likes me in that sort of state, I'm inclined to be so grateful, I'm hooked straight away. Also, I suppose a part of me was waiting for something like this to happen, but there simply hadn't been a likely candidate since Ginette. And, of course, the frightened part of me had been actively trying to avoid it, but I fell for Sally, and I could do nothing to stop it.

It has to be said there was a certain relief for me in finally allowing myself to be with a woman, And it was a very good feeling to be with Sally. I have come to realise as I've grown older that it is the person, not the gender, that matters for me.

In many ways I remained 'a small fuckable chap who drinks'

to Robin, but whereas he had a complete lack of fear about both work and life in those days, and could walk through a first night, no nerves at all, I could not. It wasn't just nerves. I took work more seriously, and certainly always felt that in order to succeed at all, I had to work much harder at it than he did.

But already, even though Robin had so much talent, and had played leads in the West End years before me, he was beginning to fall behind such contemporaries as Nigel Hawthorne and Paul Eddington. His lifestyle didn't help, but neither did the fact that he wasn't really a fighter in his work. People who find things as easy as Robin did, certainly during the early part of his career, never learn to fight in the way that the rest of us do. Although we had so much in common, our approaches to our work were diverse, and Robin used to get quite cross with me over both my being so pedantic, and my extreme nervousness.

More than anything, Sally fulfilled an emotional need for me at the time. I turned to her for understanding and I got it. She helped me to cope with all my various insecurities and was particularly supportive about my work. I told Robin about Sally almost straight away. I could have imagined doing nothing else. I didn't have any secrets from him. He was not at all fazed. In fact, he made it quite clear that he rather liked the idea. I never ceased to be surprised that the idea of two women together, and of perhaps actually joining in, seems to be the fantasy of so many men. It was certainly a fantasy of Robin's.

Sally, who, like many gay women, had once been straight, used to meet us most days in the pub, and Robin had always been terribly affectionate and good with her. She worked in central London, but was living out of town, and used to drive in and out. Then one day, she'd had too much to drink to drive, and she ended up staying the night at Bow Street. It seemed a bit daft to start trying to sort the settee out and make all that mess with bed clothes, and it felt perfectly natural for Sally just to crash out with Robin and me.

I know that the idea of three in a bed is a big turn-on for a lot of people, even if it is taken no further than that. And of course I was excited by the idea at first, or I wouldn't have gone along with it, but it also seemed like a kind of solution, albeit a bizarre one, to my various sexual and emotional dilemmas. I still loved Robin, the man who for so long had been my best friend as well as my husband, and the way in which we were growing apart distressed me greatly.

The three of us ended up living together in my little flat which, when it became known around the place, led to other men saying to Robin, "Aren't you lucky?"

I should mention that it was during the time Robin, Sally, and I were the odd threesome that I acquired a little Yorkshire Terrier, called Katie Cupcake, who liked to sleep on my head. And, I can assure you that when fighting off a complete nervous breakdown and prone to panic attacks, whilst in a state of permanent exhaustion, playing the lead in the West End, sharing a four-feet-six-inch bed in a tiny flat with two rather large people and a dog intent on smothering you, it is actually quite difficult to experience much rampant sexuality. You just don't have the energy.

What I remember most of this time with Sally, Robin and me was the enormous fun that we had, and the support that we gave each other. It was like a permanent party. We were a group already wherever we went. Perhaps incredibly, our threesome lasted seven years on and off. I can recommend it as a way of living if you have the right three people, I really can. And strange as it might seem, if Sally had not entered our lives, I really do not think Robin and I would have stayed together for nearly as long as we did,

While all this was going on and I was living what must have seemed to be this extraordinary bohemian life, I continued to work extremely hard. Of course, work has always been the one constant factor in my life. Whatever has been happening in my personal life, whatever state I've been in mentally, I always seem to have just kept on working through. I was becoming a lot stronger mentally though, partly thanks to the psychiatric treatment I received at the Middlesex Hospital.

Unfortunately, I was not in a position to concentrate solely on really good quality work, even though I was being offered plenty of it. The sorry side of show business is that the best work is often the worst paid. Robin was appearing at the Players' Theatre, which rarely pays well, whilst trying to launch a writing career. He started very promisingly, and there was certainly no doubt about his talent. However, he didn't persevere, and his early promise was never fulfilled. I therefore was the major breadwinner and unable to choose my work in the way that I might have liked.

22

"You Can't Cry, You're Market"

This was how, in the early 70s, I went into a children's TV series called *Hickory House* made in Manchester by Granada. While filming, I used to stay with my mother in her Disley cottage, where we still shared a bed. Alan Rothwell, who went on to play footballer David Barlow, the younger brother of Ken, in *Coronation Street*, was the main man on *Hickory House* and asked me to present it with him.

Unfortunately, the show was a complete disaster for me. I seemed to do nothing but get myself into trouble with the Lancashire education committee. We didn't have enough rehearsal time and the programme was always over or under running. After just half a day's rehearsal, we'd end up having to ad lib our way through. There was one occasion when we'd made two little boats, just like on *Blue Peter*. But I don't think what happened next was the sort of thing that happened on *Blue Peter*. Alan asked me what I was going to call mine just as it began to sink, so, naturally enough, I feel, I replied, "The Titanic". This went down almost as well as the ship herself!

You really weren't supposed to make cracks like that on children's shows.

There followed, thankfully, another opportunity to do some rather good work. I had a role in a prestigious production of Shakespeare's *Twelfth Night* at the temporary theatre on the site of the bard's Old Globe, which has now been so splendidly reconstructed, largely due to the efforts of director Sam Wannamaker, father of the wonderful actress Zoe, whose dream the whole project was.

It was there, on such hallowed ground, that I chalked up another memorable first. The play was directed by Michael Attenborough, son of Richard, and Alfred Marks played Sir Toby Belch. I played Maria, and I stopped the show. Literally! But I did have a good reason. The clue is the name by which the theatre became known: The Plastic Bucket. It was open-sided back then, but partially covered by a tent, which looked like a kind of mini dome and was a total water trap.

One day, we had torrential rain. The tent filled with gallons of water and the entrances to the stage began to resemble Niagara Falls. So there we were, in our costumes and wigs, with sheets of water coming down all over the place, and a nutty girl was fiddling around with an electric board that was also running with water. It was getting highly dangerous. I looked up, and there on the fast-collapsing tent-like roof, which you could see through, was this great man of theatre, Sam Wanamaker, in his underpants, bailing out with a plastic bucket. Hence the theatre's name. Apparently, this spectacle was a regular feature. This was, however, the watery equivalent of picking up grains of sand off the beach. There was no way Sam and his bucket were going to rescue us. But the sight of a half-naked Sam doing this extraordinary trampoline act above people's heads is something I shall always cherish.

However, it suddenly became very clear to me that not only were our costumes and wigs going to be ruined, not only were we all in danger of breaking our legs on a treacherous stage, not only was it impossible for the audience to hear us, but the roof was about to collapse!

So I just walked forward on stage, held up my hands and said, "That's it. We're stopping. It's not safe to carry on."

In 1974, I made another brief foray into the world of films. I was given a part in the Disney picture, *One Of Our Dinosaurs Is Missing*, which was released the following year and centred around a secret microfilm that was smuggled out of China and hidden in a dinosaur skeleton in the Natural History Museum.

I nearly went missing too – permanently!

This was another film with an impressive cast, including Peter Ustinov, Derek Nimmo, Roy Kinnear, Bernard Breslow, and Helen Hayes. I played Joss Ackland's wife, and in one scene, he takes me out for a special dinner at a Chinese restaurant, where he presents me with a rather unusual present.

"Happy birthday, darling. I bought this for you," says Joss, as a dinosaur appears in front of me.

Now the creature concerned, a 60-foot-high replica, was supposed to trundle along on a kind of track and stop a foot or so away from me. It didn't stop, though. It just came trundling on until it smashed into me.

The set was pretty solid, but almost all of it was destroyed, including the table in front of me and the chair I was sitting on. I ended up stuck under the table with this dinosaur still moving about on top of me. It was extremely frightening. I suffered a concussion and quite a few bumps and bruises. And it would have been even worse if two of the extras playing Chinese waiters had not reacted very quickly and pulled me out from the wreckage. Nowadays, an actor would probably sue for compensation. That didn't occur to me. But I did get a bunch of flowers from the dinosaur.

It was also in the early 1970s that the battle to save Covent Garden took place. This was at about the same time that Les Halles, the inner city marketplace in Paris, was flattened. And those of us who were part of The Garden, and loved it, were determined that the same thing was not going to happen in London.

Our beloved fruit and veg market moved to Nine Elms in 1974, but the battle to preserve its old home for our capital city began long before then. All the diverse characters of The Garden came together and, boy, did we fight. We battled for every brick of it. And to this day, walking around Covent Garden as it is now, I feel a certain pride that I was part of that struggle. The people who lived and who worked there were not opposed to the commercial operation being moved. We realised that such a central site was no longer feasible, but we were not prepared to let its history and architecture be destroyed.

The Covent Garden Community Association was formed. I was asked to become involved because I was quite well known, but I would have done all that I could in the fight in any case. It began in a very small way, with the association seeming something of a David against the Goliath of the big business organisations that had control of most of the property in the area. We staged candle-lit processions and I helped organize the first big demonstration, a public meeting in the Piazza.

I managed to get several public figures to speak, including the broadcaster David Jacobs, whose father had been a porter in the market. However, I didn't realise that I was going to be called upon to make a speech too. It was the first I'd ever made in my life and I had to call on both my grandfather's genes and Robin's support in the wings. I sent a message to the Greater London Council (GLC) via Eliza Doolittle, "You think you're going to get Covent Garden? Not bleeding likely!"

Everybody in the community did their bit, including many of those involved in London Theatre. Dame Peggy Ashcroft was a great supporter. The Players' Theatre put on a show to raise funds. We were determined that bureaucracy and big business would not destroy our community. The GLC insisted it would be wonderful to have parks in Covent Garden for people to sit in, but they were intending to demolish people's homes, and buildings of huge historic importance, to make way for them.

At one point, we managed to steal their so-called plan for redeveloping the garden. But in reality there were no such plans. The only plan was to flatten the place. Like everyone else, I was angry. The big landlords were offering people 30 pounds to get out of homes their families had lived in for generations. These were people who didn't realise that they could say no; who, because of their pride, refused to admit that they were in trouble. I arranged for some of them to be interviewed on *Panorama*, and gradually, the truth began to come out.

A recent BBC documentary, *The People's Piazza*, tells the story of our fight and shows footage of a campaign meeting in The Sun Tavern, in which I am featured calling out:, "We're not bloody going anywhere."

And that's exactly how it was. But strange things happened during the fight. A building in Longacre went up in flames, shortly after it had been ruled that its beautiful old facade could not be touched. It burned down on a summer's night, and I remember looking out of the window of my flat and thinking how heavy the fog was for that time of year. The street was full of smoke, of course, not fog, and it wasn't until the next morning that I realised how close the whole area had come to being burned down.

Against all odds, we ultimately won the day. We awoke public awareness to the planned destruction of this rather glorious part of our national heritage. The wonderful old buildings of The Garden were saved by a protection order issued in 1973 and quite a lot of new council housing, some of it very imaginative, was built in the area for the people who belonged to this very special community.

I remember walking through the piazza just after all the boarding had been taken down, and there was a man in a long coat with a greyhound at his feet, standing alone in the middle, playing a flute. It was like something out of a 17th-century print. It made me cry, because I thought it was every bit as important that we managed to preserve the spirit of Covent Garden as to preserve its architecture. That spirit lives on, as do the characters.

At one point, when Robin and I were going through a particularly bad patch, I was spotted in tears by an elderly neighbour who was one of my favourite Garden characters. "Come on Amanda," she said. "You can't cry, you're Market."

Now, that was a great compliment, and I still remind myself of it if ever I'm feeling upset about anything. To this day, market people retain a unique way of looking at things. I used to have 'a lady who does' of Irish descent called Catherine, whom I once asked to buy me a *Daily Mail* and an *Evening Standard*. "I couldn't get a *Mail*, so I got you two *Standards*," she informed me on her return. And that, I can assure you, is more typically Market than Irish.

I relied very much on Catherine, however, just as I relied on my neighbour, Annie, who used to guard me with her life against all evils, both imagined and real, and to whom I invariably turned when the going got tough. Catherine is no longer with us, and Annie died recently, whilst I was writing this book. There is also my dear friend Beryl, who is always there when I need her. Like me, Beryl does not have a very high opinion of her own appearance. She once asked me how I'd got on in rehearsals and I replied that I was too ugly that day to have an opinion.

"I know what you mean," she replied. "I felt too ugly today to go through the front door of my office, so I went round the back".

Then there is Mr. Kipps, who manages to stock almost everything you need in his small general store in Endell Street, and somehow contrives to survive, in spite of the nearby presence of giants like Tesco.

I am lucky enough now to have a neighbour and good friend, Maggie Crowe, who, along with her son, David, is a relative newcomer to Covent Garden, yet has immersed herself in the area in all possible ways ever since her arrival. And I believe she quite probably loves it as much as I do.

I consider myself extraordinarily lucky to have lived for so long in 'old Covent Garden' at the heart of a community unlike any other that I have ever encountered, and among such a rich variety of people who continue to make the place so special.

Playing a part in the saving of the Garden was one of the best things that ever happened to me. Another of the best moments of my life came shortly after, when in 1974 I was invited to play the lead role in a West End production of *Oh Kay!*, which had been written for Gertrude Lawrence by PG Wodehouse and Guy Bolton with music by the Gershwin Brothers.

Gertie had been my heroine since my school days. I even owe my name to her. I still keep a framed photograph of her by my side, which I always have in my dressing room when I'm working in the theatre. I was, of course, even more nervous than usual of taking on a new role, because I was stepping in Gertie's hallowed footsteps, and that meant so very much to me.

I had bumped into Guy by chance. Naturally, I hadn't been able to resist asking him about Gertie, as I always did anyone I met who had known her. But Guy was a rather gruff man, totally disinterested in the past and he just asked me, rather shortly, what I knew about Gertrude Lawrence? Without pausing to think, I rattled off a story or two. At the end of it, Guy simply asked, "Do you want to do her play?"

It was an extraordinary leap of faith. He didn't even ask me if I thought I could do it. I said yes at once, and worried about it later. *Oh Kay!* had not been revived in England since Gertie's day. I don't know that my playing it was necessarily any great contribution to the theatre, but it was certainly very special for me. I found it both nostalgic and therapeutic. Once again, I got some rather good notices. A particular favourite was from the famous Felix Barker in the *London News* which began:

"Where has Amanda Barrie been all my life? Not idle, of course, but probably denied her full chance with fugitive films and fleeting TV shadows. Last night, this enchantress with the Betty Boop eyes and mock vacant manner, landed slap bang in my lap – in all our delighted laps at the Westminster – with what was surely the performance of her career..."

And it ended: "Sweeping the evening along. Miss Barrie switches with delicious ease from sentiment (Someone to Watch Over Me) to eccentric comedy, as the bogus parlour maid with a frill cap, which, in an emergency, she pulls down over her head like a visor. Never have I seen an actress come so near the gentle ineffable charm, to say nothing of technical accomplishment,

that musical stars possessed in the inter war years. Very much
Oh Kay, Miss Barrie."

I couldn't believe that one still can't! But the notice I'm most
proud of came in the form of a letter from the great man himself,
PG Wodehouse, who'd apparently heard nice things about me
in the play from Guy.

"I can see from your photograph that you must be ideal in the
part," he wrote from his home in Long Island, New York. And
he signed his letter, "Lots of love, from Plum."

I was knocked out to receive a letter from him, even more
so by the fact that he signed himself "Plum", a nickname that
I understand he normally used only within his circle of close
friends.

I have to say that whilst I would never presume to suggest that
I was like Gertie in any way on stage, several people pointed out
to me that I did do a number of things exactly the way that she
had done them, even though I didn't know it. Gertie's long-time
chauffeur came to see the show, and afterwards he asked me
what had led me to come to the front of the stage and kneel
when I sang 'Someone to Watch Over Me'.

"I have no idea." I replied. "Why?"

"Because that's what Gertie did," he said.

I hadn't known that. I just did it.

As I opened with *Oh Kay!*, something else of profound
importance happened in my life. That was when I acquired
Katie Cupcake, the dog who was to sleep on my head. She had
been found abandoned and taken to Bow Street police station.
A policeman I knew came into the Nags Head one Sunday
lunchtime, obviously saw an easy touch, and said, "Amanda,
please, will you take this little Yorkshire Terrier we have at the
station. The last dog we had went to Battersea Dogs and Cats
Home, and I can't bear the same thing for this one."

There was a complicated procedure concerning stray dogs. They couldn't just hand Katie over to me. So they tied her up outside the police station, then they cut the string, pushed her down the steps, and said, "Oh, look, Amanda, the dog's escaped, you'd better catch her."

I had Katie for nine years, during which time she made a number of appearances on stage which she thoroughly enjoyed – unlike our Coco! I'm not quite sure how she got her name. She started as Katie and it grew into Katie Cupcake. I think it was just another of those inexplicable Covent Garden nicknames. She was a real Garden dog, and she was very popular in the neighbourhood. She liked cobbles, and was never too keen on grass.

Old ladies used to walk past us and say goodnight to Katie without bothering to address me. But then, she was very good with people and would trot off periodically to talk to her friends. I was devoted to Katie Cupcake, and I have owed her a great deal over the years.

She helped me through an awful lot of scenes in *Coronation Street*, even the later ones, when Alma was dying. It was easier somehow to think about my dog than about a person. Whenever I had to cry on camera, all I had to do was think about my Katie.

23

Absurd Antiques

I n the mid 1970s my mental health became increasingly more precarious, whilst I somehow or other continued to top the bill in the West End. My home life was deteriorating rapidly – a gradual, all-encompassing decline. Heavy drinkers invariably want their partners to join them, and it is all too easy to fall into that trap. *Absurd Person Singular* followed *Oh Kay!*, and I would only ever allow myself a drink after a show, never during the day. Meanwhile, Robin was still working at the Players' Theatre occasionally, whilst drinking more and more.

As time passed, he began to transform from the tall, handsome, vigorous man I had married into a physical wreck. He'd once been a wonderful cook, but now he scarcely ate, growing thinner and weaker.

On one occasion, as I was preparing to leave for a matinee, he collapsed – virtually unconscious – onto the floor. Thankfully, he recovered. I did love my husband, but his drinking became insurmountable. Ours had been a good, if unusual, marriage, full of laughter, until it reached the point where it was impossible even to discuss his drinking.

I still remember well a day when, rendered so distraught

by the situation, I leaned against a parking meter outside the stage door of The Vaudeville and simply broke down. I thought I would be unable to go on, but of course, I did – as always. Indeed it was my work which kept me going, and, in spite of everything, I loved being in *Absurd Person* with Paul Eddington and Millicent Martin, two great stars. Yet I was mentally exhausted, and I longed desperately for at least some respite from the emotional turmoil which surrounded me off stage.

The essence of any relationship I sought was never sexual or physical; it was usually born of a yearning for a sense of home. That was all I had ever truly wanted – a home, and someone to share it with. I hadn't realised, when I was sent to boarding school, just how profoundly I'd been affected.

Then, it became clear that Robin was involved with someone else. I still remember the depth of my loneliness. That was the beginning of the end.

Eventually, he left. He walked out of Bow Street, and I shall never forget the sight. It was like a scene from *Geoffrey Barnard Is Unwell*. He departed quietly, clutching the same battered suitcase he had arrived with all those years before, an old and honourable case that had once belonged to his father, around which he'd wrapped a tie to hold it together. I watched from the window as he walked slowly up the street. I knew how much he loved our flat, loved Covent Garden, and the peculiar little life we had maintained for so long. Indeed, how much he had loved me. It broke my heart to see him go, but there was no alternative.

In 1978, my father died at the age of 66. It was especially sad for me, as we had only just reconciled after decades of estrangement, the result of a peculiar emotional distance dating back to my childhood. My father remarried, and his second wife decided she wanted nothing to do with me – apparently, I reminded her too much of my mother. I once suggested he tell her I was his daughter, not a former lover, but it made no difference. I barely saw my father throughout my adult life, until six months before his death. He never even met Robin.

I was still also coping with the emotional upheaval of Robin leaving. Although I knew I could not have continued with him, I missed Robin and worried about him. Unsurprisingly, with all this going on, I began not to feel at my best professionally. I joined a show called *The French Have a Song for It* with Helen Shapiro. It had been a hit at the King's Head in Islington, but flopped at the Piccadilly Theatre. The show never worked for me – largely because I do not speak French and could never master the songs. Audiences left because of my French, and I was always getting laughs in the wrong places. My pronunciation would transform lines like "he got up and went out into the night" into "he washes himself", or worse. Helen Shapiro and the cast were lovely, but I never conquered the French.

Eventually, I was offered a tour of Noël Coward's *Blithe Spirit*, which I accepted, eager for escape from my life as it had become. And that was how I met the late, great Heather Chasen, who was to play opposite me. I had previously known her only from a distance as a distinguished actress with an impressive track record – star of *The Navy Lark*, and the vampish Valerie Pollard in *Crossroads*. She was strikingly beautiful, but at first I had no idea just how good she was to be with. Heather was a quintessential English eccentric – also very funny and very kind.

On our first day of rehearsal, we left together, and I noticed her eyeing a particularly lovely young woman passing by. "I saw that," I said, and we both burst out laughing. In an instant, I felt the warmth that shared laughter brings, and it always does something to my heart.

I had heard the usual theatre rumours that, though Heather

had been married, she might be interested in relationships with women – it was an open secret. She had a beautiful son, Rupert, who had played the incredibly handsome schoolboy Bobby Phillips in the film *If*. Like so many, me included, Heather's life was mixed and complex. You certainly couldn't put her in a box. Most of us are fairly complicated creatures, both physically and emotionally, yet the world has an obsession with putting labels on people. My attitude has always been: how dare anyone label anyone else.

It was not long before Heather and I became close. Ours was never a passionate affair; that was not its nature. Heather cared for me, and we laughed constantly. I soon came to love her wholeheartedly. She was, emotionally, a homemaker, though the practicalities of running a household – without being buried in debris and dogs – were somewhat beyond her. I did my best to help, redesigning her home so that, for a while at least, it became almost the sort of place where she could justifiably utter a regal 'enter' to welcome visitors.

We took an antique stall at Camden Lock on Sunday mornings, which we enjoyed immensely. Somewhat miraculously, given our other commitments, we kept it going for two years. I grew to love the company of dealers and made many friends.

On Saturday nights, after the theatre, we managed perhaps four hours' sleep, rising at four to get our stuff ready in Heather's garage. In the winter we were invariably frozen before we even loaded the car.

In retrospect, we must have been mad, staggering off to Camden Lock in the dead of night with bits of furniture on our heads after two West End shows. But it quickly became a way of life. Heather had an extraordinary eye and could have been a marvellous antiques dealer, had she wished. However, she was a compulsive buyer who could never leave things alone – I think we bought more than we sold, making profit elusive. She hated parting with treasures.

"Oh, darling, this piece is far too nice to let go. I really think we should keep it," she would say.

Through Camden, I learned much about art, antiques, and the knack of finding special things. I have always had a penchant for skips. To this day, I cannot pass one without peering in. I remember one day, driving along Harley Street, I spotted a pair of Edwardian crutches with inlaid mahogany - beautiful things. I shouted for Heather to stop, retrieved them, and strapped them to the roof rack. A few blocks later, I was shouting again, having spotted some lovely lampshades in another skip. That was a particularly fruitful Sunday. The first things we sold were my crutches, then we made about £70 from some other things I'd picked up off the street.

I discovered a true love for the business – not for the "antiques" in inverted commas that are sold in Olympia or posh Mayfair shops, which I often find pretty horrible, but for all kinds of objects, perhaps damaged and restored, that can be used to make your home look and feel better.

One way or another, Heather and I shared a crazy but delightful relationship. At one stage we were both playing the lead in different productions in the West End, yet we never seemed to have any money. As far as Heather was concerned, this may not have been connected with the lifestyle to which she aspired. She always dressed beautifully and was incredibly stylish in every way.

I will never forget having tea with her one day in what was then one of the smartest places in town – Maison Sagne in Marylebone High Street – her suggestion after she had been to the bank manager in order to get an overdraft. She had been given £40, which in those days was a big deal, for an actress anyway, so we were celebrating – with Katie Cupcake, whom I think Heather loved almost as much as I did.

"I do think one should always wear silk and cashmere, dear, don't you?' remarked Heather casually, as she summoned a passing waiter to enquire, with the air of one accustomed to being instantly obeyed, "Could I have a little more cream for the dog?"

In our financial situation, sackcloth and ashes and a cup of water would have been more appropriate, but Heather never allowed herself to be bowed down by the practicalities of life.

When I met Heather, she didn't drink, having had an earlier problem with alcohol. In support, I gave up drinking myself for seven years, and following my experiences with Robin, I was more than happy to do so. I even accompanied her to meetings of Alcoholics Anonymous. But unfortunately, Heather eventually lapsed, with fairly disastrous consequences, which led to us parting. She had previously given me the home life I always yearned for, leading to a period of my being perfectly well mentally. And she was another person in my life with whom I could have imagined being with for ever, were it not for their inability either to cope with or to stop drinking.

24

Enter Alma

In 1981, another life-changing moment arrived. I joined *Coronation Street* to play Alma Sedgwick, later to become Alma Baldwin. My initial stint lasted five weeks, and I returned briefly the following year.

My very first scene required me to act opposite my heroine, Pat Phoenix, who was, of course, the truly wonderful Elsie Tanner. Larger than life, with film star glamour and boundless energy, Pat reminded me, in some ways, of my mother. I was, understandably, overawed before I even began. But it was worse than that. As the proprietor of the café, I had to sack Elsie. I was mortified.

Coronation Street in the early 1980s was a very different place from the one I would return to later. It was governed by an old regime and a strict hierarchy. People had their adopted seats in the green room – a kind of common room for actors – and, much like with revered regulars in an old-fashioned pub, you sat in the wrong seat at your peril. Arriving as a newcomer was thoroughly daunting. And - as like my mother I had always been a Corrie fan, watching whenever I could - I immediately found myself faced with people I felt I already knew. That made me extra nervous. I had a tendency to stare at the person I was working with, thinking, "That's Pat Phoenix. I'm saying these lines to Elsie Tanner. Oh, my God." It was quite overwhelming for someone as self-conscious as I could be.

The *Coronation Street* regulars in those days really were like movie stars and that's precisely how they behaved. To me, Pat Phoenix was Rita Hayworth; Doris Speed, who played Annie Walker, was Phyllis Calvert; and Jean Alexander, who played Hilda Ogden, was Gracie Fields. However, working with them was not at all like working with the show business professionals I'd encountered so far in my career. They had all been in the series for years and enjoyed total job security – unheard of in the business, and quite unlike the way things are now, with cast members being axed all the time.

I was used to a kind of conversation rather more typical among people in the business: whether you'd seen the latest show in town, the quality of performances, and gossip about what various actors were up to. Within The Street, however, con-versation between the actors was much the same as you'd find among the regulars at the Rovers. "Are you going to Kendals at lunchtime?", "I've seen these wonderful drapes in that new shop on Deansgate."

Every afternoon back then, a huge tray of cakes and cream buns would be delivered. I was amazed to watch Jack Howarth (Albert Tatlock) fill his pockets with them every day before trotting out of Granada, pockets bulging, looking as grim as ever. Had anyone bumped into him, cream buns would have spilled from every orifice.

Anne Kirkbride (Deirdre Barlow) once astonished me by meticulously applying little black dots onto silver wrapping paper. Apparently, she wanted all her Christmas wrapping paper to match, and when the store ran out of the exact design she had chosen, she decided to improvise. Anne was always extremely industrious.

Coronation Street was a very different world for someone used to West End theatre. Newcomers were cannon fodder, really. Their job was to support the senior cast. I was well aware of this and developed a way of sliding in and out of scenes, hoping that if I wasn't noticed, I might last longer. I realised that almost all the leading characters back then played comedy, so I deliberately avoided that, even though it had always been my strength. Instead, I retreated into the shell from which Alma ultimately emerged – a quiet, sweet, gentle person whom I was then to become stuck with.

I particularly hated rehearsals, not least because they were held in a room with windows, which meant daylight. I've never been fond of daylight when I'm working; I prefer to be buried in the depths of a theatre basement. In those days, we had what was called the "tech run" – words that still send ice-cold water running through my veins. This medieval torture was a certain type of rehearsal, a word seldom used now in soap. Indeed, you have to explain to younger actors in this kind of television what "rehearsal" means. The tech run, when you rehearsed for the camera in front of all the technicians and cast, took place every Wednesday at 2pm and had its own bizarre dress code. The rule seemed to be that none of the assembled cast would ever look remotely like themselves. It was customary to dress up for the tech run, and it was built up as a big occasion. Certainly, it was unheard of to go in your jeans.

Pat Phoenix had extraordinary presence and wore the most remarkable clothes. One tech run day, she arrived dressed from head to toe in a white cowgirl outfit: a big white Stetson, a white cowgirl jacket, suede skirt, and white boots. Earlier that day, she'd been wearing a frilly shirt and an A-line suit, but that wasn't extreme enough for the tech run, obviously. So she popped up to Elite, Manchester's famous second-hand clothing shop, at lunchtime to acquire something suitably bizarre. Looking back, perhaps the most extraordinary thing of all was that nobody paid any attention to Pat's Annie Oakley look.

I also vividly remember Lynne Perry (Ivy Tilsley) wearing a black and white evening dress, a hat, and four-inch heels – all for a TV rehearsal in the middle of the day. I never slept at all the night before the tech run because I was always so nervous. In spite of these various delusions of grandeur in The Street back then, the working conditions were quite tricky. Corrie was not given its own home, Stage One, until 1990. Before that, this huge show had to be squeezed into Granada Studios amidst whatever else was being made at the time. This meant that nobody – not even the likes of Pat Phoenix or Doris Speed – could have their own dressing room. There were not enough to go round. Besides, they would all be needed for some other show when not being used by Street cast. So we shared dressing rooms and had to pack up all our belongings and take them home at the end of each working day, which was a real drag. The corridors were always full of people standing around chatting because the person with whom they were sharing their dressing room was trying to sleep. Even the green room was just a small, crowded place off the rehearsal room, where nobody had any space to themselves.

In retrospect, though, particularly compared with the way things are today, *Coronation Street* in 1981 was a doddle – an absolute doddle. The workload was easy when there were only two shows a week. Our working week didn't begin until Tuesday afternoon, when there was a read-through.

For me, one of the special joys of joining The Street was rekin-dling an old friendship with Tony Warren, the man who created

Corrie. I'd known Tony since we shared the same agent, Dorothy Macauland, whose client I was during my early dancing years. I'd last seen him as an aspiring performer, prancing around at an audition, entertaining all of us waiting in the wings. He didn't seem to have changed a bit.

During my first stint in Corrie, I stayed with my mother in Didsbury. She would bring me a bacon sandwich and a cup of tea in bed early in the morning – a time when I am never at my most awake – and while I was eating with one hand, she would take the other and guide it while I sleepily signed cheques with which she would pay her gas and electricity bills.

It was, and still is, a big thing to go into The Street, but the viewing figures then were so much greater than they are now. With no internet and just four channels on the box, Corrie's share of the national TV audience was immense. Despite having played the lead in so many West End shows, in *Carry On Cleo* and all the other films and TV I'd done, I was well aware that the exposure you got in The Street far exceeded most other areas of show business.

It still amuses me when people tell me, as they occasionally do, that they never watch *Coronation Street*, yet they know every single thing that's ever happened in it. Back in the day I used to think The Street had a lot in common with Margaret Thatcher and that many of the millions who never watched *Coronation Street* might also have been among the millions who claimed never to have voted for the Iron Lady.

Which leads me nicely, I hope, to Tony Williamson's *The Cabinet Mole*, in which I played Mrs Thatcher. People tell me that I did rather a good impression of Maggie, which I find rather disconcerting.

Around this time, I also changed my agent. Previously, I had moved from Alec Graham to Julian Belfrage, a lovely man and an absolute top agent with extremely distinguished clients like Judi Dench and Maria Aitken. He expected all his clients to wait for the right, truly prestigious job to come along. It was through Julian that I did *Early Struggles* for Stephen Frears. But if jobs of that calibre didn't come along, Julian simply insisted you wait until they did. I had to persuade him that I should go into *Coronation Street*. He'd ignored several approaches from Granada, before that first five-week stint in 1981. I was still sending my mother money and helping Robin out, and it wasn't just that I wanted to work, I needed to work, for heaven's sake. So I changed to Peter Charlesworth, also a very respected agent, but perhaps a little more commercial than Julian.

Within just days of joining Peter, and very shortly after *The Cabinet Mole*, I was offered Michael Frayn's *Noises Off*, playing Dotty Otley, which for me was an absolute joy, because the play involves more action than words. As a dancer, I felt it was made for me. If it's done properly – and this production was – it's a wonderful piece. But it's a notoriously difficult play to stage. *Noises Off* is ridiculously physical. The wings of the Savoy Theatre were like a set from *Emergency Ward Ten*; people were always hurting themselves as they leapt about.

We had a complete first aid unit lined up: bandages, ice, arnica, everything at the ready. I was, however, in my element. I particularly loved the second act, because there is virtually no speech and it's all movement. The actors have to be very fit, which I was, and my dance training really came into its own. It was so wonderful for me to be at rehearsals and not be in a panic about learning my lines, while everyone else was panicking about the moves, writing them down and trying to memorise them. I have never had to write down moves; I'd be there straight away. I've always been with movement the way the rest of the world is with words – it comes quite naturally to me.

Shortly after *Noises Off*, I went into *Stepping Out* at the Duke of York's Theatre, and during the course of almost three years with the show, my life again changed forever. Two momentous things happened. The first was that my mother died. The second was that I met the woman with whom I was to spend the next 15 years of my life.

My mother's death, at the age of 77, utterly shattered me. It wasn't just that I lost her – it was the way it happened. She was still living in a house in Didsbury with my sister Caroline, but had finally been persuaded to move to London, something she'd threatened to do forever. I was convinced she would be much happier in London, and she was actually packing up the Didsbury house when she called me in between shows one Saturday and told me she had a pain in her chest. "I'm sure it's indigestion," she said. I told her I thought she should see a doctor. "No, it'll be fine. I'm drinking hot peppermint," she replied. She just wouldn't budge. And that was when we fought.

Each year in *Stepping Out*, we had a different company, and that was the last night of the year's run. As usual, on the last night, things were a bit fraught. I was in between shows, trying to get ten minutes' sleep to keep up my energy, and I don't suppose I was at my most patient. Anyway, we rowed, and I shall always regret it. We hung up on each other, something we'd never done before, even though we spoke every day. I then had to go on stage, and when I came off, I didn't know whether to call her or not. If she'd already gone to bed to get some rest, it would have been the worst thing I could do. I was uneasy, though, with very good reason, as it turned out.

The next morning – a Sunday – my brother called to say that Connie had died. I screamed the place down. I didn't cry; I screamed. It wasn't just grief, it was frustration at the utter futility of so much of her life. She'd tried so hard to do all sorts of things. She'd been talking about moving to London for as long as I could remember, and now, just as she was going to do it, she had died.

The next day was the opening night of *Stepping Out* with the new company. I went ahead with it. I don't think it occurred to me to do anything else. I remember telling the director, Julia McKenzie, not to tell anyone else, and somehow I got through it. I was on autopilot. I had lost my best friend, my soulmate, the person who had been such an extraordinary presence in my life and who, it has always seemed to me, was responsible for everything I became.

I had always dreaded my mother's death, but to have quarrelled with her the very last time we spoke was something I would not have believed possible and something I will never quite get over. She pushed me beyond all reason as a child, sent me away to a school I hated, and on occasions drove me mad, but she was my very best friend until the end, and we never stopped laughing together. I enjoyed her company more than that of almost any other person I have ever known. When I really needed her, she would invariably turn up, always out of breath, dressed in a Sherlock Holmes hat and that cloak, ready to spring into action like Super Mum.

I have never met anyone in my life remotely like her. I find it impossible to describe her in the way she deserves. She was unique. She was my inspiration and my tormentor. She was my greatest-ever fan. I shall never forget the way she used to strike a match when she came to see me in the theatre so I would be able to see her face, nor the trouble it sometimes caused. Every time I go on stage, I still look for her, and I know I always will. I have no doubt that I owe her everything I am.

In 1988, I returned to *Coronation Street* and began what was to become a mammoth 15-year stint in the world's most popular soap. A whole new life opened up for me. However, partly because of the extraordinary exposure which The Street gives everyone who appears in it, and partly because of my personal circumstances, I found myself in a very tricky situation. I had always been fairly open about relationships to people close to me, but I quickly learned that this was no longer possible for a Corrie regular. Every hiccup in their life is front-page news. It had never really occurred to me before that what I did or didn't do in my private life could be quite such a big deal.

Almost as soon as I returned to The Street, I was hit by a double whammy: a producer I'd worked with years before, who had fallen on hard times, decided to try to sell a lurid story about Robin, Sally, and me to a national newspaper. Simultaneously, another person who worked in Corrie discovered that I was sharing my life with a woman and tipped off the press. I have decided not to name this person because of the effect it could have on others, but one day I noticed, upon his script, scribbled phone numbers for the day and night desks of the *News of the World*.

On another occasion, I spotted him jotting down the registration numbers of all the actors' cars in the car park. Suffice to say, this unsavoury character – perpetually short of money – had made a cottage industry out of selling Corrie stories to the national press. I suspect there is someone like this on most high-profile shows, where information is a valuable commodity, but I have always thought it the lowest of the low. The result of this double betrayal was the start of my being so relentlessly pursued by the press.

On one occasion, there was a knock at my hotel room door. A young woman – who later revealed herself to be a reporter for a Sunday newspaper – pushed past me, surveyed the room, flung open the bathroom door, and demanded, "Where is she?"

Then there was the reporter who telephoned me directly, having doubtless bought my number from the *Coronation Street* snitch, and asked, "Are you a lesbian?"

"Only on Tuesday afternoons," I replied.

People have often said I handled the press well during those *Coronation Street* years, but in truth, I was terrified. I was living with a woman who desperately wanted our relationship to remain secret, which only made matters worse. I used to escape to Lincoln's Inn Fields near my London flat, where I would sit and sob. I called it 'Paranoia Park'. Perhaps I was a little paranoid, but I had every reason to be. The pursuit was unrelenting. I became so guarded that even if someone innocently asked what I had done over the weekend, I found myself in a quandary. I felt I couldn't even use the word "we", not even in passing.

Of course, there were people like Barbara Knox, Sue Nicholls, Helen Worth, and John Savident, whom I trusted implicitly, and with whom I could be completely open. But to have one's private life splashed across the front pages, in the most lurid terms imaginable, would have been quite another matter. I knew, you see, that if it were me – if the thing I most dreaded had come to pass and my sexuality became tabloid fodder – I simply would not have been able to walk into the green room. It may sound foolish, but that was truly how I felt at the time.

However, I hated behaving as though I were ashamed of such an important part of my life. I never wanted to live a furtive, hole-in-the-corner existence, but the circumstances – particularly those surrounding my personal life, living with someone who insisted on secrecy – left me with little choice. That, alas, was simply how it had to be.

25

A Typical Day on The Street

I have always believed that my return to *Coronation Street*, some six months after my mother's death, was largely due to Connie. I doubt the producers ever realised it, but I don't think they had much choice. When they signed me up to play Alma again, I swear that, immediately after her passing, my mother shot off to the casting agency in the sky to demand my reinstatement. She was the original *Coronation Street* groupie. In the years between my five-week stint on the show and her death, she relentlessly bombarded Granada with phone calls, each time adopting a new persona and accent to extol my brilliance and beg for Alma's return.

I was oblivious to all this until, to my utter embarrassment, the then-producer, Bill Podmore, sought me out while I was at Granada filming an episode of the Don Henderson detective series *Bulman*, and asked plaintively, "Please can you stop your mother phoning us?"

She had somehow acquired his direct line and was calling incessantly. The truth is, I was so nebulous during that first brief stint that I doubt anyone even noticed me. Naturally, that didn't deter Connie. I was mortified. I had this vision of her on the phone, putting on a funny accent, with everyone in the Corrie office whispering, "It's Amanda Barrie's mother again."

Of course, when I confronted her, she was entirely unabashed. "It's just that we all thought you were so wonderful, darling," she said, which immediately put me on red alert.

"What do you mean, 'we all'?" I swiftly countered.

"Oh, just some of my ladies," she replied.

It transpired she had persuaded most of her hairdressing clients to join her in phoning the Corrie office on my behalf. I doubt many of them had ever seen me on The Street, but that would not have bothered Connie in the slightest. She also flatly refused to believe that Bill and his staff had any idea that it was her making the bulk of the calls.

"They'd never have known it was me, dear," she insisted. "I put on all these different accents, you see..."

"Perhaps not quite as well as you thought," I suggested mildly.

It made no difference; Connie never, ever gave up on anything. So I am quite sure she would have continued her campaign in the afterlife.

She might, however, have been less enthusiastic about my becoming a regular had she realised what a treadmill the show would become when two episodes a week became three, then four. The hours were quite demanding. We were often required to be in the studio by 7am, sometimes earlier, for make-up, and frequently didn't finish until 7.30pm. By then, both body and brain were utterly numb. You arrived at and left Granada in darkness, rarely seeing daylight at all. Mind you, it has to be said that in Manchester it is often impossible to distinguish between the two.

The numbness only deepened as time went on. Being in a soap

is like running a marathon with no finishing line in sight. When one day's filming ends, you then have to learn the next day's lines, cramming nine, ten, or even 25 scenes into your reluctant brain – all of which tend, unfortunately, to coagulate into one.

The early mornings were the worst for me. I would stagger out of bed at 5am and begin the struggle to find my features, none of which ever seemed to be present at that hour. Anyone observing would have noticed a sort of silent mouthing as I tried to get dressed and brush my teeth – part of the desperate process of memorising the next batch of lines.

At the studio, half-asleep creatures with their eyes glued shut would creep about, unrecognisable to anyone, let alone half the country. The make-up girls were expected to resurrect us daily, these poor souls radiating cheerfulness, genuine or otherwise, endeavouring to transform the walking dead not only into human beings, but into something vaguely recognisable as the stars of *Coronation Street*. There was, of course, no time for plastic surgery – unless you did it yourself – so make-up simply had to do its best.

The studio grew hotter as the day wore on, and more often than not, half my make-up would detach itself from my skin. By the time my scene arrived, I looked like Bette Davis in *Whatever Happened to Baby Jane*, and my own hasty home improvements, layered on in the semi-darkness of my rabbit-hutch dressing room, seldom helped. My hair was a particular vexation; Manchester's damp atmosphere rendered it wild and unmanageable. One minute it stood on end and I resembled Tina Turner; the next, it flattened itself, and I looked like Adolf Hitler. It fought me from morning until night, only behaving just as the day's work ended.

Throughout all this, the strange mouthing continued – a sign that a scene was being frantically rehearsed in a remote part of my brain. My dyslexia made the constant learning especially arduous. Actors are inclined to suffer from a peculiar morning fog, quite apparent when you peer bleary-eyed into the equally bleary eyes of your scene partner. At that stage, most of us could barely remember our own names, let alone those of our characters, or anything more ambitious. Shortly after being glued together by the make-up department, we were on set, surrounded by technicians and lighting men, everyone bustling to sort out the first shot of the day. Then, miraculously, everything would lurch into action, and about 10 minutes later, to our amazement, we were acting.

When any of these scenes were cleared and subsequently broadcast to millions, I often used to think it must have been done by some sort of out-of-body experience, as I still wasn't fully awake.

Everyone in The Street dreaded scenes in The Rovers, as you had to perform with the rest of the cast sitting in the booths, waiting for their turn. If you were the one who fluffed your lines, you felt an even bigger fool than usual. To have a dry - when you forget your lines - or a fluff in The Rovers Return always turned me to jelly, and I think most people felt the same. But once released from such scenes, we were so relieved that we would become reanimated, turning into rather chatty little people heading off to have coffee and smoke furtive ciggies in hidden places.

When lunch was called, it was always welcome, though back then it was almost certainly not quite what viewers might have expected. In both winter and summer, the cast of *Coronation Street* ate from a catering truck parked outside in the car park, always 50 or 60 yards from the Granada building – just far enough, in Manchester's climate, to ensure that your hair, clothes, and the remnants of your equilibrium were destroyed.

The cast braved all weathers, those wearing wigs clutching them tightly as they climbed the steps to the hatch, precariously carrying steak and chips on paper plates back to the green room. Balancing food while keeping your wig in place meant you were lucky to arrive with half your lunch intact.

It is curious how large a part food plays in producing a soap opera; rather like animals in a zoo, it sometimes seems that it's all soap actors think about. Helen Worth once said to me, "I can't understand it, but as soon as I see Stage One, I get hungry."

Older members of the cast invariably tried – usually unsuccessfully – to avoid eating, so they could continue to fit into their costumes, but temptation was everywhere. When I first joined, there was a ritual: every morning, a large chromium-plated tray covered in doilies and small sandwiches would be delivered. They all tasted the same, but as the fillings were different colours, presumably the contents varied. In an effort not to pile on the pounds, we desperate actors would eat only the insides, so in the afternoon you would see us foraging through curly bits of white bread for the odd piece of escaped corned beef or cheese. Eventually, driven by hunger, we would eat the stale bread too.

Throughout the day, the green room was dotted with prostrate bodies; some of the younger cast members would even lie on the floor. It was often rather like an airport lounge during a particularly bad flight delay. Getting home at night brought little relief. I would usually arrive at my flat just in time to see *Coronation Street* on television. On the rare occasions when I felt strong enough to go out – virtually only ever at weekends – I was so programmed to memorise any words put in front of me that I would find myself trying to learn restaurant menus.

There was one advantage to the heavy Corrie workload: unlike the terrifying experience I endured when I first joined the show, I was hardly ever nervous during my second stint. As far as I know, neither was anyone else – we were all simply too busy trying to get through it all. And in case any reader still believes there was anything remotely glamorous about being a star of *Coronation Street*, I will share one final story to demonstrate the reality.

In 1995, a lavish reception and dinner was held at Manchester Civic Centre to celebrate the show's 35th birthday. The cast was required to be present, dressed in our finest. However, the transport provided by Granada was an elderly, none-too-clean, and slightly undersized bus. We set off for this grand occasion, crammed together, some forced to stand and cling to straps. Parts of this event were televised, so anyone who watched it might be puzzled by my story as viewers saw us emerging from shining limousines. The reality was that we were merely transferred briefly into the posh cars for the benefit of the cameras.

Arguably my greatest supporter during my Corrie years was Roy Hattersley, then Deputy Leader of the Labour Party, who made headlines in 1990 when he spoke at the Edinburgh Television Festival about the wonders of *Coronation Street* in general and, it must be said, Alma in particular. Roy gave the first annual Granada Lecture at the festival. There was no second, though whether that was due to one of the country's leading politicians declaring undying love for Alma, I cannot say. He actually compared Alma to Tolstoy's heroine Anna Karenina, which led a *Financial Times* journalist at the subsequent press conference to ask if his 'post-structural analysis' was serious or ironic, and if he stood by the comparison.

More recently, in an article in *The Scotsman* headlined "Ode to Alma," Roy Hattersley wrote, "Afraid of being accused of insufferable pretension, I replied, 'Really all I'm saying is that I fancy her,' and I knew at once that my admission was a mistake.

I'M STILL HERE

Two days later, Neil Kinnock, then Leader of the Labour Party, invited me to his room for a pre-lunch drink. As I walked in, he held out his hand in congratulations. 'This,' he said, waving a copy of the *Daily Mirror*, 'is exactly the sort of down-to-earth publicity we need.' Page five of the paper was dominated by a large picture of Amanda Barrie, above which the headline proclaimed more or less: 'I fancy him too.' The actual words I have blocked from my mind. The story that followed the picture I was too embarrassed to read.

However, I do recall it provoked one of the classic moments of my relationship with Neil Kinnock. Having expressed a similar enthusiasm for Miss Barrie, he said he had admired her ever since she had appeared as the eponymous heroine in *Carry On Cleo*. Noticing my look of surprise, he added, 'Not that I ever saw the film.'"

So it seems I had two very senior Labour Party admirers. I can but cringe at publicly declaring that I fancied Roy Hattersley back, but it seemed the only polite thing to do at the time.

When I subsequently met Roy at a special Granada screening of his lecture, and later by chance in Joe Allen, I found him immensely likeable and quite charismatic. It is certainly true that power attracts.

After ceasing to be deputy leader, Roy wrote about television in several national newspapers and continued loyally to declare his devotion to me – and to Alma. He suggested he would like to be a knight on a white charger, sweeping Alma off her feet and looking after her. When Mike betrayed Alma by spending a night with a prostitute while away at a sales conference, Roy quoted Paul Newman's remark about his absolute fidelity to Joanne Woodward, "Why go out for a hamburger when you can have steak?"

The majority of those writing in the Great British Press, however, appeared to remain consistently more interested in my sexuality than the quality of my performance. So it amused me enormously to know that, while the tabloids were chasing me all over the place and door-stepping my home, there hung unnoticed in the Royal Academy, a seven-foot-high painting of me, stark naked, by Maggi Hambling, one of Britain's leading artists and proudly 'queer', the term she always uses.

This particular oil painting was among Maggi's four entries for the prestigious Jerwood Prize, which she won that year. Earlier, I had been all over the Royal Academy Summer Exhibition in watercolours painted by Maggi, which were sold to people who had no idea they had bought "Alma". I sat for Maggi frequently over a 12-month period from around 1991 to 1992, during which she produced a substantial series of new paintings and drawings of me. Some of which, I must admit, are quite raunchy – perhaps mostly so the ones in which I am not entirely naked, but wearing only fishnet tights and boots. Had the identity of Maggi's latest muse, as she called me, been revealed, our names would doubtless have been indelibly linked by all the best tabloids. As it was, I remained hidden in plain sight...

I had always been a great admirer of Maggi, and had previously bought several of her paintings. Indeed, the first two I acquired I really couldn't afford, and I had to raid my income tax money to pay for them.

It was in 1987, when I attended her exhibition at the Serpentine Gallery in Hyde Park, that I encountered her for the first time. I was nearly mown down by her as she swept up the steps, dressed in a dinner jacket, paint-spattered jeans and trainers, the ensemble topped off with a large black "I am an artist" hat. She was, as usual, brandishing her habitual cigarette, and almost set me alight as she brushed past. She didn't notice me or anyone else – we were, after all, there to notice her. As an actress, I noted that it was a very grand entrance

Meeting her properly was just as terrifying as I had anticipated. Having cavalierly committed myself to spending money I couldn't afford, I inquired of the woman running the exhibition if I could pay with three post-dated cheques. "You'll have to ask Miss Hambling," she replied, and immediately trotted off in search of her. I was aware that I was turning bright red, and I didn't think I was actually capable of facing this exotic creature, the artist, but I had no choice. A few minutes later, Maggi made another of her grand entrances; she never simply walks into a room like an ordinary human being. This time, she homed in on me.

"Now, what is it you want?" she barked.

I blurted out my request. To my immense relief, she agreed to my payment plan and then barked again, "It looks as if I'm coming home with you." A reference to the two works I had purchased. Obviously!

It was after another chance meeting that I began to sit for Maggi. In her book *Maggi Hambling, The Works* she wrote: "Amanda became my muse, a muse with a sharp eye who challenged and contributed whenever we discussed work. And I think the performer in each of us fell for its reflection. That relationship was the inspiration for the Laugh paintings."

I was highly flattered, of course. But anyone who thinks being an artist's model is glamorous has got it entirely wrong. In fact, I suspect it may be even less glamorous than working on *Coronation Street*. I discovered the two had much in common with being a chorus girl – certainly in terms of physical endurance, as one is forced to hold a single position for hours on end, all the while being directed in an entirely arbitrary fashion. I do not think I could have managed without my dance training. At least I was accustomed to aching muscles.

In spite of all that, I loved every minute of it and became utterly caught up in the creative process. It was, in its way, quite therapeutic. In *Coronation Street*, I was constantly wearing a pinny, serving up meat pies and sausage and chips from behind the counter of Jim's café. In real life, I don't think I had ever previously worn any kind of apron, and it was definitely something of a relief for an old chorus girl to be back in those fishnet tights.

26

Rover's Regulars

It is the laughter and the friendships made that I remember best and miss the most about *Coronation Street*. The Street is known for the exceptional characters that have been its essence from inception. At worst, it was an experience to work with some of them, and at best, an enormous privilege.

In particular, Corrie has long been famous for its succession of daunting grand dames of soap – beginning at the very beginning with such all-powerful doyens as Pat Phoenix as Elsie Tanner, Violet Carson as battle-axe Ena Sharples, and Doris Speed as Annie Walker, landlady of the Rovers. That tradition continued in the next generation with women like Julie Goodyear, as Bet Lynch, later also to be landlady of the Rovers. Julie was among those who grew to the size of a giant within the show. I used to reckon it must be something in the air wafting through Stage One. I always thought of Corrie as a garden in which certain plants took root and became quite exotic, growing to triple or quadruple the size of the others. The strange thing is that when they left The Street, these giants usually returned to normal size.

I was exceptionally lucky to have worked with so many of them when they were at their peak. Jill Summers, who played

Phyllis Pearce was another larger-than-life character, one of life's true eccentrics and a real favourite of mine. She was a wonderful, strong North Country woman, both as Phyllis and in real life. Her son told me that when she was dying in hospital, one of the nurses asked her if she would like a drop of brandy. Jill just shook her head weakly. Then the nurse offered her a cup of tea, and got the same weak response. Finally, Jill was offered a glass of water. At which point, a voice from the bed said, "It gets better, doesn't it?" And apparently those were her last words.

Bill Waddington (Percy Sugden) was famous for not being able to remember his lines, which was strange because he did one-man shows and was able to tell really long stories. He used to have his lines written on the inside of his cap so that when he took it off, there they were in front of him. Once, we could all see the writing on his bald head where the ink had rubbed off.

I'm aware that *Coronation Street* is often regarded as a real place, and indeed, even the cast sometimes call each other by their character names. Yet, of course, they are actors with, invariably, a very different lifestyle to the folks of Weatherfield. The Street always used to be a place you could imagine yourself being part of. And possibly one its greatest strengths over the years has always been that it might even be somewhere its viewers would like to live. Though I very much doubt that's the case anymore, now that murder and mayhem, death and destruction, seem to have taken over, with barely a hint of humour or a trace of human warmth anywhere. Virtually every Corrie character seems to be involved in a storyline centring on brutal violence or terminal illness. Instead of the old days when The Street's characters used to gather joyously in the Rovers for a good gossip, now they are constantly huddled around hospital beds watching over friends or relatives on life support machines.

Back in the day, what could have been nicer for viewers than the thought of popping into the Rovers for a drink with all those Corrie residents they felt they knew. People, who, by and large, were decent folk who liked nothing better than coping with life's ups and downs by having a bit of a laugh, and a pint or two in their local. Sadly, that's all changed. Indeed, it is possible that the *Coronation Street* of the 21st century has housed more murderers and gangsters than Belmarsh Prison.

When I was in Corrie there is little doubt that viewers really identified with the characters, and probably didn't realise just how far removed the actors mostly were from the people they represented on screen.

Helen Worth and I always had a good chat and lots of laughs when, early in my time in Corrie, we were doing scenes in the café. And I shall never forget the time she suddenly remarked, "The grouse haven't been frightfully good this year, have they?"

To hear this coming from Gail, in her pinny, was rather unexpected to say the least, particularly as she was shaking a chip pan at the time. But Helen is really a very sophisticated woman and a great foodie. Without any doubt, some of my happiest days on the show were working with her in the café. In fact, when we had to have a row during one of our final scenes together, after being told that our characters had to go their separate ways, we were so upset at the prospect of being parted that we were both close to tears. We very nearly couldn't say our lines.

Another of The Street stars from back then who was not at all what you would expect is Eileen Derbyshire, who played Emily Bishop. Eileen is one of the funniest people I've ever met. But she doesn't like being recognised, and is not comfortable meeting fans or people she doesn't know. Her behaviour could be just a tad eccentric and she used to create rather wonderful disguises. Once she arrived at Granada wearing middle eastern robes and a yasmak.

Liz Bradley, who as wheelchair-bound Maud resembled a latter-day Ena Sharples, was actually very theatrical and lived rather grandly in a big house in Hampstead with swans at the bottom of her garden. But she adored being in The Street, and it broke her heart to leave. However, she went straight on to portray Alan Bennett's mother in his play *The Lady in the Van*, with Maggie Smith in the title role. Sadly, Liz died not long afterwards, and she is another person I will always miss. But she did die in the style that she had lived – having a wonderful time in the South of France with her film director son.

Then there was Sue Nichols, of course, who still plays Audrey Roberts, Alma's best friend. When Alma moved into Audrey's house, Sue and I wanted to become a sort of double act like *The Odd Couple*, and do lots of comedy together. But it never seemed to happen, not on screen anyway. Off screen, we spent most of our time giggling in corridors.

Speaking of comedy, I do think that Jack and Vera Duckworth, as portrayed by Bill Tarmey and Liz Dawn, were quite probably the best comic pairing since Morecambe and Wise. In their case too, don't kid yourself that they were playing themselves. Bill was a gentle and attractive man with none of Jack's sometimes uncouth, rough and readiness about him. He was multi-talented and also a much-acclaimed jazz singer with a string of records to his name. Liz was one of the best clothes horses I've ever seen, and had seriously good taste. She used to work endlessly for charity, and was a successful businesswoman.

Johnny Briggs, my oft-erring husband Mike, was one of the few in the cast whom I think did rather resemble his character. Indeed, I always felt the man he portrayed and the storylines we acted out took him over a bit. Johnny could be very funny and very charming, and we always had a good time working together, but he only talked to me on set if we were doing scenes together in which we were having a nice time and getting on. If we had a quarrel as characters, he would stop talking to me. I used to say, Johnny, it's not real, you know. But it was almost as if he sometimes forgot that.

Obviously, I shared more storylines with him than anyone else in The Street, and I suppose I always rather enjoyed working with Johnny because we came from the same kind of background. We both started in show business very young, and we both liked to run through our lines together repeatedly before each scene, so that we could do it in one take if possible.

There was an episode in 1991, I think, when Mike dumped Alma for another woman, and I got to slash her duvet and cut up all of Mike's ties. I quite enjoyed that. The rather more serious aspect of that storyline was Alma getting left alone for Christmas. She was very much a victim at the time, and I was staggered by how many people identified with what was happening to her. I received loads of letters about it. I could identify with it myself because of the way I've always felt about being alone.

It was during that period that I came to properly like and appreciate the character I was playing, and allowed a lot of myself to come out in Alma, something I continued to do right up until I left Corrie. Mike and Alma reunited, of course, and their wedding day in 1992 is probably my most vivid memory of our working together. It was about the hottest day I can remember in the UK. Even compared with present-day temperatures. We were on location, filming in a real register office, and the crew spent the entire day mopping us all down and trying to stop our make-up from melting.

The other Corrie man in my life as Alma was the legendary Bill Roache, who has played Ken Barlow since the very first episode on 9 December 1960. I would imagine most people think he is very serious. He isn't. He's a great giggler, for a start, He's also another one who has various sides to him a million miles from the character he plays. He's always been rather adventurous, and, many years ago now, qualified as a Formula One racing driver. Bill is quite a man and also extremely nice. Not to mention extremely handsome. I have no idea how he manages to stay looking so young. If he could bottle the formula, he'd make a fortune.

I remain a huge admirer of Barbara Knox, (Rita), who has always been a real quality act. If Rita had not become a Corrie regular, I think she would have gone on to a spectacular career in the theatre. I saw her do a one-woman show in London's Barbican Theatre with a hundred-piece orchestra, and she was absolutely breathtaking. I reckon her singing voice is every bit as good as that of her namesake, Barbara Cook.

Yet another Corrie actor with a great voice was John Savident, (Fred Elliott), who appeared in many big musicals in the West End and elsewhere, including *Phantom of the Opera*. Once we had to spend an entire freezing, rainy night on open moorland filming the exploits of the ill-fated staff of Freshco, the Corrie supermarket, who'd been sent on an endurance trial. John cheered us all up at four in the morning with a rousing rendition of 'The Lonely Goatherd' from *The Sound of Music*. Cold as we were all yodelled along with him. It must have been quite a spectacle. Pity we didn't have an audience, really.

Then there was my very good friend Kevin Kennedy (Curly Watts). We were both Manchester City fans and had been all our lives. Like me and my entire family, Kevin knew only too well what it was like to support this thoroughly infuriating football team through all its ups and downs, trials and tribulations, and periods of total abject misery. The glory days with Pep Guardiola lay way ahead in an as yet unheralded future.

I'M STILL HERE

The Manchester glory team when Kev and I were working together on Corrie was, of course, United. And it took a man of monumental spiritual fortitude, way beyond the capacity of most mere mortals, to cope with the mockery and cruel taunts which followed Kevin through the streets of Manchester when he used to trot along to Granada carrying his little blue and white City bag and wearing his blue and white scarf. His was a special kind of courage.

27

——

A Few Scares

During my time in The Street, I suffered two serious health scares. I underwent a hysterectomy amid fears that I might have cancer. Then a little later, I became afraid that I might be going blind.

The problems I had before my hysterectomy, which included bleeding so heavily it was as if I was haemorrhaging, turned out to be gynaecological. I do very clearly remember my sheer terror. This made me particularly anxious about the effects on viewers of the way in which Alma, who, of course, died of cervical cancer, was written out of *Coronation Street*.

I vividly recall waiting for the results of my tests and how worried I was. My strongest feelings when I was acting out Alma's death was that if one woman stayed away from her doctor, because of what we were showing on screen, then that was unforgivable. It seems, in the main, the opposite happened, and that the show made women more aware. But my personal experience caused me to be especially anxious about the storyline.

Like many women, I think, I was aware for some time that something was wrong before my problem was finally diagnosed.

By and large, it was fibroids that went wrong. I had been given HRT treatment which caused my fibroids to virtually explode. There had been all kinds of minor signs, but at least two doctors and a gynaecologist said it was all nothing and put it down to the change of life. And it was quite a while before it was discovered that I had these fibroids, non-malignant growths, in my womb. By the time I was correctly diagnosed, the operation was almost an emergency. I really was afraid that I had cancer, and some of the tests came back borderline. I was in a cold sweat all the time.

The operation, thank God, was a success. It went better than I could have ever expected, even though I ended up going into the Portland Hospital the day before the 1991 Grand National, and underwent my operation on National day, which naturally infuriated me. Apparently, my last words before I went under the anaesthetic were, "Back Seagram!"

I'd already put on a hefty bet myself, and I came round just in time to see Seagram win. My bet paid my entire medical bill.

It was about five years later that I became afraid that I was going blind. I had a retina vein occlusion, virtually overnight, in my left eye. It was a blockage in one of the channels that feeds the eye, sort of like having a kink in a hose. I woke up one day, and I had a lot of black lines in front of my eye. When I learned what was wrong, I was wet through from head to foot with terror, because I was told that the same thing could happen in the other eye at any time. The treatment prescribed involved pints of blood being taken from my body and replaced with equal amounts of plasma. Whilst still continuing to work on Corrie, I underwent this treatment four times over a period of six weeks. Thank God, my bad eye has partially repaired itself, and my good one has not been affected. So far.

I have another racing story here. While all this was going on,

I backed a 100-1 horse called See Enough. When it won by five lengths, I decided that was an omen. I started talking to my eye. I called it Walter and told it what it had to do. My specialist said that on very rare occasions, your eye can make itself another channel, and if the channel points in the right direction, it can start to correct itself. So every night when I lay in bed, I would give my instructions to Walter, and when I went back to see my specialist, he said, "Something's happening. Your eye is growing a new blood vessel, and it's beginning to empty."

I think I experienced a minor miracle. I can still see, and I'm eternally grateful for that gift.

Most importantly of all, my eyesight scare did not affect my ability to work, as I had feared that it might. I not only continued in The Street, but shortly afterwards, was involved in one of my most testing storylines, physically as well as mentally.

Alma was kidnapped by Don Brennan, played by Geoff Hinsliff. I had not really worked with Geoff before, but discovered that not only was he a very good actor, he was also a very nice guy, which was all for the best, considering the demands that were made of us! The storyline culminated in an hour-long special that mostly took place in Don's taxi.

In order for us to produce this extra-long episode, as well as all the others, the filming had to be done at night between 6pm and dawn. We also needed to be in the studio from dawn, so the schedule was even more gruelling than usual. It was really important to get through all the scenes as efficiently as possible.

But we were doing these highly charged, emotional scenes in a motor car with a cameraman and a sound boom squashed in with us. I had to act terrified and burst into tears while looking at Geoff with a cameraman crawling over him and a huge sound boom sticking up between his legs. We did it, though, and I think we managed virtually every scene in one take.

There was little margin for error. Filming had to end promptly when dawn broke, it wasn't just daylight that was the problem, but the sound of birdsong. The birds of Manchester – yes, there are some – became our biggest enemy that week.

Weather conspired to make things more difficult. It tipped down with rain. Of course! There is one scene where Alma tries to run away from Don, and I had to crawl up a steep, muddy hillside. Every time I tried to grab a sod of earth, it came away in my hand and I slipped backwards down the hill.

On screen Don was seen driving his car into the murky waters of Salford Quays, and then Alma pops up miraculously, more or less unscathed. In order to film this, I underwent the most frightening ordeal of my acting career. I was told that it had been arranged for us to film in a police diving tank, and that I would merely be required to submerge myself briefly in the water while standing on a platform. We were driven to Liverpool, to a place where police divers are trained. I had imagined the kind of neat, sanitized tank generally used for these kinds of scenes in films. What I was faced with was an expanse of black water, about the size of six Olympic swimming pools, 16 feet deep and covered in debris. I had to climb down two ladders tied together, the drop being too big for just one, in the dark – because the whole storyline took place at night. I then had to walk out onto a kind of pipe just a few inches wide, into the water. Because I was not likely to stay submerged for long enough without help, chains were fitted around my ankle to weigh me down. I must have been mad to go through with it.

I was genuinely scared, but I did it. I shuffled out on this pipe and submerged myself in the water. The next shock was that it was absolutely freezing. My poor heart had been nearly boiled in *Carry on Cleo* and was nearly deep, frozen in *Coronation Street*. No wonder, albeit many years later, I've had to have heart surgery. I almost passed out, but I did it. I plunged myself underwater and emerged as Alma escaping from Don's car – the only bit the viewers saw.

When I crawled up that ladder again, I was taken into a caravan and rubbed down with towels, which reminded me of my childhood experiences on Llandudno beach.

Later that day, I realised both my eyes had turned blood red, a side effect of being plunged into freezing water that nobody had told me about, and which frightened me even more than it might have done otherwise, considering my recent eyesight scare. Thankfully, all was well, and I received a letter of thanks from Carolyn Reynolds, who was the producer then, and various other Granada executives. So that was all right then…

When your entire life has been taken over for so long by one of the most extraordinary and all-encompassing jobs it is ever possible to have, moving on is a huge step to take.

However, I was quite sure, as the new millennium dawned, that leaving Corrie was the only decision to make. I suppose I'd been thinking about leaving for about two years. I knew it was probably about time that I set foot back into the world. Also, common sense tells you when something is over.

One of the things about *Coronation Street* is what the people in it describe as their hooks. If you are part of a family, if you've got a husband, a wife, a grandparent, children, or cousins, they are your hooks because they create storylines for you. If you happen to be single, or in my case, married to Mike Baldwin, which was practically the same thing, most of the time you are not in that position. Mike would kick me out, or we would fall out over one of his affairs, and I was left pretty much alone as a woman of a certain age. And in a soap, usually all they can think to do with you in that situation is to palm you off with some man, with whom you eventually disappear and, probably, you go off to live on an island or something of that ilk. And that will probably be the end of you. I didn't want that to happen. But I could see it coming. So I decided I would jump before the time came for me to be pushed. And I actually asked them to kill Alma, because I thought that if she remained alive, and I was ever asked to make one of those returns that people do, the temptation might be there. I didn't want that. Because it would never be the same to go back.

However, during the first year of the new millennium, life went on pretty much as usual. Even after I made the decision to leave The Street. Of course, for a long time nobody outside Granada and the Corrie inner circle knew about it.

We filmed the death scenes at the beginning of 2001. It was quite an experience. There I was departing this world in a tragic deathbed scene with more people sitting on my bed than you can possibly imagine. Cast and crew!

It was like the death of some great royal personage, with all concerned gathered round. Alternatively, there was an element of how many people can you get into a telephone box about it. I was most concerned about lying absolutely still and looking as if I wasn't breathing. Dying does take acting to its limits.

Alma's best friend Audrey, played by Sue Nichols, who is a good real-life friend of mine, was a constant presence at my deathbed. They were all fussing over Alma, getting her cups of tea that she couldn't possibly drink, and trying to talk to her. Alma was beyond answering through most of it. I just lay there. In a way, I was not dramatically involved to any great degree in my own exit.

Which might explain that no 'best exit' award came remotely near me. Something which, under the circumstances I really cannot quarrel with.

However I was somewhat amused – I think – when the best exit at the British Soap Awards for the year I left Corrie went to a dog! Bracken, the little Yorkshire Terrier that was Batley in *Emmerdale*, even attended the ceremony and was given a standing ovation when he was taken to collect the award by his on-screen owner. I like dogs a lot. Particularly Yorkies. And I was very happy for Bracken, honestly. But I did consider entering myself for Crufts the following year...

The thing that really annoyed me was that I didn't even get any repeat fees for my final episode because only my nose was in shot.

My last day on set was partly like every other day and partly like no other day. It was extraordinarily emotional. I was leaving behind such an enormous part of my life. A certain routine, so many friends and, it has to be said, a financial security very rare in our profession.

It began with the usual 7am make-up call, and then, until mid-afternoon, I lay on Alma's deathbed. This had a strange reality to it, maybe because I really was going, inasmuch as I was leaving Corrie after so long, albeit, hopefully, not leaving the world. I remember thinking, Amanda, this is not a good moment to start method acting.

Actors who leave Corrie after the sort of stint I had are always given a generous farewell gift by the rest of the cast. Helen Worth, to whom I was probably closest of all, was given the task of buying my gift.

She couldn't think what to buy me so asked me what I wanted. I said, well, I'm going to an antique fayre at the weekend, shall I just buy something? Helen said that would solve her problem and be absolutely wonderful.

The cast are always generous in these situations. I duly acquired a beautiful 17th century mini figurehead which had come off a galleon, probably from around the window to the captain's cabin. Helen was thrilled, as was I.

So when we completed Alma's deathbed scene, she was temporarily resurrected in order for those assembled to bid me a fond farewell. I sat up in bed, while they all clapped and started to say their goodbyes, and Helen handed me the farewell gift which, as far as I knew, nobody else was aware that I had acquired for myself. Being Helen she had wrapped it beautifully,

I opened it and expressed my thanks and delight, both absolutely genuine, whilst my screen husband, Johnny Briggs looked on in bewilderment.

"What's that dirty old bit of wood you've got?" he asked.

Eventually, I got out of bed. I went back to my dressing room for the last time. I changed into my own clothes. I walked out of Stage One, the home of *Coronation Street*, for the last time. And I bought everybody a farewell drink in the Old School, Granada's social club.

Then I stepped out into the unknown. And what a step it proved to be.

PART FOUR
My 90th Year

28

—

Tigger in a Flying Jacket

So here I am in my 90th year, looking back at the times I have had. Twenty-five years into a new millennium, 11 years married, and living the kind of life I had always yearned for. With the most unlikely person, that former red-top journalist whom I met for the first time when I was in *Coronation Street*.

I almost never did interviews then, for obvious reasons, but I had been persuaded that I could trust Hilary, who had promised only to write about my early life in Soho. She kept her word. I liked what she wrote, and was quite tickled by the headline – *The Secret Life of Corrie's Alma* – which I did not doubt was a deliberate spoof.

I had repeatedly refused to do promotional interviews, even though we were supposed to, but at that time we had a lovely publicist on Corrie, Peter Mares, whom I sat next to at a Granada dinner and, quite accidentally really, told about my early life in Soho.

He thought that would make a really good story, which would be safe for me and great publicity for Corrie, so he sounded out Hil, who at the time was Showbusiness Editor of the *Daily Mirror*. And he asked her if the Soho showgirl story would be enough for her. She was aware of what he meant by that, of course, because pretty much everyone in Fleet Street seemed to know about me. She was very enthusiastic about the idea and said it would be enough. Peter told me that he trusted Hilary. "You can trust her too, Amanda, she will do a good job, and everything will be fine," he said.

So I said I'd do it. I'd turned down everything for so long, I felt I more or less had to. I still had misgivings, but not for a fleeting instant did I imagine where this interview might lead…

I met Hil for the first time, and all three of us went to lunch. We Corrie actors were always chaperoned by a press officer when we gave interviews back then. Not that it seemed to make much difference a lot of the time.

Over a meagre luncheon meeting, not a lot more than an hour, Hil managed to get out of me so many stories about my Soho life, being a showgirl at Winston's, and all manner of other things, that she succeeded in writing a three-part series for the *Mirror*, complete with that headline, *The Secret Life of Corrie's Alma* – which may or may not have been deliberately misleading…

A few months later she approached me again to do a sort of Grand National special, to tie in with the April 1992 race. She offered to take me to see Red Rum, three times Grand National winner, a truly magic horse and a legend on four legs.

I went along with it, partly because I knew I would be going with someone who also happened to be quite horsey and had her own horse at the time. I wouldn't have liked to have visited Red Rum with anyone who didn't appreciate horses.

So we drove out to Ginger McCain's stable, where Rummy lived in cherished retirement, and we spent most of the day there. Ginger gave me a piece of Rummy's tail, and we had photographs taken which I cherish to this day.

We got another spread in the *Mirror*. The headline was *Eat*

Your Heart Out Mike, and Hil's opening paragraph began: *For Coronation Street Star Amanda Barrie it was love at first sight.*

She was of course referring to my feelings for Rummy.

We had dinner together that night in a Manchester Chinese restaurant, and I think we both enjoyed each other's company. But that was that. Everything went silent for quite a long time. Indeed it was 10 years before we were in touch again. Ten years before Miss Bonner had her Road to Damascus moment outside The Opera House

Which led to our night of just talking and talking until dawn, and my realising that she had stolen my heart. And, indeed, learning soon afterwards that the same thing had happened the other way round. I had stolen Hil's heart too.

We both seemed to take it for granted almost at once that we were going to be together. And Hil was probably even more surprised than I was, because she had always been straight.

However, at first, this was in many ways a torrid time.

We were of a certain age. We had previous lives. For all sorts of reasons there was a relatively short period before we could be open about our relationship. Our feelings for each other were powerful, but we did try to cause as little hurt as possible.

We spent as much time as we could together in my Covent Garden flat, a lot of it trying to work out what to do next.

Of course, Hil and I were both anxious at the time about our relationship becoming public knowledge. Neither of us were ready. I still wasn't quite sure if I would ever be ready as the past continued to weigh heavily on my shoulders. But we knew, because of who we were, a soap actress and a journalist, also of interest to Fleet Street if only for gossip value, that our story was going to come out sooner or later.

We were well aware that we didn't have the luxury of just going along quietly and keeping our private lives private.

So Hil decided to grasp the bull by the horns and tell the handful of people who were really important to her about us. Which totally astonished me. I wasn't at all sure she knew what she was doing. I told her to be careful, that in my experience they may not react how she thought they would. And she said that if that turned out to be the case, then they weren't the friends she believed them to be.

However, the fox still had its head down quite a bit. After all, I was used to being with somebody who hadn't even told her family what our relationship was.

The first people Hil told were her longest-standing friend, Jean Carr, with whom she had shared a flat when she was just 18, and Jean's husband, Louis Turner. She visited them at their North London home, and they went out to dinner at a local Thai restaurant where, for all her bravado, Hil found that she couldn't quite get the story out. She kept stumbling over the words.

Finally, Jean said, for which we will both love her forever, "So Hilary, what is this all about? Are you trying to tell us that you've changed your sexuality? I say, Louis, pass me some more of those prawns; aren't they wonderful?"

It was a fabulous reaction.

Hil continued to tell other close friends and family. She took Maggie Forwood, another long-standing chum from her newspaper days, to Sheekey's to break the news. And before poor Maggie had time to take it in, I arrived, hot-footing it from rehearsing that year's ITV pantomime. Now that must have been a real shock. But Maggie remained unfazed, and I seem to remember us having quite a nice time together.

Whilst we expected that word would get out about us sooner or later, we hadn't expected it to happen quite as quickly as it did. Hil rang her hairdresser one day to make an appointment and he responded immediately by telling her he'd just been hearing all about what he called her "exciting new life."

He was quite a well-known celebrity hairdresser, and it turned out that he was sitting on a Mediterranean beach with Barbara Windsor and another actress who at the time was with the same agency as me. Apparently, someone at the agency, who was one of the very few people then who knew about Hil and me, had behaved rather badly and gossiped about our relationship. Which of course, was just the beginning…

Hil always reminded me of Tigger back then, because she seemed to bounce everywhere. She bounced into rooms and bounced out again, bounced off to do a job. Bounced all over the place. And I remember telling her how much I would hate it if she lost her bounce. However, I didn't think she really understood what I meant. And in a way I think it was easier for Hil to be open about us than it was for me, because I'm that much older, and for so much of my life it was such a stigma to be gay. Some of that sort of stuck with me, hence my fox thing. Hil had no knowledge of living with the fear of becoming publicly known to be gay, in times when the consequences could be awful. And I was afraid she was going to find out that it could still be pretty daunting, which would have been so sad.

But I was probably not yet fully aware of how much times were changing. That fox with his head down still lurked within me. And I was genuinely worried about Hil.

The extraordinary thing was that she didn't lose her bounce, and to my utter amazement, as soon as and whenever she could she went round quite openly saying this is my partner. No, we don't want a twin-bedded room, we'd like a double please. She didn't seem to have much of a problem changing from being straight actually. And was often quite reckless. My jaw dropped, because I'd been creeping around for ages, and there was this newcomer who seemed to have picked it up quite quickly and was somehow ahead of the game.

Before I was publicly out, we even went for a little weekend in Paris, where I wasn't known, of course, and we went to a club for gay women. Hil found it online. Not me. This wasn't something I tended to do. But Hil was quite determined to pay it a visit.

The place seemed to be mostly full of women who looked pretty miserable. Something I reckon used to quite often be the case with gay women. And not so surprising really when you consider what we had to put up with. Then in bounced Tigger and they just flocked around her, which gave me a bit of a start. I felt a bit left out actually! But Hil was having a lovely time and smiling at everyone. Madam La Patrone even came across and gave us a bottle of wine. I thought, watch out for the trees, baby. Gay women are supposed to have a history of getting struck by lightning and hit by falling trees. I don't think that's based on any factual evidence at all, but nonetheless…

Indeed, there was no lightning, but Hil was soon to experience how things could still be when we were together in Bradford where I was appearing at the annual pantomime at the Alhambra Theatre, my first proper job after coming out of Corrie.

Pantomime people weren't ever going to be prejudiced about anything, certainly not Hil and me. Everybody in the cast immediately accepted us as a pair.

But it was in Bradford that we were first pursued with true persistence by the press. The word had found its way off that Mediterranean beach, across the Bay of Biscay, along the English Channel and up the River Thames to London, landing somewhere along the embankment just a hop and a skip from Fleet Street, the home of the Great British Press. Apparently, we were the talk of every newsroom. And they were after us with a vengeance.

The phone calls came first. Almost entirely to Hil on her mobile, partly because they all had her number as she was still a working journalist, but also simply because she was one of their own. And mostly she was called by editors. I was mildly miffed by this, actually, as I'd always previously been landed with the Manchester second stream.

We were in our hotel room one morning when the calls began to come. We sat around for a bit discussing what we could do about it, if indeed we could do anything. But at the same time Hil, who had been working on a new novel whilst she'd been with me in Bradford, was packing up her manuscript to send off to her publishers. You didn't email electronic copies of books back then. So after a bit, off to the post office she trotted. Wearing the leather flying jacket which was one of her very favourite items of clothing.

When she returned I thought she was looking a tad pale and she told me she reckoned we were being door-stepped – Fleet Street speak for when photographers and reporters stake out their targets. A black Mercedes with tinted windows was parked up outside our hotel. Hil was fairly sure it was part of a newspaper door-stepping operation.

And she was one who should know, of course. This was the first time that she had been door-stepped by the press, but iron-ically, she had previously stood on a doorstep or two herself.

It indeed proved to be the case that the black Mercedes contained representatives of the *News of the World* on our trail, who may or may not have snatched a picture of Hil in her flying jacket, the significance of which was totally lost on her.

Meanwhile at the Alhambra, everyone was wonderfully pro-tective of us. Whilst at the same time more than a tad mystified. Particularly the kids, who couldn't understand in the first place why the press were chasing us, indeed why the sexuality of two old women would be of interest to anyone: and in the second place, why these two old women were worried about it. Us being together was so not a big deal to them, straight or gay. The straight ones would say casually, "Oh yeah, I tried that once, but it didn't do anything for me."

The transition was already well under way with the young. Which I had not noticed until that pantomime because I had been closeted away in Corrie, with its own particular values and constraints back then, and further constrained by being in a relationship with someone who seemed determined to keep our relationship secret for ever.

In the dawning new world, this transition was a bit like a forest fire. It moved at extraordinary speed.

Hil did have one wobble. In my dressing room on the day she realised that she really might soon be all over the *News of the World*. There was yet another call from a journalist she actually knew quite well, and I realised that she was fighting back tears. She had found out the hard way that writing tabloid stories is one thing, suddenly becoming the subject of them is entirely another. Briefly I wondered if she might run. Instead, she phoned the late Richard Stott, her former editor at the *Daily Mirror* whom she both liked and greatly respected, explained the situation to him, and asked his advice.

"I'm thinking the best thing might be just to tell them the truth," she said.

"Bonner, have you taken leave of your senses?" boomed Stotty, as the whole of Fleet Street called him.

Hil recovered well – and quite quickly – after that. She told them nothing, and went nowhere. It seemed I was stuck with her.

With the help of some highly placed friends, we managed to avoid publication of anything at all at the time, although the

News of World did later print a fairly ambiguous story about us accompanied by a rather unattractive picture of Hil in her flying jacket – glowering at the camera she had correctly suspected was aimed at her from behind the Merc's tinted windows.

Now, as far as I'm concerned, a flying jacket was always considered more than a little bit of a hint in the gay world. Of course, Miss Bonner didn't understand that at all.

"I just really like my flying jacket," she said.

Upon which I'm afraid I had to reply, "Yes dear, and so do all the girls…'

29

———

Married at The Lane

W hat I have now is all that I ever wanted. I have a very happy home life with the person I love. I seem to fit into the world quite comfortably at last. I am no longer a creature apart.

Sometimes, it's the silly things that make life what it is.

Hil in the kitchen preparing supper, pausing to wave a sharp pointed knife in my direction, and asking, "Are we going to get married, or what?"

Obviously, I replied, "Or what?"

Sitting at the table one night after we'd been told we could no longer have the little Jack Russell we were expecting to buy, before we found Coco, I asked Hil, "Are you very disappointed?"

"Well, not that much," she replied. "To be honest, I never really wanted a Jack."

"Neither did I," I replied in some surprise. "I thought you did?"

"No," she said. "I thought you did."

Ever since, misunderstandings in our household have been known as Jack Russell moments.

"I look 90 today," I remarked grumpily one morning last year, having not yet given much thought to the momentous birthday approaching.

"Yes, well, you very nearly are," responded Hil, barely even glancing towards me. I never get any respect.

In spite of various Jack Russell moments, on 12 September, 2014 we married at the Theatre Royal, Drury Lane, a stone's throw from our London flat, and probably my very favourite theatre – the steps to which I had knelt upon all those years before as a young dancer, and prayed to be given the chance to remain in the world of theatre for the rest of my life.

I had been in panto in Lowestoft over Christmas 2013, as the Fairy Godmother in *Cinderella*, and our Dandino mentioned in passing that he had recently been married at The Lane – something I didn't even know was possible. I called Hil straight away and said, "That's it, we can get married at The Lane! You fix it and I'll be there!"

So she did. She's always been better at that sort of thing than me.

We had been discussing possible wedding venues, without coming up with anything that seemed right. We'd even thought about marrying abroad, but there often seemed to be questions about the legality of same-sex marriages overseas.

Marrying at The Lane was beyond perfect. We even had perfect weather. The sun shone all day, and we had the use of the newly renovated terrace overlooking Catherine Street, just a stone's throw away from the site of Hil's Road to Damascus moment all those years before.

Our dear friend Andrew Robley, a truly wonderful singer, sang 'Love Changes Everything'. It was fabulous, and very apt, though I have to admit that it was Hil's choice. She is the soppy one.

Indeed she was just a tad emotional on the day. She cried through much of the proceedings.

Chris, the ever-present, was, of course, one of our witnesses, along with our great friend Alan St Clair, sadly no longer with us. They walked us through the gathered throng in the Grand Salon towards the registrar who promptly dubbed them 'the bridesmaids', and referred to them as such throughout the proceedings.

Another dear friend, Guy Black – created Baron Black of Brentwood in 2010, and in my opinion, definitely the most impressive peer since Southend – made a speech about us so eloquent and complimentary that neither Hil nor I recognised ourselves. Guy was, of course, accompanied by his husband Mark Bolland, the former deputy private secretary to the king, famously credited with restoring the tarnished images of both Charles and Camilla. Mark has been made even more famous by the Netflix series *The Crown*, in which, however, he is portrayed by an actor neither as handsome, obviously, nor as tall!

Stephanie Beacham arrived clutching the most enormous bouquet of flowers which she presented to us. They were glorious, and Hil and I were delighted. Only later did we learn, from another guest, that Stephanie had been given the flowers on breakfast television that morning. We have not previously let on that we know that! So should she read this book, Miss Beacham will learn for the first time that she was found out! However, Hil and I thought it was extremely funny, and of course, no less than one would expect of a Costa Con.

A number of actors were there – including Helen Worth, playing truant from Corrie, Tracie Bennett, playing truant from rehearsing I've forgotten what, Sherrie Hewson, hot footing it from *Loose Women*, John and Carol Challis, John Lyons and his wife Ann – a total of around 120 people from all walks of life. There was me, as usual, thinking nobody would come. But they did. And it was a great day.

We invited a selection of pantomime people, including a few ugly sisters, all of whom arrived looking like the smartest most debonair chaps about town you have ever seen.

The redoubtable Heather Chasen was present, being even grander than usual, and asked, with her nose right up in the air, "Who are all these boring men in suits?'

I told her the last time she'd seen them they'd been wearing full slap, multi-coloured wigs, and high heels.

Heather, who behaved exactly as she pleased through her entire life, insisted on smoking in spite of being continuously asked not to. Finally, an exasperated waiter picked up her smouldering cigarette from the ashtray by her side, dropped it elegantly into her glass of champagne and, with something of a flourish, removed both!

In September last year we celebrated our 10th wedding anniversary with a weekend in Paris. Chris drove us there, bless him! He picked us up from our Covent Garden flat, we crossed the channel through the Euro Tunnel on LeShuttle, we stayed in a lovely little hotel in Saint Germain, we visited the Palace of Versailles, we ate and drank excessively, we thoroughly indulged ourselves. Indeed it could be said we lost our heads in Paris. There's a history of that of course...

30

Blue at Heart

Sport has always been very important to me, and it is important to Hil too. Which is all for the best, as I don't think I could live with anybody who didn't love sport. The year 2016 brought huge joy to me and the entire Broadbent family, when Pep Guardiola came to Manchester City and began a resurrection on a monumental scale, culminating, in 2022/23, in City winning the treble – the European Cup, the FA Cup, and the Premiership – then the following season winning the Premiership again for a record-breaking fourth consecutive time. If you cut me open down the middle you would find Manchester City written on my heart. Only people who love sport the way we do will understand the joy of it. And the heartache on occasions...

Hil wasn't particularly into football before we met, but she has become a genuine City fan. She is now almost as devoted to the blue people as I am, largely, she says, because of the pleasure she gets from watching the really beautiful football they play under Pep. Well, most of the time, parts of last season were not quite so good... But we'll be back.

We watch the girls too, of course. Manchester City women

are one of the dominant teams in the Women's Super League, finishing fourth this season, when they were also League Cup runners-up, FA Cup semi-finalists, and Champions League quarter finalists. As I write, the England women's football team have just become champions of Europe for the second time, in a tournament watched by an incredible 500 million people worldwide – exceeding even the 365 million who watched the women's Euros three years ago when England won for the first time.

Cricket has always been Hil's great sporting passion, and I honestly believe that if she could, she would watch every ball played in every game in the world.

A while back now we met the equally cricket-mad Sir Tim Rice at an Oldie of the Year lunch, and having talked cricket with Hil for half the afternoon, he promptly invited us to his box at Lords to watch a day of test match cricket. For a dreadful moment I thought Hil was going to kiss him. Since then, clearly being a glutton for punishment, Tim has repeated the invitation. I still won't let Hil kiss him...

My love for horse racing continues. And, just like all those years ago with Sid James when we were filming *Cleo*, I still have my betting buddies. Number one is a venerable racing man called Simon Crockett, whom I attempt to consult before every big race. But obviously I need an appointment. Simon and his wife Susie, also a racing woman who has spent much of her life working with horses, are special and much-loved friends – upon whom we know we can rely absolutely. Although I fear the same cannot always be said about Simon's racing tips...

I attended Royal Ascot for the first time in 2015, having been put up for membership of the Royal Enclosure by the legendary Martin Pipe, 15-time champion national hunt trainer. I'd never really wanted to go before, possibly because I didn't have a clue what to wear. But 2015 was different, we had married the previous year and our wedding clothes seemed to fit the bill pretty well. Wardrobe sorted. We attended in good company with Martin and his wife, Carol, and a group of horsey chums including George and Angie Malde, owners of one of the all-time great national hunt horses, Bonanza Boy. The Maldes are loyal friends both to people and to horses. When Bonanza Boy quit racing they gave him a pampered retirement at their Exmoor home, where he lived to the age of 30. If only more owners would take the same care of their racehorses in their old age.

Hil always says that she noticed a dramatic increase in my interest in her after I learned that the Pipes were her neighbours in Somerset. Complete rubbish of course.

But it has to be said we have shared wonderful times with the Pipes – Carol is a famously splendid hostess – over the years. Not least, in 2008, the quite thrilling return to their Nicholashayne yard of the David Pipe trained Grand National winner Comply or Die.

Also present that night were two other great Somerset friends and neighbours, Barry Bryant and Colin Sully. Colin is director of business resilience for a huge international company – and no, we don't have a clue what the hell it means either. Barry, now retired, spent his working life in the same crazy business as me. For many years he was theatre producer Cameron Macintosh's number one stage manager. His life is rather different now. Colin and Barry live in an old manor house surrounded by an eclectic selection of animals, including chickens, ducks, geese, and a shire horse. Most of which, with the exception of the shire, are often to be found in their kitchen. They are the kindest and most generous of people, and we honestly don't know what we'd do without them.

Another important part of our life together for 16 years of love and joy was our dog Coco. We lost her 18 months ago, and will always miss her. Dogs are often inclined to home in on one person. Coco was always really Hil's dog, loved, worshipped and adored Hil, whom she followed everywhere. Until she was quite an old dog, if Hil left her in the car with me, even if she was only filling up with petrol, Coco would howl. Throw back her head and howl. She would also sit by the front door and whimper if left alone with me in the house. This was totally humiliating. Particularly because if she ever had anything wrong with her Coco would come straight to me. I was her first responder.

And I always worried about her, far more than Hil ever did. I am known for worrying, and I'm also believed to be, by Hil anyway, a bit of a witch. I do have the odd premonition of doom...

Soon after Coco arrived as an eight-week-old puppy I became convinced that she was going to get out of the garden of our Somerset house, which is built on the side of a hill, onto the garage roof. I told Hil so repeatedly. But My WiFi was having none of it.

"Don't be ridiculous," she said. "There's a fence fixed into the ground, a hedge, and a length of chicken wire across it all. There is absolutely no way Coco is getting on to the garage roof."

But one day Hil returned from a trip to the shops to be greeted by an ecstatic tail wagging gleefully whimpering puppy on that garage roof threatening to throw itself off to get to its mummy. Hil leapt to the rescue which she completed successfully, but not without acquiring a selection of scratches and bruises negotiating the fence, the hedge and the chicken wire. Coco, of course, was unharmed.

On another occasion, in London, Hil had a dental appointment. Coco was not invited! But somehow or other our canine

Houdini managed to get out of the flat and took off after its mother. With me in pursuit through the heart of Covent Garden. Wearing a see-through dressing gown. And nothing else!

Like all dogs, I think, Coco thoroughly enjoyed the period of lockdown brought about by the Covid pandemic – because their people were captive. And it has to be said, and I'm slightly embarrassed by this because I know how much a lot of people suffered, Hil and I also thoroughly enjoyed Lockdown, which we spent in Somerset.

We had both worked constantly throughout our adult lives, in quite stressful occupations – even before adulthood in my case. Neither of us had ever had a break beyond holidays. No gap year, that was for sure!

In some ways, it was a bit like that social occasion you've been dreading which is suddenly cancelled at the last moment and you breathe a huge sigh of relief. That's what Lockdown felt like to me. Everything stopped for a moment. Quite a long moment.

Our good friends and neighbours up the road, John and Maggie Flaherty were kindness itself and regularly delivered groceries from Waitrose where Maggie worked. Hil's vegetable garden thrived with the extra attention she was able to give it, and the glorious sunshine of that spring meant that crops came to fruition earlier than usual, providing us with a continual supply of fresh garden produce.

Everything we needed was at hand. We had rather a wonderful time at our little Georgian house with its turquoise pretend-Maldives indoor swimming pool – which I always insist be kept at 31 degrees. The enforced isolation made it feel like we were living on an enchanted island looking out over our garden and our field and the Blackdown Hills, rather than the sea.

Lockdown was one of the best times of my life.

We even sat in the garden and painted, something we'd meant

to do together for years, producing two water colours of our beautiful espaliered Comice pear tree in full bud.

I don't think we felt as alone as some people did. While our face-to-face social contact was limited for the duration to drinks with our lovely neighbours, Sue and John Biffen, at the hole in the hedge – which Hil carved out specially for the purpose through the tall laurel hedge dividing our properties – we were constantly in touch with those closest to us by phone or Zoom. We spoke to Chris every day, of course. We always do.

Lookdown disrupted family life for almost everyone, of course. And family becomes more important than ever as you grow older, I feel. They are the only people who have always known you. You go your separate ways, you follow different paths, and then you seem to come full circle.

During lockdown my nephew Jamie started phoning me every day at 11am. He still does. Every single day without fail. Full of apologies if he is early, or knows he is going to be late. I don't think he quite realises how much this means to me, and to Hil. She addresses him simply as 'Nephew' and considers him to be every bit as much her nephew as he is mine!

I am also constantly in touch with my brother Chris and my sister Caroline.

Into his 80s now, brother Chris still looks immaculate and extremely dapper. In spite of major health problems over the years, I don't feel that my brother has changed much from the lad who, in his early teens, came to stay with me in London, while I was hopping about as a dancer. He loved clothes and shopping, two things we have always had very much in common. I clearly remember taking him shopping once and buying him an antelope coat – which seems really awful now – and some winkle-pickers, a pair of the most pointed shoes you have ever seen. Full of great pride he proceeded to trip all the way down Oxford Street. We went on to the 2i's Coffee Bar in Old Compton Street, which was a haunt of the Beatles at the time. We also used to go to the pictures a lot, have a Wimpy on the way in, a Wimpy on the way out, then go on to another film, and maybe yet another Wimpy and yet another film. I'd love to do it all again.

Caroline, I think, is probably the sanest of us two sisters, which is not saying much. She is so efficient at almost everything, and so good at all the things that I'm not good at and at organising me. I am lucky to have her. In return for her constant assistance, I frequently give her as many clothes as she will take off me. Clothes are my great weakness, and I never have enough room for half of what I own. So Caroline is doing me a favour. She's another one who hasn't changed much with the years. She also once made a remark about my mother I will never forget, when Connie was having a health issue. "She's the only person I know who can have an asthma attack and eat a chocolate biscuit at the same time," said Caroline. It was true too.

I just wish my brother and sister and Jamie all lived next door.

31

—

Death Comes First

As you grow older, arguably the greatest sadness is the people you lose along the way. In this millennium I have lost a number of people who were very special to me. Some of them tragically young,

My nephew Adam died in 2013 aged just 45. He had been diagnosed with cancer two years earlier at 43, which came as an enormous shock to the entire family. Adam was the sweetest person in the world, and he dealt with his terrible illness as, to my utter amazement, so many people seem to, with courage and humour.

He spent the final weeks of his life in a hospice in Macclesfield, cared for by staff whose kindness and sensitivity were quite overwhelming.

The last time we visited him he still laughed at my totally inadequate jokes. When Hil and I stepped out of his room into the corridor, knowing we would never see him again, we were both fighting back tears. A passing nurse, who had previously confessed that she watched all the soaps and had never missed an episode of Corrie, adding, "I'm deep as a puddle, me," stopped to speak to us.

She uttered no platitudes. Instead she just said, "Crap, innit?"

If I ever had to go into a hospice I would like to be looked after by that woman.

A second big shock was receiving a letter from Adam three weeks after he died. Apparently, he had left similar letters to everyone close to him. Our letter began "to my two dotty aunts". I don't think I've ever cried so much in my life. It was wonderful to receive but so bittersweet.

Adam and his letter also, by default, gave Hil the story and title for her next crime novel. It transpired that his funeral clashed with a test match at The Oval for which my cricket-mad WiFi had tickets. And it was The Ashes! England versus Australia! The pinnacle of international cricket.

I told her I would go alone, but that was never going to happen. It was as important for Hil to be at the funeral as it was for me.

"Of course I'm going to be there, death comes first," she said.

What? Now this was just the most bizarre remark. Death comes first? Goodness knows where that came from. It couldn't possibly have been from Adam. Obviously. Hil doesn't believe in that sort of stuff. But we both agreed that it would be a pretty good title for a crime novel.

And so, Hil's next book was born. It's plot centring around a letter written by a dead man. It was duly called *Death Comes First*, and was, of course, dedicated to dear Adam. *With thanks for the inspiration you never knew you gave me*, Hil wrote as part of the dedication.

Adam's death was just the beginning of a truly terrible time for my family.

Two years later, Jules, wife of my nephew Jamie, died suddenly aged 39. She'd been to her doctor with a chest infection, but nobody realised just how ill she clearly was. She'd always previously appeared to be a particularly fit and healthy young woman.

Jamie and Jules had shared a little cottage just outside Leeds with their four children, they each had a son and daughter from previous relationships. There wasn't much room, but everything was always immaculate. After all, Jamie is a man who colour-codes his tee shirts! Jules and Jamie were an incredibly close couple. After her death, Jules' two children went to live with their father, and Jamie's life was turned upside down. He remains one of the nicest, kindest people I know, and I am full of pride and admiration for the way he has coped with such tragedy.

There was more to come. Not long afterwards, my sister-in-law Ed, wife to Chris and mother of Jamie and Adam, was diagnosed with a rare form of cancer. She died in 2017, aged 72.

It was a truly terrible five years. But I do think it might have been a factor in bringing the remaining Broadbents closer together.

Not long afterwards, in 2020, we also lost Alan St Clair, another friend who, to all intents and purposes, was family. He was an extraordinary one-off character with a splendid handlebar moustache which made Poirot's look a bit ordinary. An artist of considerable talent, he was also, in his day, arguably the most famous barman in London. Latterly he was the bar manager of The Chelsea Arts Club, but everywhere he worked became Alan's personal club. He was very grand and came from a quite remarkable family, his ancestors having built Rosslyn Castle in Scotland, its famous chapel made even more famous by Dan Brown, in his novel *The Da Vinci Code*, as a possible site of the Holy Grail.

Alan once remarked on having originally come from Normandy in France, and when I enquired further it transpired that the St Clairs had once owned the whole of Normandy.

I shall miss Alan always.

I'M STILL HERE

When one is in one's 90th year, your own health is likely to be an issue. By and large I have been fortunate in that regard until this year when I do seem to have rather fallen apart.

I haven't been seen much on television so far in 2025, but I have made appearances in two very important theatres, alongside two magnificent leading men. In fact, arguably the most important I have ever played opposite.

My first appearance of the year was in an operating theatre at London's famous St Bartholomew's Hospital. known to all as Barts, where my leading man was consultant cardiologist Dr Mike Mullen. I was aware that he had performed the same heart procedure I was to undergo on the Duke of Edinburgh. Obviously, I relinquished top billing to him. My second appearance was in another operating theatre at the Royal National Orthopaedic Hospital, where I underwent a hip replacement, and my leading man there was orthopaedic surgeon Mr Will Aston. To whom I also relinquished top billing, of course.

Clearly, 2025 has been the year of the op.

I had for some time been struggling with a hip which had grown increasingly more painful, eventually reaching the stage where it really no longer worked as a hip. I put it down almost exclusively to all those high kicks, splits and can cans I performed in my younger days finally catching up with me. I had also been coping for several years with a naughty little valve in my heart which was slowly closing up, to the extent where it prevented me from having hip surgery until I first had heart surgery.

This led to quite a considerable period of time during which I was passed about from one medical professional to another, whilst I staggered around the place desperately trying not to let it show that there was anything at all wrong with me. In public at any rate. And, of course, I refused point blank to use a walking stick.

I developed a few tricks. The feeling of being totally unable to move, as anyone who has suffered from anything like this will know, is at its greatest when you try to stand up having been sitting for a while. So, once I had somehow hoisted myself more or less upright, I would insist that whoever I was with indulged in loud conversation with me, whilst all concerned pointed out objects of interest, a painting, the view from the window, almost anything, as the alternative reason for remaining stationary, as opposed to real one. That I was temporarily rooted to the spot.

I would also make Hil, or any other companion, proceed before me downstairs so that I would have someone to break my fall should I topple over. I'm not sure about the wisdom of this particular plan, but fortunately it was never tested.

I was admitted to St Bartholomew's Hospital in March this year, where my valve was replaced using a procedure called a TAVI, a transcatheter aortic valve implantation. But I still had to wait until my heart was deemed suitably recovered for me to undergo the required hip op.

Having a TAVI turned out to be one of the most extraordinary experiences of my life. The procedure does not involve cutting open the chest and is minimally invasive. A catheter is inserted through the femoral artery in the groin and up your body to your heart in order to fit a new artificial valve, most usually made from pig tissue, inside the one that is no longer working properly.

I was awake throughout. Properly awake. I was given only a local anaesthetic. Not even a sedative! If all goes well with a TAVI, quite frankly, it can be considerably less of an ordeal than the average visit to a dentist. And mine went extremely well, thanks to wonderful Dr Mike, undoubtedly one of the best in the world at this still relatively new procedure, and to our dear friend Professor Charles Knight, who just happens to be Chief Executive of Barts, and put us in touch with Mike. Charlie is very important in our lives as, it should be said, is his husband Peter Probert who was instrumental in getting Hil's first play, *Dead Lies* produced. Hil always says it would never have happened without Peter.

There were one or two surreal moments during my TAVI. I was told that my knickers were about to be removed and asked where I would like them put.

I replied, "You can put them on eBay as far as I'm concerned."

And I got a pretty good laugh. Which always pleases me greatly. It is a bit of an obsession of mine, that if it's possible to play any situation for laughs, I will.

The truth is that I was worried sick about having this procedure. I knew that it had an excellent success rate, but the very idea of someone poking about with my heart frightened me, not to mention the list of things that can go wrong, even if only rarely, which you are presented with in advance.

Thankfully, the op went like a dream. I believe Mick Jagger has also had a TAVI, by the way. But, so far, my rendering of 'Satisfaction' has not improved.

I was in hospital for just two and a half days. Our wonderful friend and neighbour Maggie came with Hil to Barts to pick me up, and took a photo of us standing outside the main entrance. I came out feeling like a new woman, but eventually decided to keep the one I'd got...

Maggie is always there for us, as is her son David, who does so much for us, and whom we love dearly. I even forgive him for being an Arsenal supporter. We couldn't do without either of them.

Five days later I asked to be taken for Sunday lunch at the Ivy. The new addition to my heart behaved perfectly. I did, however, avoid the roast pork, one of my favourites, out of respect.

I shall always be grateful to Mike and his team for ensuring "I'm Still Here" and hopefully will be for a bit longer yet.

And also for making me well enough to give Will Aston, one of RNOH's leading surgeons, the chance to make me properly mobile again.

For my hip replacement operation, and because I once had a bad experience with a general anaesthetic, even though I would now be regarded as fit to have one, I chose an epidural. This is a regional anaesthesia administered via injection into the back. They also give you some kind of happy pill.

You are, however, fully aware of everything that is going on, but you feel no pain and are totally unbothered by the whole experience.

Though I do remember being aware of Will going at it hammer and tongues during the operation. There was a lot of noisy bashing, scraping, and sawing. Indeed I thought it sounded rather as if he was excavating an extension to the Channel Tunnel.

As I write, just over a month has passed since the op. I feel well. I am now walking about assisted by just one crutch. And I am determined that by publication day of this book, three days before my birthday, I will be walking not only without aids, but also in a sprightly fashion. Maybe even capable of dancing a few steps. But if I do the splits it will be totally by accident...

32

The Future?

I f I were to sum up my 90 years, I don't believe I have gained any wisdom, nor had any great thoughts which could change the world. When I look around me and watch the news, and I consider those 90 years, my only thought is pure gratitude for the life I have been given.

And I wouldn't mind having a few more years. Not at all. Just so I don't miss anything.

I can't stop thinking about the future, which might seem strange for someone of my age. But, you see, I tune into the news constantly. I've been the same since I was a child in the war, huddled with my family around our radio. I watch the news on TV whenever I can, otherwise I have it in my ear. At night I go to sleep – eventually – with an ear-phone in, listening to the news. I am a total news junkie and I absolutely have to know what is going on in the world.

So what really pisses me off is the thought of what I will miss knowing about when I permanently depart.

I mean, will actors all become AI? Will our profession be overtaken by a mishmash of robotic creatures? Will it translate to sport, so poor dear Hilary won't know whether or not she's watching real cricketers? Will she be able to tell the difference? I want to know.

As has already been established, sport is very important to me. I've come to watch flat racing more than national hunt because, by and large, the horses don't get hurt, and every year I follow the progress of the youngsters leading up to the next classics. I can't bear the thought of not knowing who will win the next Oaks and Derby.

And I'm worried about what the future might hold for Manchester City. Will they stay in the top rank of Premiership and European football? Or will they have one of their slumps. You can never be sure with City. Even under Pep.

I want to know.

And what about my beloved news bulletins on TV and radio? What about fake news? It's sometimes hard to tell the difference now. How fake is the news going to become? God knows what it will be like in the future. Will we need to treat all news on every media outlet like a Netflix drama? Will we learn to cherry-pick the facts? Or will we come to accept that nothing in the world is real any more?

I want to know.

Will people be so addicted to mobile phones and tablets – and believe me I'm a bit of an addict with my phone – that we will not communicate directly at all, but just sit there talking into a phone? Already, people are inclined to point their phone and take a picture rather than look at things.

How might that affect relationships? Will we just send texts and voicemails and post videos on Instagram? Will we stop touching each other except in a medical emergency. And how might that affect procreation?

I want to know.

The whole world seems to be in a crazily dangerous state,

frightening way beyond anything I have witnessed in my 90 years since World War Two. How did we finish up with the quite awful leaders we have? How did we choose them?

In the future, are there still going to be political parties as we know them? What about parliament and congress and so on? Will bodies like these even exist? Or will all countries be run by some sort of disembodied AI creation in charge of everything and everyone, communicating with the people only by social media posts from unidentifiable sources?

I want to know.

For how long will we still have royalty in this country? Will we just replace the lot of them with some huge AI figure-head creation? If running true to form in this age of celebrity – of which I know I am a part but I do not think I have ever aspired to be what I clearly am not – an AI amalgamation of famous people from all walks of life, dead or alive: Churchill, Chaplin, Marilyn Monroe, David Beckham, Taylor Swift, Abraham Lincoln, Queen Victoria? Will it be like a Michelin Man football mascot, and will it trundle out onto the balcony of Buckingham Palace and wave to the crowd, which will promptly drop to its collective knees?

Would it, could it, could any of this, be much worse than what we've got at the moment? And am I going too far?.

I want to know.

I wonder if we are ever seriously going to try to save our planet? If so, why is all that money being spent on getting to Mars? Have you looked at Mars? I have the NASA app on my phone. I've looked at Mars a lot. Why would anyone go there? There's nothing on Mars. They haven't even got a Marks & Spencer.

Can we please instead spend all that money on this wonderful earth we've been gifted. It makes me mad. We're like kids who were given a beautiful Christmas present and jumped on it and broke it. Are we really going to try to mend it?

I want to know.

Possibly the first time I fully realised that I was no longer troubled by that blessed lurking fox was when I received my *Attitude Magazine* Icon award for outstanding lifetime achievement in 2016. The fox was still there, but he had become my friend, and I was happy for him to be there when I made my way onto the stage.

We should all remember that animals and people usually become how they are treated. The fox within me was no longer cowed, afraid, and given to aggression. He had his head up, and was wagging his tail.

The late great Paul O'Grady presented me with my award and there were many people in the audience whom I deeply admired, people who were clever and funny, people who successfully lived their lives in their own way. A lot of them were gay, of course, but far from all. And as I stood on stage next to Paul – a married woman accompanied to the event by my wife – it occurred to me finally that I really did have absolutely nothing to be ashamed of or feel guilty about. I had grown a new skin. I no longer had any secrets.

I thought, oh my God, I made it. I'm completely guilt-free, I'm utterly shame-free, and I'm totally comfortable within myself. I'm also quite proud to have gotten this far.

I had lived under a cloud for so much of my life. It's hard to relate what it is like when you suddenly lose a burden like that. You feel released from everything. The sense of freedom is enormous. It really is like being reborn. It cleanses you. It's an exorcism. It's therapeutic.

Attitude is the UK's best-selling gay magazine, and the world's biggest LGBTQ media brand. Its award put a sort of exclamation mark at the end of a very long chapter.

I was a little overwhelmed, though. I had to make a speech, and I don't think I did it very well. What I tried to say was, that for me getting an award for being gay was like getting an award for breathing.

There is one last thing that has to be said. Not a day goes by when I do not think about how lucky I have been to ultimately find the love of my life.

I love Hil to bits and cannot envisage life without her.

She's my best friend, my chef, my television engineer – she's really good at sorting out TVs – and of course, she's my ghost-writer.

So this is highly embarrassing for her, because I am saying it out loud, and Hil is sitting next to me, writing it down. Or I hope she is.

She is also positively cringing. And she's protesting! She's arguing with me again. I'm going to have to speak to her sharply.

"Shut up, Hil. This is my book, and I mean what I'm saying. Oh, and darling, put the kettle on…"

.